P9-DXQ-796

THE BASIC/NOT BORING MIDDLE GRADES LANGUAGE ARTS BOOK

Grades 6–8+

Inventive Exercises to Sharpen Skills and Raise Achievement

Series Concept & Development
by Imogene Forte & Marjorie Frank

Incentive Publications, Inc.
Nashville, Tennessee

Acknowledgement:
Many thanks to Joy MacKenzie,
whose adapted exercises
are included in this book.

Thank you to the students
who contributed works to this book.

Illustrated by Kathleen Bullock
Cover art by Mary Patricia Deprez, dba Tye Dye Mary®
Cover design by Marta Drayton and Joe Shibley
Edited by Angela Reiner

ISBN 0-86530-458-0

2 3 4 5 6 7 8 9 10 06 05 04

PRINTED IN THE UNITED STATES OF AMERICA
www.incentivepublications.com

TABLE OF CONTENTS

INTRODUCTION

Do basic skills have to be boring? Absolutely not! Mastery of basic skills provides the foundation for exciting learning opportunities for students. Content relevant to their everyday life is fascinating stuff! Kids love learning about topics such as UFOs and weather maps, famous quotations and seashore sounds, detectives and mysterious characters, peculiar laws and mind-blowing trivia, foreign words and surprising sequences, and more. It is on acquired knowledge bases that they develop basic skills which enable them to ponder, process, grow, and achieve school success.

Acquiring, polishing, and using basic skills and content is a cause for celebration—not an exercise in drudgery. *The BASIC/Not Boring Middle Grades Language Arts Book* invites you to celebrate with students as you help them sharpen their abilities in the essentials of language arts.

As you examine *The BASIC/Not Boring Middle Grades Language Arts Book,* you will see that it is filled with attractive age-appropriate student exercises. These pages are no ordinary worksheets! *The BASIC/Not Boring Middle Grades Language Arts Book* contains hundreds of inventive and inviting ready-to-use lessons based on a captivating theme that invites the student to join an adventure, solve a puzzle, pursue a mystery, or tackle a problem. Additionally, each fittingly illustrated exercise provides diverse tools for reinforcement and extension of basic and higher-order thinking skills.

The BASIC/Not Boring Middle Grades Language Arts Book contains the following components:

- **A clear, sequential list of skills for 6 different content areas**
  Checklists of skills begin each content section. These lists correlate with the exercises, identifying page numbers where specific skills can be practiced. Students can chart their progress by checking off each skill as it is mastered.

- **Nearly 250 pages of student exercises**
  Each exercise page:
  . . . addresses a specific basic skill or content area.
  . . . presents tasks that grab the attention and curiosity of students.
  . . . contains clear directions to the student.
  . . . asks students to use, remember, and practice a basic skill.
  . . . challenges students to think creatively and analytically.
  . . . requires students to apply the skill to real situations or content.
  . . . takes students on learning adventures with a variety of delightful characters!

- **A ready-to-use assessment tool**
  Six skills tests, one for each content area, follow each series of exercises. The tests are presented in parts corresponding to the skills lists. Designed to be used as pre- or post-tests, individual parts of these tests can be given to students at separate times, if needed.

- **Complete answer keys**
  Easy-to-find-and-use answer keys for all exercises and skills tests follow each section.

HOW TO USE THIS BOOK:

The exercises contained in *The BASIC/Not Boring Middle Grades Language Arts Book* are to be used with adult assistance. The adult may serve as a guide to ensure the student understands the directions and questions.

The BASIC/Not Boring Middle Grades Language Arts Book is designed to be used in many diverse ways. Its use will vary according to the needs of the students, the form of instruction, and the structure of the learning environment.

The skills checklists may be used as:

. . . record-keeping tools to track individual skills mastery.
. . . planning guides for the teacher's instruction.
. . . progress reports to share with parents.
. . . a place for students to proudly check off accomplishments.

Each exercise page may be used as:

. . . a pre-test or check to see how well a student has mastered a skill.
. . . a tool around which the teacher may build a mini-skills based lesson.
. . . one of many resources or exercises for teaching a lesson or unit.
. . . a way to practice or polish a skill that has been taught.
. . . a review of a skill taught earlier.
. . . reinforcement of a single basic skill, skills cluster, or content base.
. . . a preview to help the teacher identify instructional needs.
. . . an assessment for a skill that a student has practiced.

The exercises are flexibly designed for presentation in many formats and settings. They are useful for individual instruction or independent work. They can also be used under the direction of the teacher with small groups or an entire class. Groups of exercises on related skills may make up the practice materials for a series of lessons or may be used as a unit enhancement.

The skills tests may be used as:

. . . pre-tests to gauge instructional or placement needs.
. . . information sources to help teachers adjust instruction.
. . . post-tests to review student mastery of skills and content areas.

The BASIC/Not Boring Middle Grades Language Arts Book is not intended to be a complete curriculum guide or textbook. It is a collection of inventive exercises to sharpen skills and provide students and teachers with tools for reinforcing concepts and skills, and for identifying areas that need additional attention. This book offers a delightful assortment of tasks that give students just the practice they need—and to get that practice in a manner that will definitely be remembered as non-boring.

As your students take on the challenges of the enticing adventures in this book, they will increase their comfort level with the use of fundamental reading, writing, and language skills and concepts. Watching your students check off the skills they have sharpened will be cause for celebration!

READING COMPREHENSION

Skills Exercises

THE WORKS OF BEN Jonson

SKILLS CHECKLIST FOR READING COMPREHENSION

✔	SKILL	PAGE(S)
	Determine the meaning of words and phrases	18
	Paraphrase a written text	18
	Explain uses and meanings of words from a text	18, 21, 40, 51, 55
	Identify literal main ideas	19
	Identify supporting details	19, 22
	Identify the author's point of view	19, 36, 46, 47
	Identify implied ideas	20, 21, 35
	Read to find answers to questions	22
	Identify elements of a story	23
	Explain sequence of events	24–26
	Choose the best title for a selection	27
	Identify cause-effect relationships	27
	Distinguish between facts and opinions	28, 29
	Summarize a written text	30
	Identify the theme of a written piece	30, 54
	Make generalizations based on material read	31
	Draw logical conclusions from written material	32, 33
	Predict future actions or outcomes	34
	Make connections between fiction and real-life situations	35
	Compare and contrast written pieces	36, 52
	Identify the tone of a written piece	36, 52, 54, 55
	Evaluate ideas, conclusions, or opinions from a text	37, 38
	Make judgments about ideas or concepts in a text	38, 39
	Find information in written material	40, 41
	Make use of graphics to understand a text	42, 43
	Interpret charts and graphs	44
	Identify and interpret symbols	45, 51
	Identify figurative language	45–48, 56
	Explain techniques used by a writer to communicate a message	45–57
	Identify many literary devices (such as similes, metaphors, personification)	45–57
	Identify bias in written materials	48, 49
	Identify stereotypes in written materials	49, 50
	Identify persuasion in written materials	50
	Identify the author's purpose	51, 54
	Identify techniques that develop characters	53
	Explain personal responses to written material	58

RULES TO LIVE BY

It's great fun to play around with sophisticated words that are not normally used in everyday conversation. Below is a collection of phrases, written in "snooty" language, but offering some good, sound advice. Match each sophisticated phrase with its contemporary, vernacular translation. (If you don't know what *vernacular* means, look it up. By the time you get through with this page, it should be a word you will never forget!)
Write the number of each "snooty" phrase next to its matching translation in ordinary language.

1. Sustain thyself by engorging a goodly portion of the nutritious elements.
2. When the gray aurora dawns in the eastern hemisphere, rouse yourself to a vertical position.
3. Render to each homo sapien his rightful appurtenances.
4. Avoid premature surrender to excessive anticipation.
5. Please refrain from making your bowler a depository for sputum.

6. Ambulate with extreme vigilance.
7. Avoid contumelious comportment.
8. Never extricate foreign matter from your proboscis.
9. Shield your oral aperture when forcibly expelling from the same.
10. Regard with deference and esteem those who are your predecessors.

_____ A. Cover your mouth when you cough.
_____ B. Eat to live.
_____ C. Be patient.
_____ D. Don't be rude.
_____ E. Watch your step.
_____ F. Don't spit in your hat.
_____ G. Get up in the morning.
_____ H. Respect your elders.
_____ I. Give everyone his own stuff.
_____ J. Don't pick your nose.

Name

GET AHEAD!

People do not like headaches. But have you ever wondered how headaches feel about people? An eighth grader wrote this clever essay that will give you some clues.

____

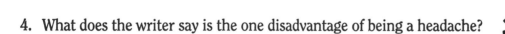

Fortunately, a headache never has difficulty finding a good home. A toothache has to hope for a vacancy in a holey molar. An earache must wait for a cold day to chase down hatless children, but I just move into a head any time.

Even if an earache is lucky enough to catch an ear, he has the most cramped quarters in which to live. And imagine how confining it is to be a toothache, trapped inside a bicuspid! Neither has as much room as I, and I don't have to tolerate either bad breath or sticky, yellow wax!

A headache can easily find lodging in any head that has a problem (and most people have plenty of problems!). Why, I've lived in some of the best heads—presidents, movie stars, and even athletes—I have known many of them intimately. I've met more people than any other ache around. Most of them I like, but the person I wish never to meet is the one who invented aspirin!

1. From what point of view is the essay written? ________________________
2. What is the main idea conveyed by this essay?

   ____
3. List at least three details that support the main idea you have written above.

   ____

   ____

   ____

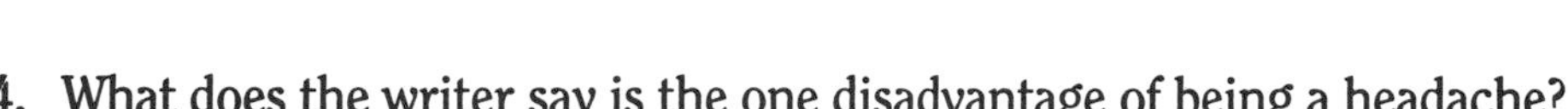

4. What does the writer say is the one disadvantage of being a headache?

   ____
5. Which title below do you think best fits this piece? Write it on the line above the essay.
   - Go to the Head of the Class
   - Down with Aspirin!
   - Advantages of Being a Headache
   - Heads I Have Met
6. Explain your title choice.

Name ____

WANTED: TOP-QUALITY PERSON

In this famous poem, Rudyard Kipling describes what it takes to be a "real" or high-quality man. It seems he was writing to his son or some other young man; however, the qualities he describes are not specific to any gender. Today, we could read this poem as addressed to anyone—male or female. Several qualities he mentions are:

A. self-confidence	C. self-control	E. perseverance
B. patience	D. long-suffering	F. humility

However, these words do not appear in the poem. Underline in the poem the phrase(s) that describe each of these qualities and mark those lines with the appropriate letter.

"IF —"
BY RUDYARD KIPLING

If you can keep your head when all about you
Are losing theirs and blaming it on you;
If you can trust yourself when all men doubt you
But make allowance for their doubting too;
If you can wait and not be tired by waiting,
Or, being lied about, don't deal in lies,
Or, being hated, don't give way to hating,
And yet don't look too good, nor talk too wise;

If you can dream—and not make dreams your master;
If you can think—and not make thoughts your aim;
If you can meet with triumph and disaster
And treat those two impostors just the same;
If you can bear to hear the truth you've spoken
Twisted by knaves to make a trap of fools,
Or watch the things you gave your life to broken,
And stoop and build 'em up with wornout tools;

If you can make one heap of all your winnings
And risk it on one turn of pitch-and-toss,
And lose, and start again at your beginnings
And never breathe a word about your loss;
If you can force your heart and nerve and sinew
To serve your turn long after they are gone,
And so hold on when there is nothing in you
Except the Will which says to them: "Hold on."
If you can talk with crowds and keep your virtue,
Or walk with kings—nor lose the common touch;
If neither foes nor loving friends can hurt you;
If all men count with you, but none too much;
If you can fill the unforgiving minute
With sixty seconds' worth of distance run —
Yours is the Earth and everything that's in it,
And—which is more—you'll be a Man, my son.

Name

A WORD TO THE WISE

WIZARD WISDOM

"A stitch in time saves nine." "Fools rush in where angels fear to tread." "Look before you leap." These are some of the many proverbs or wise sayings we hear or read often. These quotes express ideas far deeper than the literal meaning of the words. For instance, the first saying below does not apply only to the task of gathering eggs from a hen's nest and putting them in a basket. What is its hidden or deeper meaning?
For each saying below, write your own explanation of its implied (hidden) meaning.

1. Don't put all your eggs in one basket. ______
2. Every cloud has a silver lining. ______
3. The nail that sticks up will be hammered down. ______
4. A bird in the hand is worth two in the bush. ______
5. Beware of wolves in sheeps' clothing. ______
6. The early bird gets the worm. ______
7. The squeaky wheel gets the oil. ______
8. Strike while the iron is hot. ______
9. Look before you leap. ______
10. A fool and his money are soon parted. ______
11. Fish and visitors smell in three days. ______
12. A rolling stone gathers no moss. ______
13. Keep your head in a crisis. ______
14. A stitch in time saves nine. ______
15. You made your bed—you lie in it. ______

16. Which two sayings are very similar in their meaning? #'s ______ & ______.

Name ______

PUZZLEMENTS

Don't be fooled by the two simple paragraphs below. They are a lot trickier than they might look! However, if you both read and think carefully, you should have no trouble straightening out the puzzling questions.

Kristy is the third daughter of a doctor, but the doctor is not her father. She has one younger brother, Mike, and three older brothers. Joseph is Mike's father. He is an engineer and has seven children.

1. Who is Kristy's father? ____________
2. How many sisters does she have?_____
3. Are the sisters older or younger? ____________
4. How many brothers? ____________
5. What does Kristy's mother do for a living? ____________
6. Who is youngest in the family? ____________
7. How many people are in the family? ____________
8. What detail in this paragraph did you not need to answer the above questions? ____________

Peter's Uncle Dap is his mother's brother. He lives next door to Jamie's Aunt Tess who is her mother's sister. Jamie is Peter's sister. Marty is Jamie's brother.

9. Who is Peter's aunt? ____________
10. Who is Jamie's uncle? ____________
11. Does Dap have a brother? ____________
12. Is Tess Dap's Aunt? ____________
13. How many people in the story are related to Jamie? ____________
14. What detail of the story is not helpful in sorting out relationships? ____________

Name ____________

STORY BUILDING

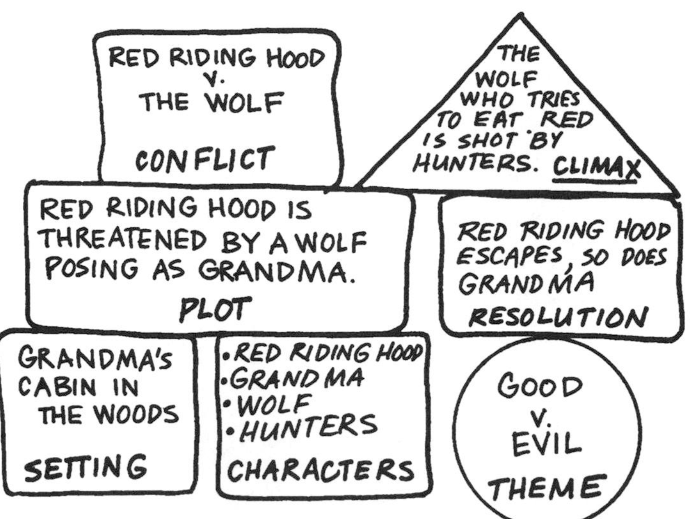
RED RIDING HOOD
V.
THE WOLF
CONFLICT
THE WOLF WHO TRIES TO EAT RED IS SHOT BY HUNTERS. CLIMAX
RED RIDING HOOD IS THREATENED BY A WOLF POSING AS GRANDMA.
PLOT
RED RIDING HOOD ESCAPES, SO DOES GRANDMA
RESOLUTION
GRANDMA'S CABIN IN THE WOODS
SETTING
•RED RIDING HOOD
•GRANDMA
•WOLF
•HUNTERS
CHARACTERS
GOOD
V.
EVIL
THEME

Elements of a Good Story

Setting - When and where the story takes place
Plot - Main events of the story
Conflict - A problem around which the story centers
Climax - The turning point (point of greatest intensity) of the story
Resolution - The ending—tells how the problem is solved
Theme - The main message of the story which illustrates a universal truth
Characterization - The way the players or the characters of the story develop through what they say, what they do, and what others say about them

It is easy to identify the parts or elements of a good story. They are the same, whether it is a nursery tale or a long novel. Sharpen your identification skills by reviewing the elements of the familiar "Little Red Riding Hood" story. Then use the second set of blocks to recreate the story of "The Three Bears" or any other story you have read.

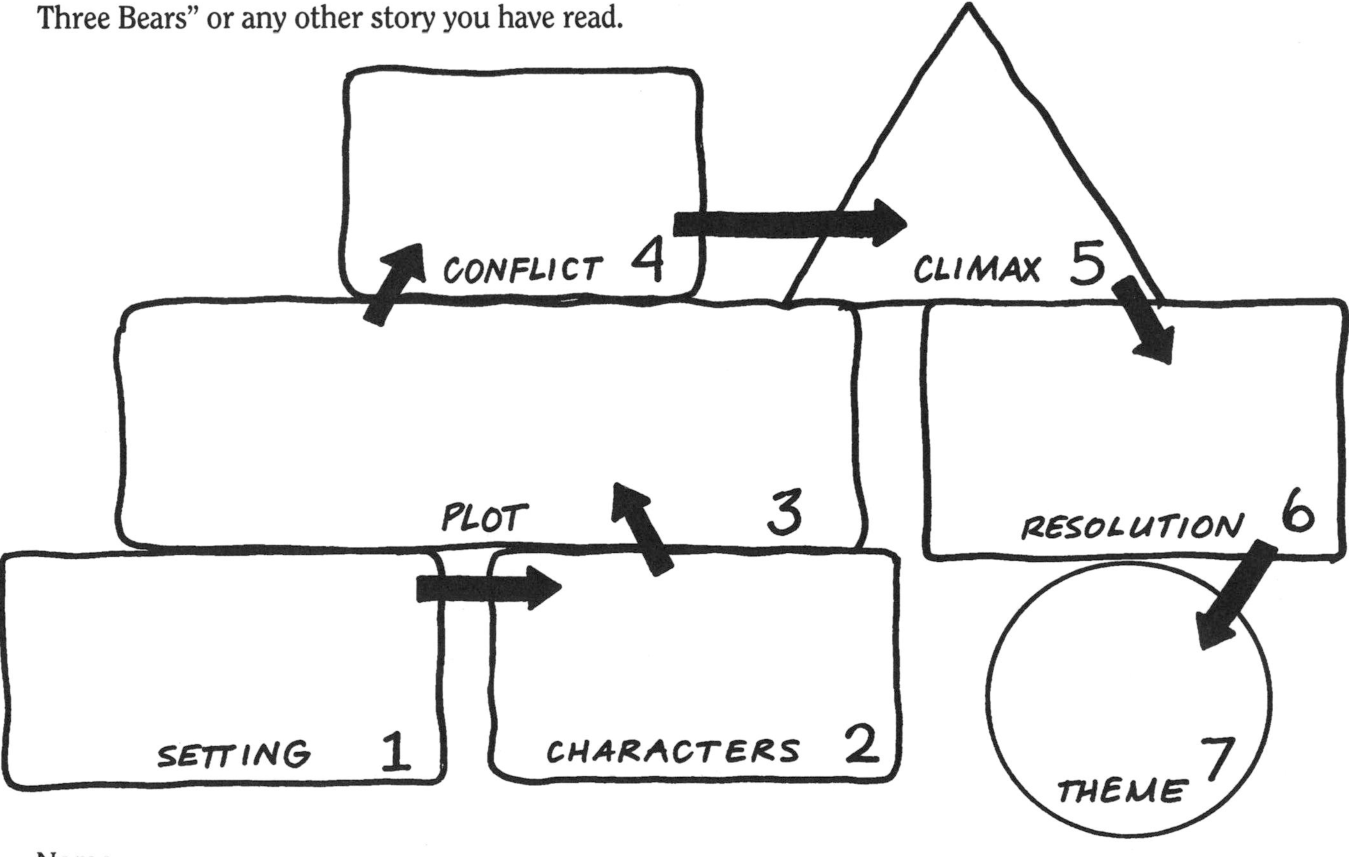
CONFLICT 4
CLIMAX 5
PLOT 3
RESOLUTION 6
SETTING 1
CHARACTERS 2
THEME 7

Name

A FAMOUS LINEUP

A sprinkling of curious tidbits of information makes an otherwise boring collection of facts far more fascinating. Across the centuries, historians have written volumes about famous people. But only the cleverest of these writers have presented information in a way that is fun to read.

Read these excerpts from the works of a young, modern-day researcher. Then see if you can create a timeline that shows the order in which the famous subjects of this research lived and worked. Use the space provided on the next page (page 25).

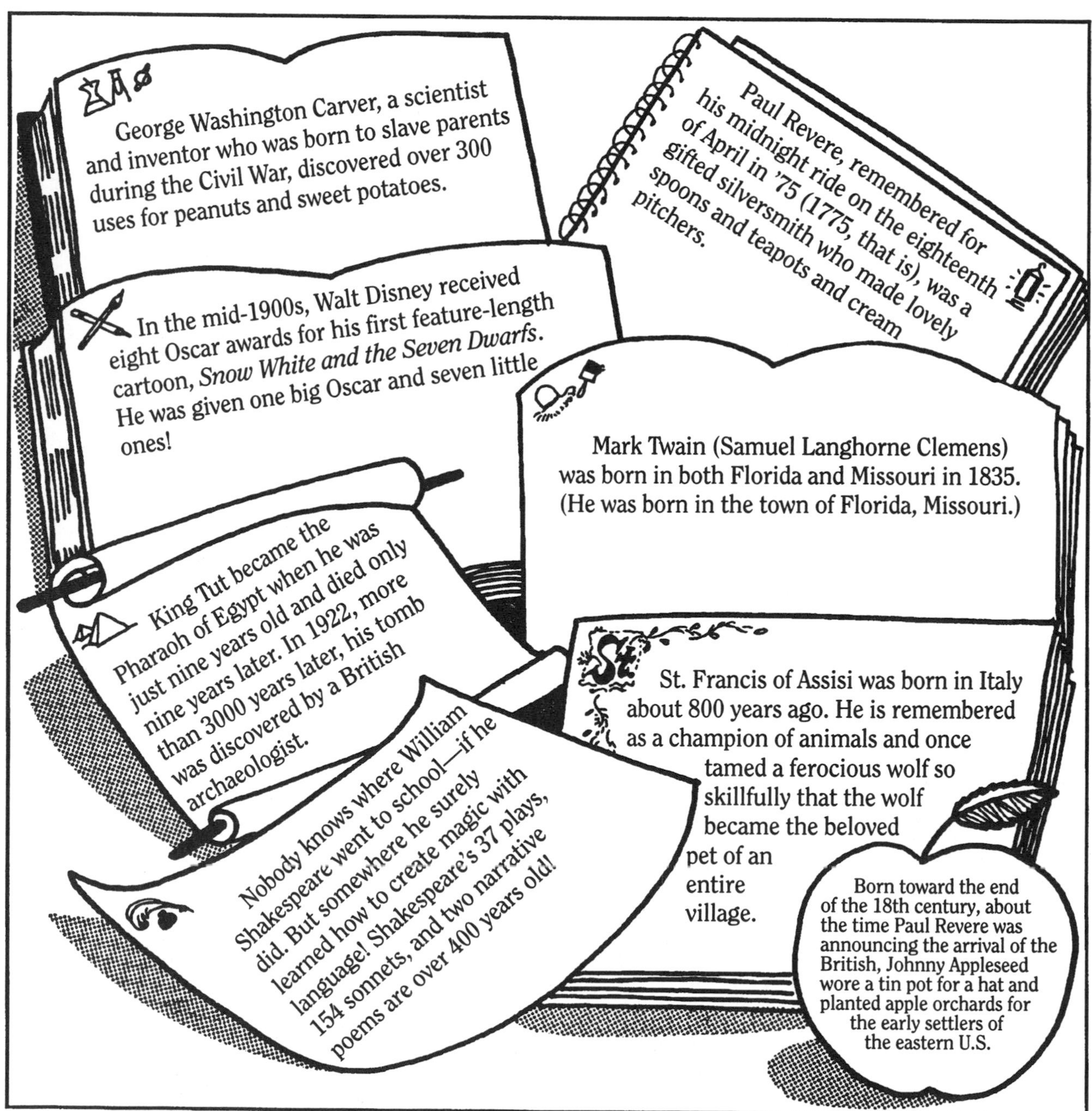
George Washington Carver, a scientist and inventor who was born to slave parents during the Civil War, discovered over 300 uses for peanuts and sweet potatoes.
Paul Revere, remembered for his midnight ride on the eighteenth of April in '75 (1775, that is), was a gifted silversmith who made lovely spoons and teapots and cream pitchers.
In the mid-1900s, Walt Disney received eight Oscar awards for his first feature-length cartoon, *Snow White and the Seven Dwarfs*. He was given one big Oscar and seven little ones!
Mark Twain (Samuel Langhorne Clemens) was born in both Florida and Missouri in 1835. (He was born in the town of Florida, Missouri.)
King Tut became the Pharaoh of Egypt when he was just nine years old and died only nine years later. In 1922, more than 3000 years later, his tomb was discovered by a British archaeologist.
St. Francis of Assisi was born in Italy about 800 years ago. He is remembered as a champion of animals and once tamed a ferocious wolf so skillfully that the wolf became the beloved pet of an entire village.
Nobody knows where William Shakespeare went to school—if he did. But somewhere he surely learned how to create magic with language! Shakespeare's 37 plays, 154 sonnets, and two narrative poems are over 400 years old!
Born toward the end of the 18th century, about the time Paul Revere was announcing the arrival of the British, Johnny Appleseed wore a tin pot for a hat and planted apple orchards for the early settlers of the eastern U.S.

Use with page 25.

A TIMELINE OF FAMOUS FOLK

Use with page 24.

LISTEN, GUYS,
I WANT TO READ MY 154th SONNET. WHAT DO YOU SAY?
APPLESAUCE!
PEANUTS!
GET ME A HORSE, QUICK!
I'M A WRITER, TOO.
MUMMY!!
MERCIFUL HEAVENS.
My best friend is a very famous mouse!
SQUEAK

Name

BORROWED TROUBLE

LET ME TELL YOU,
LET ME TELL YOU . . .

Have you ever had this experience? You meet a friend who is so excited that as she tells you what's happened she gets the events completely scrambled up. You couldn't possibly understand the story! Being able to relay events in the order they happen is an important skill. If you can't do it—no one is going to figure out what happened when.

Read the story below and follow the instructions to develop your storytelling skills.

As Albert rode home on the school bus, he thought about the wonderful time he'd had at the class picnic. There had been lots of food and games, but he'd enjoyed the softball game most of all. Since he'd borrowed his older brother's ball and brought it for everyone to use, the kids let him be a team captain, and his team had won. Later his friend, Ralph, asked Albert if he could borrow the ball and bring it back to him at school the next day. Albert had agreed and was feeling extra good that he had made Ralph happy.

When the bus stopped, Albert stepped off whistling. As he walked toward his house, he saw his brother and three friends sitting on the front porch. All the boys had bats and gloves and looked as if they were waiting for something. Suddenly Albert felt sick. He realized that they were waiting for him to bring back the borrowed ball . . .

Write the order of events, so far, in the unfinished story. When you have made a list of them, add to the sequence to show how you would finish the story.

1. ____

2. ____

3. ____

4. ____

5. ____

6. ____

7. ____

8. ____

9. ____

10. ____

Name ____

FLIP-FLOP

Jason mistakenly ate a grub worm which inhabited a large tomato he had cut up for his salad. He got sick!

Jason became ill when he discovered one half of a grub worm in his salad.

FLIP
CAUSE: JASON ATE A GRUBWORM
MMMM
EFFECT: HE GOT SICK
FLOP
EFFECT: JASON BECAME ILL
GROAN
CAUSE: HE DISCOVERED "½" A GRUB WORM
LADIES AND GENTLEMEN, PLEASE.......
...DON'T TRY THIS EXPERIMENT AT HOME !

Cause and effect in relationships can happen in either of two ways. The cause may be stated, followed by the effect, or they may flip-flop, as in the example above, and the effect may precede the cause.

Before each pair of sentences below, write **C-E** if the order of the sentences is cause-effect, and **E-C** if the order is reversed.

_____ 1. Jessica's parents sold her drum set. It was responsible for more noise than they (and the neighbors) could bear.

_____ 2. Brandon left his towel on the beach. A helpful lifeguard took him to the lost and found.

_____ 3. Hundreds of hikers were stranded in an early season snowstorm. National Park rangers had to work many hours of overtime in rescue efforts.

_____ 4. Lisa got a poor grade because she didn't do her homework.

_____ 5. In spite of the howling storm, Tom was warm and cozy in his tent. A bear had snuggled up next to him.

_____ 6. The students snickered when Mike entered the room. Later, he discovered his clothes were not properly zipped.

_____ 7. Several mice had escaped from the science lab; thus the seventh graders were doing most of their studying sitting on tabletops.

_____ 8. The class gulped audibly when they saw Miss Benson's purple-streaked hair.

_____ 9. Rosa's bank account was empty after she bought her skateboard.

_____ 10. The principal started interrogating students after she found the flag in the locker room and the volleyball uniforms flying from the flagpole.

Name

FACT FINDER

"He's the funniest guy in the school!" "Mara's the best player on the soccer team!" These sound like statements of fact, but they are opinions. If you lined up all the guys in the school, asked 100 people to vote for who was funniest, and all 100 voted for one boy, then would the first statement become a fact? If you collected the statistics on every game the team had ever played and showed that Mara's stats were better than everyone else's, would that make the second statement a true fact? What about all the players who supported Mara, passed her the ball, defended against the other team, and without whom she could never have scored any goals?

Telling the difference between statement of fact and opinion can be tricky. Read the following "factual" report, written by a young visitor to the state of Hawaii. Underline or highlight any sentence or part of a sentence that is opinion rather than fact.

Hawaii is the newest of the fifty United States and is the most beautiful state of all. It is 6,450 square miles in area and is the 47th largest state. It is actually made up of a chain of islands, and is the only state in the union completely surrounded by water. No wonder it is the favorite playground of mainland Americans! The many beaches and miles of warm surf, moderate temperature, the long hours of sunshine, beautiful sunsets, and brilliantly colored flowers that bloom year round have made this state into a tourist spot sought out by people from all over the world.

Main products of Hawaii are pineapple, sugar cane, tropical fruits, coffee, macadamia nuts and fish. Recreation and tourism are the main sources of income for many islanders. The first settlers to Hawaii brought much of their Polynesian tradition to the islands. Their dances (including the hula), religions, chants and customs contribute much to the beauty and richness of island life. Over the years, new arrivals have come to seek their fortunes, build homes, and raise families, so the culture has taken on additional facets and flavors. For this reason, modern Hawaii is sometimes referred to as the "population melting pot of the world," making it a fascinating place to live and a delightful place to vacation.

1. How many phrases contain opinion?

   ____

2. Think of a good title for this report:

   ____

   ____

   ____

3. Tell why each phrase in answer #1 is not a fact.

   a.______________________

   b.______________________

   c.______________________

   d.______________________

Name ______________________

U.F.O.

(UNEARTHING FACT & OPINION)

How well can you differentiate between fact and opinion? Below is a mixed list of facts and opinions. Identify each statement with an **F** (if it's a fact) or an **O** (if it's an opinion).

Have someone time you to see how long it takes. Ready—set—go!

_____1. Girls are braver than boys.

_____2. Blue and yellow make green.

_____3. A dog will attack you only if you act afraid.

_____4. Bread can be made from water and flour.

_____5. Frogs are amphibians.

_____6. Colorado has beautiful mountains.

_____7. Today, computer E-mail is the most efficient means of communication.

_____8. Julius Caesar was a Roman citizen.

_____9. My father is 40 years old.

_____10. The nation's worst problem is crime.

_____11. All Americans should be patriotic.

_____12. If you eat your vegetables, you will be healthy.

_____13. You will love my grandmother's cooking!

_____14. Teenagers love to dance.

_____15. The best skiing is in the Swiss Alps.

_____16. There are twelve months in a year.

_____17. Boys keep very messy bedrooms.

_____18. Democracy is the best form of government.

_____19. Ghost stories are scary.

_____20. The United States is bigger than England.

_____21. This lesson is easy.

TELL US EVERY FACT YOU KNOW

Check your answers. Then ask a friend to do the activity. Who is faster at unearthing fact and opinion? Who is most accurate?

Name ________________________________

A BELLY LAUGH BALLAD

A ballad is a poem or rhyme that tells a short story and is meant to be sung. Many ballads are love stories or tragic stories of death and betrayal. A few are humorous. Here is a very funny English ballad, written on a universal theme. Some of the words have been paraphrased from Old English. You will be able to figure out the others!

GET UP AND BAR THE DOOR

It fell about tne Martinmas time,
And a gay time it was then,
When our goodwife got puddings to make,
She'd boiled them in the pan.

The wind so cold blew south and north.
And blew into the floor;
Quoth our goodman to our goodwife
"Get up and bar the door."

"My hand is in my housework,
Goodman, you may see
And it will not be barred for a hundred years
If it has to be barred by me!"

So they made a pact between them two,
They made it firm and sure.
That whoever was the first to speak
Should rise and bar the door.

Then by there came two gentlemen,
At twelve o'clock at night,
They could neither see house nor hall
Nor coal nor candlelight.

They called, "Is this a rich man's house,
Or do you say it's poor?"
But ne'er a word would one of them speak
For barring of the door.

And first they ate the white puddings
And then they ate the black:
Tho the goodwife thought much to herself,
Yet ne'er a word she spake.

Then said one robber to another
"Here, man, take ye my knife;
Do ye take off the old man's beard
And I'll kiss the goodwife."

"But there's no water in the house,
And what shall we do then?"
"We'll use the pudding water
That boils in the pan!"

Up then started our goodman.
An angry man was he.
"Will ye kiss my wife before my eyes
And scald me with pudding bree?"

Then up and started our goodwife,
Did three skips on the floor;
"Goodman, you've spoken the foremost word;
Get up and bar the door!"

I WILL NOT SPEAK A WORD!
NOR SHALL I...

1. What is the theme of this ballad?

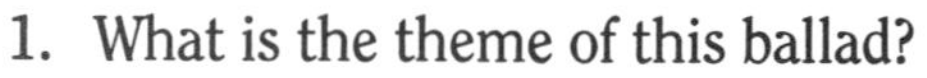

2. What serious point or moral is made by this funny story?

3. Use the back of the page to write a brief summary of the story in this ballad.

Name

LAWMAKERS GONE LOONY?

In the state of North Carolina, it is illegal to sing out of tune! There was once a law in Boston, Massachusetts, that said no one could take a bath in that city without a written prescription from the doctor. A Carmel, California, law prohibited women from taking a bath in a business office! Some of these laws are still on the books, although they may no longer be enforced. Pretty silly, aren't they?

People need laws to help them live together safely and harmoniously, but some laws are very peculiar. It boggles the mind to figure out what their purpose might have been.

Below is a list of laws that were actually enforced at one time in the United States. Read the laws. Think about why each law might have been written. Can you generalize what kinds of goals lawmakers had in mind when these laws were first enacted? At the bottom of the page, name three or four general purposes for making such laws. Then categorize each of the laws below by labeling them with the letter of one of the purposes you wrote.

A LIST OF PECULIAR LAWS

_____ Walking with your shoelaces untied was against the law in Maine.
_____ If you were over the age of 88, it was illegal to ride a motorcycle in Idaho Falls, Idaho.
_____ In Phoenix, Arizona, all men were required to wear pants when they came to the town.
_____ In New Jersey, you were breaking the law if you delayed a pigeon.
_____ Trapping a mouse without a hunting license was against the law in California.
_____ In Maine, it was against the law to set fire to a mule.
_____ At one time, you would break the law in Louisiana if you whistled on Sunday.
_____ All beavers in Connecticut have the legal right to build a dam.
_____ In Minnesota, women's underwear and men's underwear could not be hung on the same clothesline together.
_____ It was against the law in Oxford, Ohio, for a woman to undress in front of a photograph of a man.
_____ Blowing your nose in public was against the law in Waterville, Maine.
_____ A dog has a legal right to bite, according to law in Colorado Springs, Colorado.

Done at last!

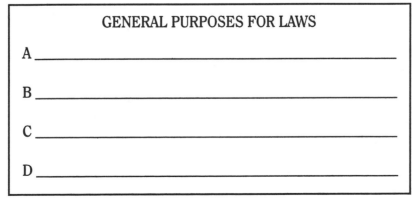

GENERAL PURPOSES FOR LAWS

A _______________________________________

B _______________________________________

C _______________________________________

D _______________________________________

Now, Now! Mixing "un-mention-ables" on the line is illegal in Minnesota, Mrs. Swensen.

Name

TALES THAT TEACH

A hungry wolf could not find enough to eat. He saw a flock of sheep nearby, but they were so carefully tended by the shepherds that he could not safely steal in to grab his dinner. One night, he came upon a sheepskin that had been left by one of the shepherds. He placed it over his body and sneaked quietly into the pasture, taking his place amidst the crowded flock, unnoticed by the shepherds. And soon, he led a little lamb away to slaughter.

The next evening, he became braver and followed the shepherd back to the fold with the flock, dreaming of a tasty overnight feast. But the shepherd decided that he would have mutton for supper, and when he went with his knife to the fold, guess which was the first "lamb" he came upon! The lamb he killed turned out to be the wolf!

The logical conclusion or lesson that one may learn from this story is a deceiver often brings himself to destruction.

Carefully read the next story and see if you can draw the conclusion that the writer intended.

There was once a man who owned an amazing goose. Every morning, he visited the nest, and the goose had laid a golden egg. The man sold the eggs in the market and began to get rich. But soon, he became impatient; the goose laid only one egg a day and he wanted more money faster. Suddenly an idea came to him. He would cut open the goose and get all the eggs at once. But of course, when he cut the goose, he found not even one egg, and his wonderful goose lay dead!

1. What is the logical conclusion or lesson in this tale?

 ____

Find the book *Aesop's Fables* and read these four tales: "The Lion & the Mouse," "The Boy Who Cried 'Wolf!'" "The Fox & The Grapes," and " The Ants & the Grasshopper." For each item below, write the name of the tale that reaches the conclusion or lesson shown.

2. Some people pretend to despise what they cannot obtain.

 Title:______________________________________

3. Liars cannot expect to be believed, even when they tell the truth.

 Title:______________________________________

4. You reap what you sow!

 Title:______________________________________

5. A kindness is never wasted.

 Title:______________________________________

DON'T MESS WITH ME!

Name ______________________________________

THE DEAD TELL TALES

Tombstones often tell stories about the lives of the people who lie under them. Some of the epitaphs or inscriptions of long ago seem very peculiar by today's standards, but they give us some fascinating information about the people of those times. Read each inscription below and answer the question that follows.

A. Abel Silas McMahon, 1884, age 2 years

In a moment he fled;
He ran to the cistern and raised the lid—
His father looked in, then did behold
His child lay dead and cold.

How did little Abel die? ____________________

____

B. Elisha Woodruff, 1816, age 70

How shocking to the human mind
The log did him to powder grind.
God did command his soul away
His summonings we must all obey.

What caused Mr. Woodruff's death? ____________

____

C. Seth Miller, 1848, age 46

My wife from me departed
And robbed me like a knave
Which caused me broken hearted
To descend into my grave.
My children took an active part
And to doom me did contrive,
Which struck a dagger to my heart
Which I could not survive.

What were the circumstances that lead to Seth's death?

____

____

D. Sally Dughy, 69 years old

In the midst of society she lived alone.
Beneath the mockery of cheerfulness, she hid deep woe.
In the ruin of her intellect, the kindness of her heart survived.
She perished in the snow on the night of Feb. 25, 1854.

What deductions can you make about Sally's life from her epitaph?

____

JIM
1800
1801
LIFE IS SHORT
JOE
1800
1899
LIFE CAN SPAN A CENTURY

THE STORY OF BROTHERS

E. Joseph Hill, 1826, age 65

My sledge and hammer be reclined
My bellows too have lost their wind;
My fir's extinguished, forge decay'd
And in the dust my vise is laid.
My iron's spent, my coals are gone,
The last nail's drove, my work is done.

Can you guess Mr. Hill's profession? ____________

____

F. Caroline Newcomb, 1812, age 4 mos.

She tasted Life's bitter cup
Refused to drink the portion up
But turned her little head aside
Disgusted with the taste and died.

What is implied about the reason for this child's death?

____

____

G. This inscription was found on the tombs of two teenagers who died in 1814.

How many roses perish in their bloom,
How many suns alas go down at noon.

Write your own interpretation of those lines.

____

____

____

Name ______________________________

THE END FROM THE BEGINNING

It's always fun to hear the beginning of a provocative story and then guess what the ending might be. "Hints" may be suggested or implied, but not revealed in the opening lines. Sometimes you have to "read between the lines" to find these hints.

Below are the beginnings of several very famous poems. Read these opening lines, then use the space provided below each partial poem to write what you think the outcome or ending of the poem might be—or could be. If you wish, you can research the real poem to find out how the original author ended it. (Your idea does not have to agree, but it would be interesting to compare the two outcomes.)

From "The Raven" by Edgar Allen Poe

Once upon a midnight dreary, while I pondered, weak and weary,
Over many a quaint and curious volume of forgotten lore —
While I nodded, nearly napping, suddenly there came a tapping,
As of someone gently rapping, rapping at my chamber door.

____

____

____

____

From a limerick in Edward Lear's *Book of Nonsense*, 1846

There was a young lady whose nose
Continually prospers and grows;
When it grew out of sight,
She exclaimed in a fright,

____!

From "The Highwayman" by Alfred Noyes

The wind was a torrent of darkness among the gusty trees.
The moon was a ghostly galleon tossed upon cloudy seas.
The road was a ribbon of moonlight over the purple moor,
And the highwayman came riding—riding—riding —
The highwayman came riding, up to the old inn-door.

____

____

____

____

Name ______________________________________

LOOKING IN THE MIRROR

Literature is like a mirror. As we read, we often see ourselves or situations from our world. Through thousands of years of civilization, human beings don't seem to change very much. That's why stories that were written long ago still apply to us today.
Below is one of Aesop's famous fables.

One fine day in the late fall, a family of ants was busy drying and storing the bits of grain and seeds they had gathered during the long summer months when a very hungry grasshopper approached them and begged for a bite to eat.

"What?" cried the ants, surprised. "Where is the store of food you have made for the winter? What have you been doing this whole long summer?"

"I didn't have time to collect and store food," explained the grasshopper. "I was so busy making music, that before I realized it, the summer was gone by, and now I have nothing available to feed myself and my family."

"So you were busy making music, were you?" replied the ants. "Very well, while we enjoy the winter feasting on what we have labored so hard to collect, you shall dance to your music!" And they turned their backs on the grasshopper and went on with their work.

Use the space below to make a list of situations in which human beings behave very much like the ants and the grasshopper. Be able to explain your choices to a friend or your classmates.

FEED THE GRASSHOPPER

A CRUMB FOR A TUNE?

Name

IT CAN HAPPEN . . .

Now and then, you read something that just seems to reach out and grab you by the heart—it stops you and makes you think. Often your response is, "Yes, that's how I would feel if that happened to me . . ."

Two young writers created the pieces on this page. The first is by a third grader, the second, by a high school student. As you read them, take notice of the similarities and differences between the two works.

I.

There is a strange quiet in your house.

Your father is reading the newspaper, but not turning any pages.

Your mother is fixing dinner and slamming every cupboard door she opens. Nobody notices that you didn't hang up your coat. Nobody reminds you to practice the piano. That's how to tell there is an argument going on between your parents.

II.

About every two years, my Aunt Ruth would go out and buy a new navy blue suit to be laid out in. She said it was important to look your best at your funeral. And every time we visited her house, all the cousins peeked in her closet and giggled at the lineup of unworn suits she had collected over the years. We laughed because Aunt Ruth was so young and sparkly—not the kind who was, at all, ready to up and die.

I remember how I grew up and got to be a teenager. But I don't remember how lively Aunt Ruth got to be this old, grey lady, lying so very still in a navy blue suit.

1. Identify the tone of the two pieces (honest, anxious, morbid, friendly, distraught, realistic, sarcastic, frivolous, etc.).
   a. Tone of # I. ______________________
   b. Tone of # II. ______________________
2. Which piece would you characterize as most moving or poignant? __________
3. Which has more tension? ______________________
4. Which seems to have taken place over a longer period of time? __________
5. In which piece is the writer mainly an observer? ______________
6. What is the point of view of # I? ______________________
7. What is the point of view of # II? ______________________
8. Which is NOT a true statement? Circle one.
   a. Both pieces are about the same subject.
   b. Both pieces are apparently a result of experience.
   c. Both pieces speak about a child's view of adults.
   d. Both pieces deal with an emotional event or crisis.

Name ______________________

WE THE PEOPLE . . .

VOTE
THIS MEANS YOU

On a certain day in November, millions of Americans stand in lines to vote for their preferred candidate. All evening long, they sit with bated breath and crossed fingers, watching a 13- or 19- or 22-inch screen as slowly, one by one, each state of the union turns a different color, showing which candidates won which votes.

Three months later, a young man—or maybe an old one—either ordinary looking or very handsome, Catholic or Protestant, liberal or conservative—steps up on a Capitol Hill platform and places his right hand on a Bible (should he be an atheist, it makes no difference), and swears to uphold the Constitution of the United States, which he, most likely, has never read.

Four years, he works long and hard, breaking most campaign promises he made. He fights with Congress and frequently disrupts prime-time television to deliver lengthy speeches on the American economy or to explain to the American people why it is their duty to help some other country who would rather we didn't.

America, land of the free, home of the hypocrite.

– Lindsey Williams, grade 12

1. Do you think that this piece is a fair representation of the election of a U.S. president? Why or why not? Explain your response.

   ____

   ____

2. Choose the word that best describes the tone of this piece: (Circle one.)
   objective critical cynical supportive light-hearted

3. What specific words or phrases in the writing contribute to this tone?

   ____

   ____

4. Is the article convincing? Why or why not?

   ____

   ____

5. Summarize the main message of the article in just one sentence.

   ____

   ____

6. Which statement can you best support?
   _____ a. The author is obviously ignorant about the U.S. democratic process.
   _____ b. The author sees the democratic process as lacking in integrity.
   _____ c. This article has no truth in it.
   _____ d. This article very accurately portrays the decline of democracy.

Name ____

GOOD INTENTIONS OR INVENTIONS?

People often misuse words with which they are familiar, but don't quite "have a handle on." Unwittingly, they substitute a word they know, a word that has a very different meaning. See if you can catch the misused word in each quote and replace it with the word intended by each speaker. (Circle the word, and write the correction in the space at the end of each sentence.)
By the way, these misused words are called "malapropisms." This word originated from a character in Sheridan's *The Rivals* named Mrs. Malaprop whose misuse of words created a humorous effect.

1. Man paying his hotel bill: "I'm here to pay my accidentals." ____________
2. Modern athletes have longer careers than athletes of the past because of Arabic exercises. ____________
3. Speaker at an awards banquet: "I want to congratulate each of you for having extinguished yourselves." ____________
4. This event is unparalyzed in the state's history. ____________
5. We need to set a predicate of excellence in performance. ____________
6. On a restaurant menu: "Dreaded veal cutlet with potatoes in cream." ____________
7. School looking for volunteer teachers: Tudors needed! ____________
8. Abe Lincoln signed the Emasculation Proclamation, which freed the slaves. ____________
9. We were laughing historically at my mother's new hairdo. ____________
10. Motorists need to stop for presbyterians walking across the street. ____________
11. Governments ruled by kings and queens are called mockeries. ____________
12. There was little water, so farmers had to irritate their crops. ____________

911
There goes the ambience

Can you think of a few more malapropisms?

____

____

____

Name ____________

OOPS!

IT'S DÉJÀ VU ALL OVER AGAIN
MADAM De BUNKUM

Explain what's wrong about each of the following statements.

1. Four people were killed, one seriously, and eight more received slight injuries.

   ____

2. One word sums up the responsibility of any vice-president, and that word is "to be prepared."

   ____

3. A bachelor's life is no life for a single man.

   ____

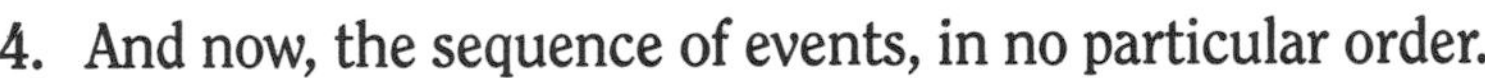

4. And now, the sequence of events, in no particular order.

   ____

5. Today is an absolutely perfect day, and it's going to be even more perfect tomorrow.

   ____

6. These are so valuable, you should buy hundreds and save them for your ancestors.

   ____

7. It's permanent for now.

   ____

8. He's overpaid, but he's worth it.

   ____

9. Sign on a London street: No entry except for access.

   ____

10. Space is almost infinite.

    ____

11. Here is a plan for having some spontaneous fun.

    ____

12. It's déjà vu all over again!

    ____

Name ______________________________

CAMPUS NEWS

Vol. 90 Issue 13 September 27

SPEAKING OUT ON HOMEWORK

by Sara Frank

An adult work day is eight hours. The work day for a high school student, especially a serious student, often exceeds that by two or more hours. Why should 14-to 17-year-olds have heavier workloads and work expectations than working adults?

How much homework should be given to high school students is a much debated issue these days. I would like to argue that high school students are given altogether too much homework. Students at Ashland High School say they average about 3 hours of homework per school night. That averages out to about 45 minutes per class. Often it is more than that—an hour or more for each class. In addition, they put in several hours each weekend on long-term assignments, book reports, and projects. Most kids also take part in after-school activities such as sports and clubs or jobs, which take up the afternoon and early evening. This doesn't leave many hours free before bedtime, and what time there is must be crammed full of homework. What this adds up to for many students like myself is that they start the day on the bus at 6:50 A.M. and arrive home at about 7:15 P.M. This means that after over 12 hours of school and school-related activities, they begin 2–3 hours of homework.

Teachers and many parents say that kids need a good amount of homework to help the learning process. They say kids need to practice what they learned in class that day. But shouldn't most of the practicing of new skills be done in the presence of the teacher? Since most high school classes meet 250 minutes or more a week (that's over 4 hours for each class), it seems that practice and at least a good part of individual homework could be done in class.

Doctors agree that teenagers need 8–10 hours of sleep a night to stay healthy. With such busy schedules, this amount of homework is hard to fit in with an adequate amount of sleep. High school kids today get worn out, tired, and sick because of the stressful, busy lives they lead. The many hours of homework each week really add to the stress. It robs kids of time to relax, socialize with friends, and do activities with families. It adds a lot of tension to their homes and lives. Teenagers need time to relax and have fun—which is what being a teenager is all about.

I don't believe that eliminating homework altogether is the solution. I am only arguing for a reasonable work load for teenagers. I recommend that teachers just should give less homework. They should teach as much as they can in class so kids can still learn, and have students do work in class where they can supervise and give them help. Teachers need to recognize that we are still kids and need to live a little. It might be good for them to think about whether it's healthy and helpful to learning to have teenagers working 12-hour days. Without the homework load, kids will be able to relieve some of the stress of being in high school. I believe that this, in turn, will actually help them learn better in school. They'll be more alert and healthy because they'll have a sane and enjoyable workday.

1. According to the author, how much time do teenagers spend on homework each week? _______
2. What main arguments does the writer use to substantiate her opinion? _______________
3. If the writer has 3 hours of homework on a given night, how long would that make her "workday" (counting bus ride?)_______________________________________
4. What does the author list as the losses to a teenager due to the long school schedule?

   ____

5. Explain the meaning of the word "turn" as used near the end of the last paragraph.

   ____

   ____

DOG WILL EAT HOMEWORK FOR BISCUITS

Name ____

IN NEED OF A CURE

Over the years, people have had all sorts of interesting remedies for various ailments—wrapping bacon around a sore throat, spreading cow manure on boils, curing a cough by drinking water in which you've soaked toenails—and such. Some are serious; some are rather humorous. Read these cures (written by kids) for common maladies, and answer the questions below.

If acne troubles you, one of these might work:

1. Wash your face every morning with prune juice.
2. Put toothpaste on each spot.
3. Rest 20 minutes a day with wet lettuce leaves lying across your forehead, nose, chin, and cheeks.
4. Rub strawberries or cucumber slices on your skin.
5. Wear a large hat.
6. Wear a high collar.
7. Grow your bangs very, very long.

GUARANTEED
CURE FOR ACNE
TRY IT TODAY

Find a good, healthy cow. Follow her around. (Not too closely.) Scoop up a small amount of cow manure. It won't take much, but it does need to be fresh. Mix this with cream cheese to make a smooth paste. Spread this on your face. Leave it on for 45 minutes each day, then wash it off. If it doesn't work, the cow will take back the manure.

Are you looking for a remedy for troublesome acne?
Alas, my friend, there is none.
Once you've tried them all, and given up—try this!
Glue a chocolate chip to each spot on your face, and nobody will notice the acne.

A BIG HAT HIDES A MULTITUDE OF FLAWS.

Acne troubled me for years; I couldn't find a cure.
I finally bought some paper bags; they did the trick for sure.
I cut some holes for eyes; I cut some for my ears.
I put one on each day for school; it served me well for years.

1. How many different cures are suggested for acne? __________
2. How many ideas are suggested that are not intended to cure the acne but to disguise or distract from it? __________
3. Which "cures" could be serious—and might actually work? __________
4. Which "cures" are probably intended only to amuse readers? __________
5. In the selection about chocolate chips, why do you think the author has used the word "Alas!"?

____

Name __________

ADVANTAGE OR AD NAUSEUM?

The mailboxes of the western world are filled daily with all kinds of advertising and informational pieces. Some pieces attract readers; others disgust the receiver. Many offer a variety of choices and incentives to purchase, join, or subscribe. It's crucial to read ads carefully, so you know what you're getting for your money. Below is an ad designed to attract teenagers to join a teen health club. See if you can read and interpret it to answer the questions on the following page (page 43).

$60
$5 a month
Basic Membership
Ashland Teen
Fitness Center
Includes unlimited use
of all exercise facilities
(except pool) for one
year and subscription
to KEEPFIT
monthly newsletter
Keepfit
$84
$7 a month
basic membership
PLUS unlimited use of
SWIMMING
POOL
$96
$8 a month
Includes above PLUS a
Speed Demon
tank suit with
monogrammed ATFC logo
ATFC
$108
$9 a month
Includes above
PLUS 1-year
subscription to
TEEN FIT
magazine
Teen Fit
$120
$10.00 a
month
above PLUS
invitation for 2
to monthly
DANCE CLUB
dance parties
$132
$11 a month
Above
PLUS 4 all-day,
free passes to
Wet & Wild
Water Park
$144
$12 a month
Includes everything
PLUS 10 free
GUEST
PASSES
PASS
PASS
FOR MORE INFORMATION, RATES,
AND HOURS: PHONE 541-489-0101
FAX 541-489-0102 E-MAIL
TEENFIT@ ATFC.COM.

Use with page 43.

Name

Use with page 42.

Join Now and Receive A
free BONUS gift
YOUR CHOICE
T-SHIRT (S-M-L-XL)
WATER BOTTLE
ATFC
ATFC

Join by March 1

1. What tactics does the ad use to attract teenagers to join the fitness center? ______________________________

2. What subscription comes automatically with all memberships? ______________________________

3. What e-mail address can you use to get the center's hours? ______________________________

4. What monthly fee must you pay to get the magazine subscription? ______________________________

5. What membership benefits do you NOT get if you join at the $10 a month level? ______________________________

6. If passes to the water park cost $15, how much do you save on water passes by joining at the $132 price? ______________________________

7. What benefits would you get for $12 a month that you would not get for $9.00 a month? ______________________________

8. Tickets to the DANCE CLUB parties cost $8 a couple. What do you save by getting these free with a $120 membership over what you'd spend on a $108 membership? ______________________________

9. Which level of membership most interests you (and why)? ______________________________

10. Do you think this ad will be effective in attracting teenagers to join the center? ______________ Explain your answer. ______________________________

11. What must you do to get a free T-shirt or water bottle? ______________________________

Name ______________________________

WHOLES & HOLES

It's Saturday morning. A group of middle-school friends who spent the night at Chad's house woke up to a breakfast of hot chocolate, donuts, and donut holes. Chad's mom could hardly believe the number of donuts and holes these guys consumed! See if you can find on the charts below the information needed to answer the questions that follow.

Donuts Consumed

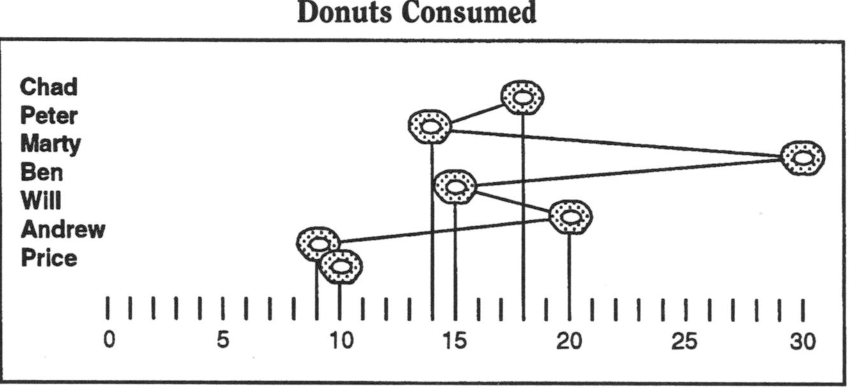
Chad
Peter
Marty
Ben
Will
Andrew
Price
0
5
10
15
20
25
30

Holes Swallowed Whole

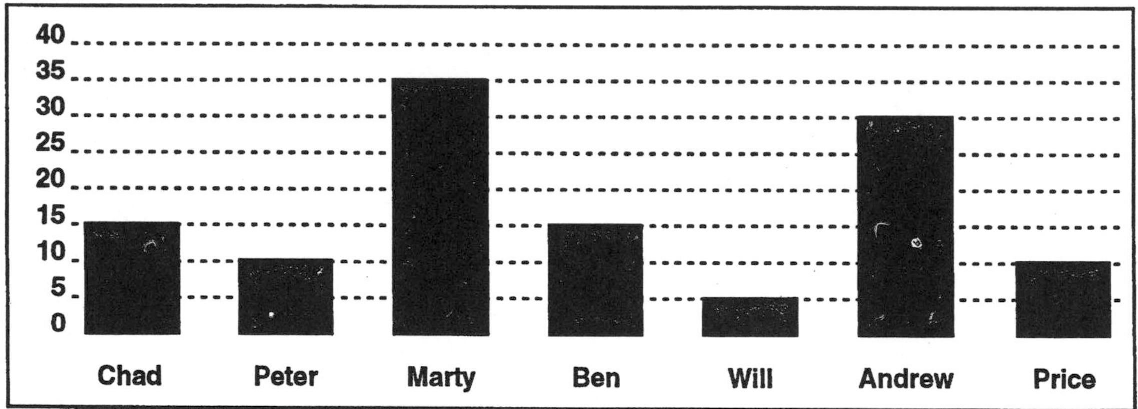
40
35
30
25
20
15
10
5
0
Chad
Peter
Marty
Ben
Will
Andrew
Price

1. Who ate the most donuts? ____________
2. Who ate the fewest holes? ____________
3. Who ate the same number of holes and donuts? ____________
4. Who's the most likely to be "stuffed"? ____________
5. Who ate $\frac{1}{3}$ as many holes as Andrew? ____________
6. Who ate twice as many donuts as Andrew? ____________
7. How many whole donuts were consumed by the boys? ____________
8. How many dozen holes did they devour? ____________
9. Who ate more wholes than holes? ____________
10. Who ate more holes than wholes? ____________

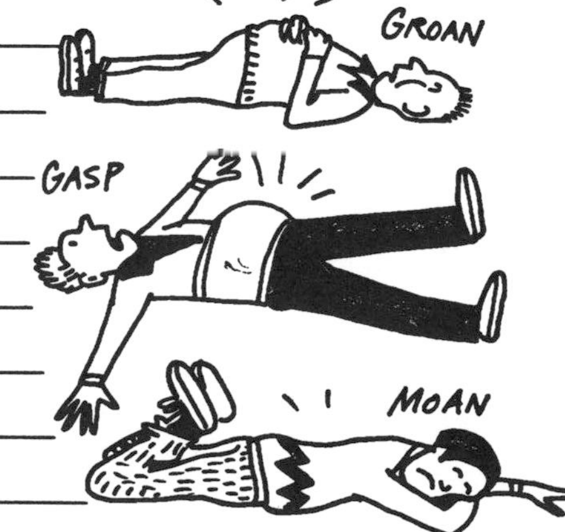
GROAN
GASP
MOAN

Name ____________

FAIR OR FOUL?

Okay, so you can read words! Let's see how sharp you are at interpreting symbols to gain information about the weather.

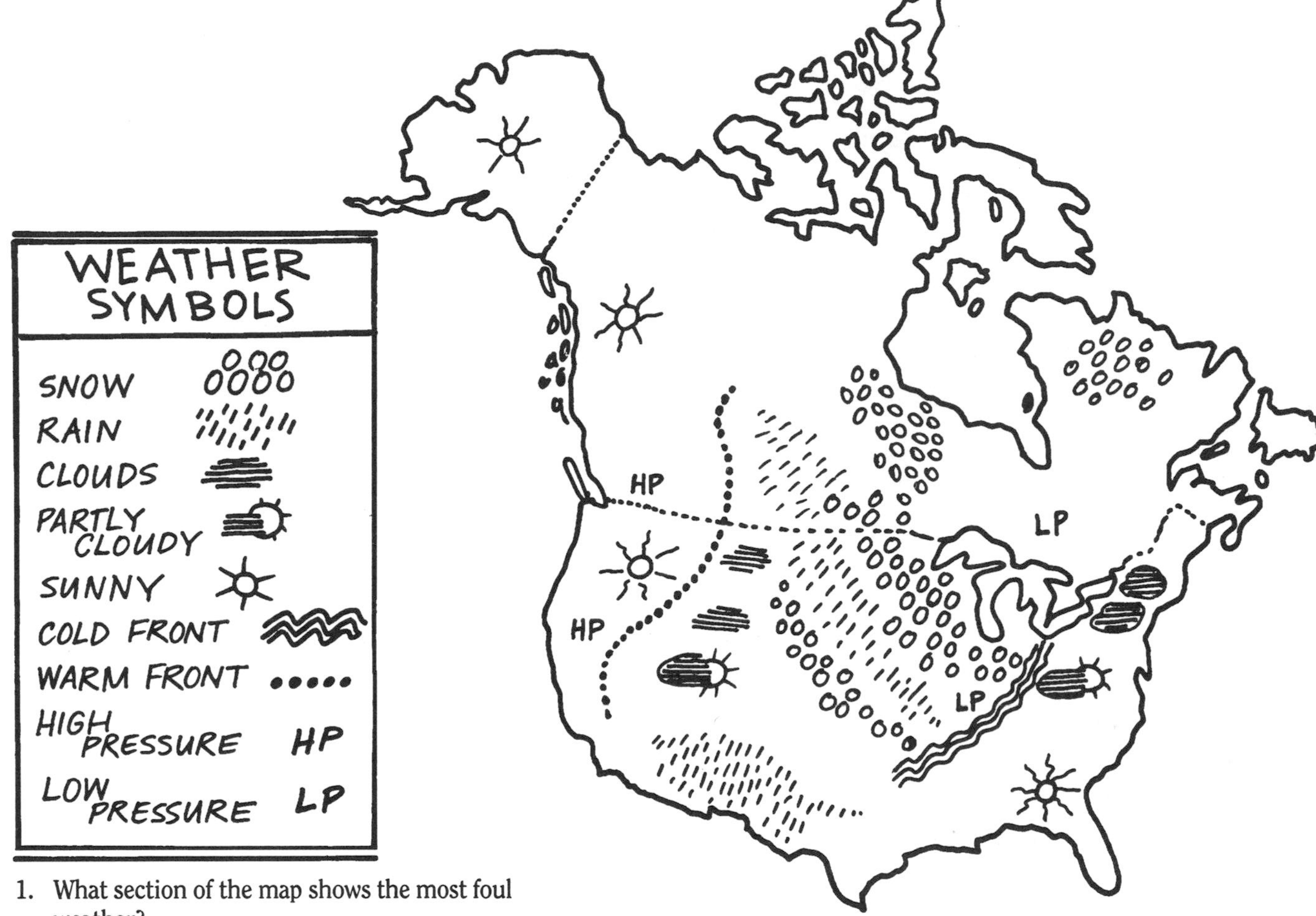
WEATHER SYMBOLS
SNOW
RAIN
CLOUDS
PARTLY CLOUDY
SUNNY
COLD FRONT
WARM FRONT
HIGH PRESSURE HP
LOW PRESSURE LP
HP
HP
LP
LP

1. What section of the map shows the most foul weather?
   N.W. United States / S.E. Canada / N.E. United States / S.W. Alaska / Central United States

2. What section shows fair weather?
   S.W. United States / S.E. United States / N.E. Canada / N.E. United States

3. What type of front is crossing the U.S.–Canadian border?
   high / cold / warm / rainy / clear

4. Where is a high-pressure system located?
   N.W. United States / N.E. Canada /
   S.E. United States / Central U.S. / S.W. Canada

5. What kind of weather exists in the S.W. United States?
   snow / sunny / partly cloudy / rain / heat wave

6. When the cold front moves past the Great Lakes area, what do you predict will happen to the temperatures in the central southeast United States?

   ____

7. What sections of the United States have some spots that are partly cloudy?
   Northwest and South / Western mountains and Central East / Midwest and Southeast / Southwest and Northeast

8. Which of these sections are not showing precipitation?
   S.E. United States / Great Lakes, U.S. region / U.S. Central Plains / N.E. Canada

Name

DOUBLE VIEW

The pieces below were written by high school students. Read both pieces carefully and then . . .

- On the line above each piece, create an appropriate title.
- Identify a single technique used by all three writers.
- Name other literary techniques used by individual authors.
- Decide from what point of view each piece is presented.
- Identify the experience being described by the author of each piece.

Record your responses in the spaces provided on page 47.

I. ______________________________

Temperatures rising at high noon,
Dry, parched, cracking lips
Yearn, burn and turn for
The drips of the succulent shimmer
Of the shimmy sham spam thing-a-ma-wham-bam
Liquid ice.
Trying to halt the frying,
Keep me from dying
While I am sighing, but not lying
About the stream that springs up . . . goosh, goosh, goosh
And cleanses my mouth
Like a spout
That makes me shout
To all about.
Energizing, Revitalizing,
Recognizing that what I need
For survival and revival equals
Two hydros plus one oxy!

— Matt Lehman

II. ______________________________

Every time the phone rings, your heart skips a beat. You have begun to absent-mindedly write senseless poetry again. Your heart feels so full that you are afraid that it just might burst. Your body feels strange and incomplete. You seem to forget more than usual. You notice every red car that passes and hope it might be his. Your auditory senses have improved one hundred percent, except when you are talking to him—then you can't even understand your own words. This is how you know if you have developed a crush.

— Kate Anderson

Use with page 47.

Name ______________________________

DOUBLE VIEW, CONTINUED

Use with page 46.

1. A single technique that is used by both authors is ______________________

2. Some other literary techniques, used by individual authors are:
   I. ______________________
   II. ______________________

3. From what point of view is each piece written?
   I. ______________________
   II. ______________________

4. Explain the experience being described in piece I.

5. Explain the experience being described in piece II.

Name ______________________

ANONYMOUS PORTRAIT

Often an author will create a piece from his or her personal bias. In an effort to engage the readers, stereotypes may be used in the description of a character or a group of people to persuade the audience to share an opinion or merely to amuse them. See if you can identify the writer's attitude and purpose in this piece.

Sleepy-eyed, they enter the learning establishment at 7:43, meeting only the absolute minimum dress code requirements. In first period, they do their homework for second period, and in second period, they do their homework for third period . . . the vicious cycle goes on and on. Their bodies shift on a dime from being goofy and rambunctious to lethargic and sloth-like—being either uncontrollable hellions or stoic sleepers who couldn't care less if the world were ending in two minutes.

Yearning to be revolutionaries, they desire, at once, to be unforgettably awful, lovable, and admirable. This all-inclusive cult, holding the inferiors at bay, evolves into a tightly-knit squadron, struggling together toward tomorrow's aspirations, preserving its identity by body-slamming underclassmen against lockers and by exemplifying the carpe diem philosophy to its max. They are thrill-seekers, determined to suck the marrow out of life—a group of individuals, ascending the social ladder, overcoming numerous obstacles to become the few, the proud, the elite . . . .

— Matt Lehman, senior

1. What do you think is the writer's intended purpose? ______________________________

____

2. What is the tone of the piece? ______________________________

3. Does the writer express a bias? If so, what is it? ______________________________

____

4. Identify and underline the specific words or phrases that create stereotypic images. ______

____

5. About what group of people do you think the piece is written? ______________________

6. Give the piece a fitting title. ______________________________

Name ____

NOT YOUR USUAL GRANDMA

A mother wearing an apron, a little boy with mussed hair and dirty hands, a little girl with an angelic smile and a pink bow in her hair, a college professor with unkempt hair and glasses on his nose, a secretary filing her nails, a teenager on the phone—these are all stereotypes of people as we expect them to look and act in certain life roles. Of course, all mothers don't cook, all little boys are not covered in dirt, all little girls are not neat and bowed . . . but that doesn't stop the stereotypic image.

See if you can recognize stereotypes in the following items. Star all items that reveal a common stereotype. Then use the reverse side of the paper to write a description that dispels or is in striking contrast to each of those images.

1. The grandmother donned her glasses and nightcap and her wolf mask, pulled the quilt up under her chin, and called her grandchildren in to kiss her goodnight.
2. Tracy smoothed her blond ponytail and flashed a smile at the new senior quarterback. "Will I see ya' tonight?" she teased, as she bounced toward the cafeteria.
3. Grandmother appeared at the front door in her freshly starched apron, her white hair drawn tightly into a bun. "Children," she called. "It's time for milk and cookies!"
4. As soon as Dad finished cleaning up the kitchen, he was off to pick fresh raspberries for the tarts he had planned to make for supper.
5. The old man sat in quiet seclusion on his porch. Now and then, he would cock his head to catch the sound of a chirping bird or a chattering squirrel.
6. "Jumping Jehoshaphat!" exclaimed the old lady. "It's the first time I've ever gotten to ride behind a good lookin' man on a Harley!"
7. The CEO of a Fortune-500 company ran her delicate hand along the smooth edge of the impressive boardroom table. "Gentlemen!" Her young, vibrant voice was one of authority.
8. He swaggered into the bar, slid his denim-clad body onto the leather stool and hung the heel of his size 14 boot on the foot rail. "What's up, Jake? How's it goin' in Guitar City?" queried the bartender.
9. The preacher pounded the pulpit and railed against the evils of tobacco chewin', smokin', and drinkin'.
10. Sirens of the approaching ambulance whirred in the distance as the neighborhood bully knelt beside the still figure of a tiny girl, stroked her head softly, and fought back the tears.

Name

A SYSTEM IN NEED OF REPAIR?

The passionate, thought-provoking essay you are about to read was written by a fifteen-year-old African American boy. Read it carefully to determine what message he is trying to convey to his readers. Write your answers to the questions below on the back of this sheet of paper.

A long time ago, you could walk down the street at night, in any American city, and you wouldn't have had to worry about your life being in danger. But in the last ten years, walking the street at night has become a game of Russian roulette.

The justice system has exercised almost every known power it has to stop crime and yet, the innocent often suffer while the guilty go free. In American it is not what crime you commit; it's how much wealth or power you have. Crime lords have broken practically every law; yet they are rarely brought to justice. The homeless, on the other hand, are constantly harassed by the police. When the upper classes demand the law, the cops respond in a flash, but when the poor and working classes need help, it takes the "overworked, underpaid" hours to come—if they show up at all. This is the harsh reality of the American system of justice.

YES, YOUR HONOR!
I FOUND 27 HOT CATS
IN HIS POSSESSION!

Our leaders believe that the only way to reduce crime is to install curfews, increase education, and convince citizens to get involved in their communities. But such ideas will only take care of the superficial troubles; the root problem still flourishes. For the danger doesn't hide on dark streets; it lurks in the dark hearts of men who are ignorant of or unwilling to acknowledge an absolute moral system of right and wrong. One study suggests that crime didn't begin its present upward swing until after prayer was removed from public schools. Of course, that is just one indicator; a connection between a morning prayer in a 6th grade classroom and a major change in the crime rate seems a far stretch, but is one of those small steps taken by a group of leaders that can become a big step for all mankind. After all, evil thrives when good men do nothing.

- Dennis Upkins

1. What bias is evident in this essay?
2. Do you think the writer supports his bias with evidence?
3. Do you agree or disagree with his premise, stated in the first three sentences of the third paragraph? Why or why not?
4. What is the underlying message Upkins wishes to impress upon the reader?
5. In your opinion, is the essay persuasive? (Does the author convince you that most of what he says is true?)
6. Do you think your answers are influenced by your awareness of the writer's racial heritage? Why or why not?
7. Circle each word that demonstrates a bias or prejudice. Beside each circled word, write a plus (+) if you think the bias is favorable and a minus (–) if unfavorable.

heathen	obese	valueless	fashionable	beneficial
show-off	free thinker	across the tracks	comfortable	blue-collar
customary	independent	crackpot	nerd	guaranteed
elegant	old-fashioned	goody-two-shoes	out-of-date	upper class

Name ______________________

A POISON TREE

When an author wants to moralize or teach the reader a lesson, he or she often weaves the lesson into a story with the use of symbols that hopefully will grab the reader's interest and help to strengthen the lesson. William Blake, a famous English poet of the eighteenth century, uses a startling tale to warn his reader. Do you think his title is a good attention-grabber?

A Poison Tree

I was angry with my friend:
I told my wrath, my wrath did end.
I was angry with my foe:
I told it not, my wrath did grow.

And I watered it in fears,
Night and morning with my tears;
And I sunned it with smiles,
And with soft, deceitful wiles.

And it grew both day and night,
Till it bore an apple bright.
And my foe beheld it shine,
And he knew that it was mine,

And into my garden stole
*When the night had veiled the pole;**
In the morning glad I see
My foe outstretched beneath the tree.

** pole: sky*

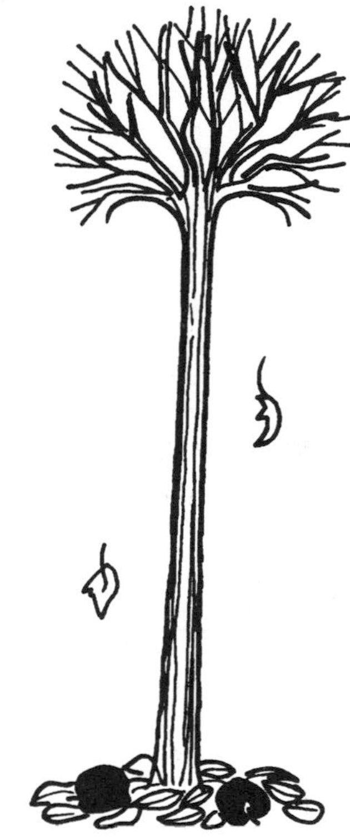

1. Determine the meanings of the words below and write them in the space provided.
   wrath ______________________ foe ______________________
   deceitful wiles ______________________ veiled ______________________
2. What occurred when the speaker expressed his anger? ______________________
3. What happened when he did not? ______________________
4. What "grows" out of the speaker's anger? ______________________
5. What symbol is used to represent this result of his anger? ______________________
6. In what other famous story is this same symbol used? ______________________
7. Why do you think the enemy comes into the garden? ______________________
8. What happens to the enemy in the garden? ______________________
9. Which statement best expresses the poet's message? (Circle the correct answer.)
   a. It is wrong to get angry.
   b. Anger, kept to oneself, can fester and cause tragic results.
   c. Good friends always tell one another when they feel anger between them.

Name ______________________

NO NEED TO
USE THAT
'TONE'
WITH ME,
MARY!

WATCH THAT TONE!

The tone of a literary work is the writer's attitude toward the subject and toward his or her audience. A writer's tone may be friendly or hostile, intimate or distant and formal, serious or flippant, etc. Think how you might describe the tone of each work below. Beside each work that is familiar to you, write a word or phrase that describes the tone of that work.

Adventures of Huckleberry Finn ______________________________

A Separate Peace ______________________________

Diary of Anne Frank ______________________________

Les Miserables ______________________________

Anne of Green Gables ______________________________

My Antonia ______________________________

Mary Poppins ______________________________

Pocahontas ______________________________

Cry the Beloved Country ______________________________

To Kill a Mockingbird ______________________________

The Wind in the Willows ______________________________

The Borrowers ______________________________

Little Women ______________________________

Cheaper by the Dozen ______________________________

The Black Stallion ______________________________

The Red Pony ______________________________

Alice in Wonderland ______________________________

The Hobbit ______________________________

Choose one of the pairs of literary works **or** substitute any two familiar works you know that are similar in subject. Identify the tone in each piece and then write a paragraph in which you compare and contrast the tones of the two pieces. Use the back of this page.

Name ______________________________

MEET CHAUCER'S NUN

A writer may use a number of techniques to develop a character.

1) By making a direct statement about him or her
2) By showing character indirectly through action, thought, or dialogue
3) Through observation and comment made by others in the story
4) By using physical appearance and habits of the person to reveal his or her character

Geoffrey Chaucer, the second most famous British writer of all time (Shakespeare is the first) was a master of characterization. In *The Canterbury Tales,* he parades a variety of 29 characters past the eyes of his readers. Here's a paraphrase of one of his characterizations—that of the nun who traveled to Canterbury with a group of pilgrims.

In this piece, Chaucer uses three of the techniques mentioned at the top of this page. Show which lines of the poem demonstrate each technique by writing the appropriate number after each line.

1. There was also a Nun, a Prioress. ________
2. Her smile was very simple and quite coy. ________
3. Her only oath by which she swore, "St. Loy!" ________
4. And she was called by Madam Eglantyne . . . ________
5. So dainty were her manners when she dined ________
6. No morsel did she let fall through her lips, ________
7. The sauce her fingers touched, just at the tips . . . ________
8. So tender was she that she could not keep ________
9. Composure at a trapped mouse, she would weep ________
10. If it were squealing, wounded, dead, or bleeding ________
11. Her little dogs she often was seen feeding ________
12. With roast, or milk, or pieces of white bread. ________
13. And deeply grieved was she if one were dead . . . ________
14. Softly on her face her veil did lay ________
15. Her nose was tiny and her eyes were gray; ________
16. Her dainty mouth was smallish, soft and red, ________
17. And smooth and fair, unweathered, her forehead . . . ________
18. A stylish cloak she wore with stately charm. ________
19. A coral trinket graced her comely arm. ________

I WEPT WHEN I SAW A LITTLE MOUSE BLEED TO DEATH IN A TRAP.

Name ________

INVITATION TO THE GREAT OUTDOORS

IT'S SUCH FUN TO BE
MOTHER NATURE!

Can you keep a secret? Then follow me
Through meadows and woods to the open sea,
Through craggy cracks in city walks,
Through fields of scraggly, huskery stalks.
Run with me through Seasons' doors
And sneak through chinks in cabin floors,
Fly up and away to starlight skies,
Slide back on shadows just your size;
And then . . . then you'll begin to see
The secret . . . Shhhh. . .'tween you and me. . .
That the best, most beautiful, greatest stuff
Of which there's NEVER not enough,
Comes from Nature's lovely store;
Her shelves are filled with fun galore!
And except for things like paste or glue,
An occasional jar or worn-out shoe,
Perhaps some soap or snips of string,
You needn't have another thing —
'Cuz the lady who paints the day's sunrises
Has a zillion more surprises . . .
So leave your paper and pencil chores
And follow me to the great outdoors!

1. What is the theme of this poem? ____________________
2. What is the author's purpose? ____________________
3. Which word best describes the tone of the poem?

   serious   playful   scolding   flippant   superstitious

4. If there is personification in the piece, write an example of it here: ____________________
5. If there is a simile in the poem, write an example of it here: ____________________
6. Write examples of other figurative language in the poem here: ____________________
7. Find at least three examples of alliteration: ____________________
8. Identify the rhyme scheme of the first 10 lines: ____________________

Name ____________________

GREEN ISN'T SO BAD!

What comes to mind when you hear the word **green?** Do you think of negative or yukky stuff such as sickness or slime or jealousy? Or do positive ideas, smells, tastes, sights, and feelings such as spring, mint, youth, fresh veggies, or newness come to your mind? A group of kids pooled their individual lists of green ideas and wrote this collective poem.

1-Green is the rhythmic chirping of crickets,
2-The way a pickle pinches your tongue,
3-And the dentist's fluoride treatments.

4-Green is mold and jealousy.
5-And the velvet stretch of a golf course.
6-Green is having the flu in math class.

7-Green stains the seat of your baseball pants,
8-Paints a forest of pine trees,
9-Drips slime on a slippery frog,
10-Dots a pond with algae,
11-Lends the music to a rushing stream.

12-Quiet is green
13-So is spinach, St. Patrick's Day, a lizard, and loneliness.
14-You are green when your heart is broken.

15-Green is sour.
16-Green is cold and crunchy
17-You can take green to the bank!

The poem is full of rich imagery and poetic devices. Identify the lines in which you find . . .

A. Personification: lines ____________________

B. Sensory images: lines ____________________

(things you can taste, hear, smell, see, touch)

C. Emotion or feeling associated with green: lines ____________________

D. Alliteration: lines ____________________

E. How would you characterize the tone or mood of the poem? ____________________

F. What is the meaning of the last line? ____________________

Name ____________________

THE SKELETON IN YOUR CLOSET

Do you know what it means to "have a skeleton in your closet?" Not literally—but figuratively? This young math student tells about the day a skeleton fell out of his closet.

GUESS WHAT ?
THERE IS
A
SKELETON
IN
YOUR
CLOSET.

Everyone thinks I'm the big cheese in math class. But the real truth is that I have to beat my brains out on every assignment. Today the cat got out of the bag. Everyone saw right through me.

It was a lousy day anyway. I was down in the dumps the minute I woke up. Studying last night wasn't worth a hill of beans, and I knew I'd be in a pretty pickle when I got to math class. My brother was getting in my hair and driving me up a wall. Mom was fit to be tied when he and I got in a big fight. She almost bit our heads off.

On my way to school, it was raining cats and dogs, so my bike slipped on a corner and I bit the dust. At school, the math teacher was pretty burned up because none of us had finished our homework. I shook in my boots as he passed out the test because I knew I was in hot water. I was especially up a creek on the algebra problems. I blew the test.

I kept a stiff upper lip at school, but I sure needed to let off some steam. I held my tongue until I got into my room where I could throw things and scream my head off. One shoe went through the window—and now I'm really in the doghouse!

This piece is loaded with figurative language. Underline or highlight each example of figurative language in the story. Count them. How many did you find?

Choose one of the paragraphs above and rewrite it in your own words. Try to use fresh, creative expressions instead of the phrases you marked above.

____

____

____

____

____

____

____

Name ____

PORTRAIT OF AMERICA

In the paragraphs below, two high school students (one a football player, the other an artist) draw very similar geographical pictures of the United States. Each creates a series of lovely images using figures of speech and sensory imagery. As you read, see if you can identify the primary literary device used by both writers.

FROM SEA TO SHINING SEA

In the tranquil forest of Vermont, stalwart, fragrant pines climb to the sky. Spanish moss covers ancient trees who spread their way from the Atlantic, across the Deep South, to where white sugar sands meet the transparent blue waters of the Gulf Coast. Rich golden grains, kissed with sunlight, stretch their arms across the Midwest toward winding, western rivers which twist through deep canyons, frantically searching for the perilous sea. Steep slopes, candy coated with a layer of snow, rest in the heart of Colorado before they make their last majestic rise toward the Pacific's blue and white, sun-crested waves. America—painting its way from sea to shining sea!—Paul Armstrong

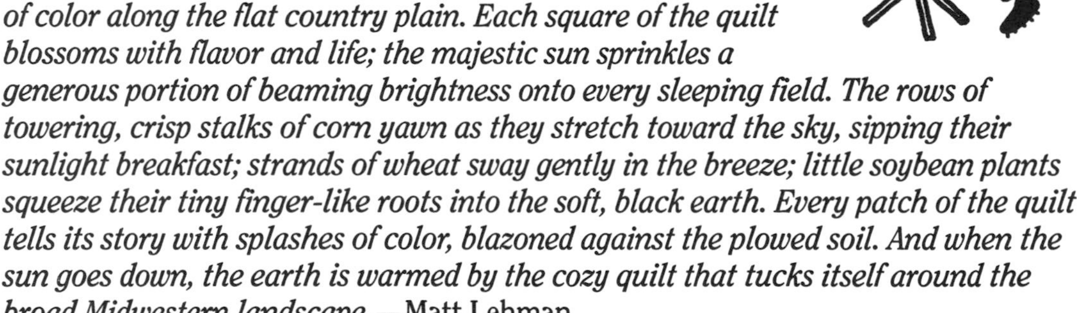
10

THE HEARTLAND

Early in the morning, the sun's golden rays peek over the symmetrical maze of crops; each section is a part of a giant, multi-colored quilt. A farmer peers out the farmhouse window and stares for miles at the beige, brown, maize and green patches of color along the flat country plain. Each square of the quilt blossoms with flavor and life; the majestic sun sprinkles a generous portion of beaming brightness onto every sleeping field. The rows of towering, crisp stalks of corn yawn as they stretch toward the sky, sipping their sunlight breakfast; strands of wheat sway gently in the breeze; little soybean plants squeeze their tiny finger-like roots into the soft, black earth. Every patch of the quilt tells its story with splashes of color, blazoned against the plowed soil. And when the sun goes down, the earth is warmed by the cozy quilt that tucks itself around the broad Midwestern landscape.—Matt Lehman

1. What is the primary poetic device used by both authors? ____________________
2. Which author used an extended metaphor? ____________________
3. What comparison is made by the metaphor? ____________________
4. Underline each individual, figurative phrase in both pieces. ____________________

Can you guess which author is the football player? Probably not—though you have a 50-50 chance! Both write with tender sensitivity and joyous exuberance!

Name ____________________

STOP THE CDS!

11777 Amazon Parkway
Deerfield, Illinois 60015

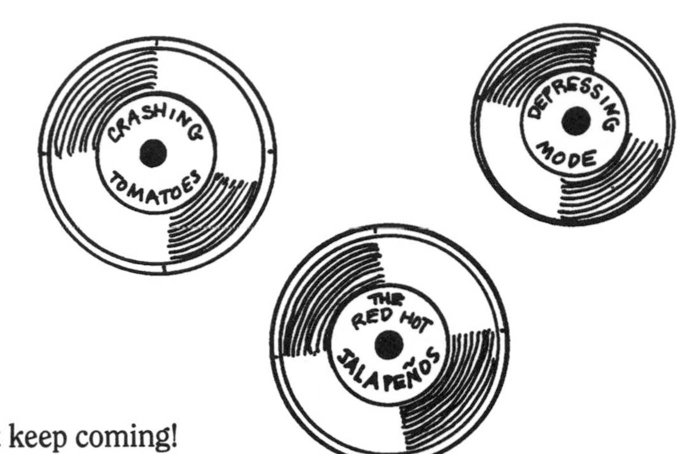
CRASHING TOMATOES
DEPRESSING MODE
THE RED HOT JALAPEÑOS

A.G.G. Music Company
1414 West Broadway
New York, New York 14415

August 15

To Whom It May Concern:

Please! Stop the CDs! They just keep coming!

I joined your CD program 6 months ago. I fulfilled my membership obligations a long time ago. I have paid all my bills. Furthermore, I have asked four times for you to cancel my membership.

But you just keep on sending me CDs and more CDs and bills and more bills. I'm sick of it. How can I get you to stop?

Do I have to get a lawyer?
Do I have to put a notice on the Internet about how lousy a company you are?
Do I have to dump old CDs on your lawn?
Do I have to write to the Better Business Bureau?
Do I have to call the president?

What will it take?

If there is a way to get you to stop sending CDs, sending bills, and sending nasty letters because I haven't paid the bills—PLEASE let me know.

Pretty Disgusted Cynthia

1. What do you think about the way Cynthia has chosen to communicate her opinions and feelings to the music company?

___

2. What do you like best or least about her letter?

___

3. How would you handle this same situation?

___

Name ___

READING COMPREHENSION ASSESSMENT AND ANSWER KEYS

A FAIRE HISTORIE OF GOOD QUEEN BESS BY WM. SHAKES-PEARE

READING COMPREHENSION SKILLS TEST

Each correct answer is worth 2 points.
Total possible score: 100 points.

Read these 5 poems and answer the questions below.

A.
I'd sooner romance a gorilla
Or go to a dance with Godzilla
I'd sooner agree to be King Kong's mate
Than find stewed tomatoes on my plate.

B.
The main thing about celery
is not the green
or the crunch
or the crisp
or the munch
The main thing about celery
is the thing
that stays with you
long after the celery is gone.
The main thing about celery
is
the strings.

C.
You need to have a stomach strong
To eat my mother's cooking.
Or else, bring a dog along
To feed it to when she's not looking.

1. What is the common theme of all the poems?
2. Which poems have a humorous tone?
3. Write a phrase from the sausage poem which has strong imagery.
4. Which poems use internal rhyme (rhyme within a line instead of at the end)?
5. Which 2 poems contain the greatest number of descriptive words about their subjects?
6. Which poems make use of questions?

D.
Don't expect me to eat oysters
because
The taste I could not stand
I'd rather swallow goldfish live
Or chew handfuls of sand.
I'd eat my walkman, eat the tapes
Chew my earphones any day
But put an oyster on my tongue
Are you kidding? No way!
You can torture me with scorpions,
Hang snakes from all my walls
Fill my bathtub with piranhas,
Push me over Niagara Falls.
You can swear to light my underwear,
Dunk me in boiling water to my hips.
No matter what you threaten—
Oysters will never touch these lips.

E.
Have you ever really looked at a sausage?
A slimy brown sausage, a hot blunt stinky sausage
With little pieces of grainy fat stuck in on the sides
A gushy fuzzy with mold reeking sausage
A wrinkly crinkly scabby sausage
Have you ever really looked at a sausage?

Name

A wall of water—it's the big wave that surfers wait for and thrill to ride. Millions of them all over the world rush into wild surf day after day—looking for that perfect big wave. Sometimes these perfect waves are as high as 30 feet!

And when they find it—how do they ride it? The idea is to ride along the vertical face of a big wave just ahead of the crest of the wave—the place where it is breaking. Of course, the surfer needs to stay ahead of that crest and not get crashed under it!

Surfers start by kneeling or lying on the surfboard and paddling out to the area beyond where the waves are breaking. Here they wait for the right wave. When a surfer sees a good wave coming, she turns and paddles furiously toward shore, trying to move as fast as the wave. If she times it right, the wave will pick up her surfboard and carry it along. At this point she stands up on the board at the top of the wave and rides it down the wall or vertical face of the wave. She actually gets going faster than the wave is moving. She must keep an eye on the wave's crest and turn the board so she stays ahead of it. If she gets it right the surfer can get a nice ride for several minutes—moving at a great speed—up to almost 10 miles an hour. Or, if she doesn't get it right, she can be be wiped out—sent smashing to the ocean bottom by the tremendous heavy weight and force of a monstrous wave!

7. What is the first movement of the surfer when she sees the right wave coming? ____________

8. What part of the wave does the surfer ride?

____

9. At what point in the process does the surfer stand up?____________________

10. What does the article tell about the size of surfboards? ____________________

11. What will happen if the surfer doesn't stay ahead of the breaking crest?____________

12. Which is the best title for this piece?__________

a. Why Surfing Is Dangerous

b. Surfing Is Fun

c. Riding the Wall

d. The Structure of a Wave

Off Her Rocker

Mother has lost all her marbles and flipped her lid! That's what we've decided. By 10 o'clock this morning she had blown her top 8 times. When the baby dumped his cereal on his head, she lost her cool. When Jenny put the cat in the washing machine, she got madder than a wet hen. And when Tommy ate her lipstick, she screamed bloody murder.

I think it was the toilet paper fort in the living room that was the last straw. She ran around yelling her head off about how we were pushing her over the edge and driving her up the wall. We tried to cool her down, but she sat outside for hours even though it was raining cats and dogs. When she came in, she wandered around in a fog the rest of the day. I tried to keep a lid on the little kids.

When dad got home, he was out in the cold about her bad day. So when he shouted, "Happy Birthday, dear, how does it feel to be over the hill?" he didn't understand why she went totally bananas and crowned him over the head with the frying pan.

THESE KIDS ARE DRIVING ME UP THE WALL!

13. How many figures of speech are used in this piece? ____________________

14. In paragraph 2, what does "keep a lid on" mean?

____

15. What figure of speech used in this piece means "didn't know anything"? ____________

16. What is meant in the first sentence by "Mother has lost all her marbles"?____________

17. What is the meaning of "crowned" in the last sentence? ____________________

18. Which figure of speech means "getting old"?

____

Name

TO TATTOO OR NOT TO TATTOO?

Tattoos have been around for hundreds of years. They've been found on Egyptian mummies, dating back to 2000 B.C. Ancient Greeks, Germans, Japanese, British, and people of many ancient tribes have used tattoos for various purposes. Often tattoos were (and still are) a mark of rank in society or a mark of membership in a particular group, tribe, or gang. Some tattoos were worn as protection against evil or ill fortune. Others showed courage. Tattoos were used to brand criminals, or to serve as disguises. But mostly, through history, tattoos have been used for decoration.

Today, tattoos are becoming popular as a fashion item of body decoration. The incidence of tattoos among many age groups is on the rise. Since the 1980s, women have been using the tattoo process for permanent eyeliner or lip color.

What, exactly is a tattoo? It is a permanent design decorating the human body. Tattoos are made by cutting or pricking the skin and inserting a colored dye or pigment under the skin. The modern tattoo process uses electric needles. In the past, instruments such as knives, thorns, and sharpened bones were used.

Is it a good idea to slice your skin and put color under it permanently? Many doctors don't think so. Serious side effects often accompany tattoos. Besides plaguing infections and eye damage from the permanent eyeliner, cancers have been linked to tattoos. Contaminated needles and equipment can also spread serious diseases, including AIDS. Many parents are irate that a child can get a tattoo without parental permission. A parent's signature is required in most states for ear piercing for a minor—yet kids can get tattoos without parental permission. One of the major concerns about tattooing is that there are no controls or restrictions on the process. No training or licensing is required for those who do it. As a customer seeking a tattoo, you cannot be sure of the person's ability, experience, carefulness—or of the safety or cleanliness of their equipment and supplies.

So think about this: when you get a tattoo—what else are you getting?

19. Which is *not* one of the reasons mentioned for tattoos?

    a) decoration b) disguise c) to frighten enemies d) protection e) membership in a group

20. What kind of tattoos are mentioned as relatively recent developments? ____________________

    ____

21. Tell two dangers of tattoos described in the article. ____________________

    ____

22. What is the meaning of "irate" as used in paragraph # 4? ____________________

23. In your own words, briefly explain how a tattoo is done. ____________________

    ____

24. What is the meaning of "contaminated" in paragraph #4? ____________________

Name ____

CASE OF THE SABOTAGED LOCKERS

The mascot of the Northfield High School Rams, a small live ram, disappeared during the second half of the Homecoming Game. Frantic fans and school officials searched the football field, stands, concession booths, and locker rooms for hours—and found nothing. But on Monday morning, inside the school, some clues began to turn up. Five students whose lockers, numbered 116–120, were all in a row, reported that the locks were stuck and they couldn't get into their lockers. Furthermore, some strange sounds, smells, and liquids were emanating from the lockers. These were a curious mix of animal sounds and smells, food smells, and mysterious liquids dripping out. Authoritative school administrators and custodians flew into action, cracking open lockers and interrogating students—including the owners of the lockers: Matt, Michelle, Andrea, Scott, and Tara. This is what their investigations revealed:

- The custodians found one strange item in each locker.
- In locker # 119, custodians found a frightened, messy, squeaking rat.
- The ram was not in locker #117.
- Matt's locker is between Michelle's and Andrea's.
- Tara's locker has the lowest number.
- The locker next to Angela's held a large sausage-garlic pizza.
- Locker # 118 did not have any food in it.
- A bag of melting snowballs caused the liquid oozing from Scott's locker.
- The locker hiding the ram was next to a locker with 10 containers of Chinese food.
- Angela's locker is next to Tara's.
- The owner of the locker between the Chinese food and the rat is the culprit who kidnapped the ram and put all this other stuff in the lockers.

25. What is the only written fact found out about Matt? ______________________

26. Which locker numbers could not have held the ram? __________ and __________

27. Which event happened fourth of these five? ________
    a. Football fans searched for the mascot.
    b. The Homecoming Game halftime occurred.
    c. Students found their lockers broken.
    d. The ram disappeared.
    e. Pizza was found in a locker.

28. From the written facts, which locker could not have been Scott's? ______________

29. What three roles did school officials take? ______________________

30. What is the meaning of the word "emanating" as used here? ______________

31. How many places were searched before Monday? ______________________

Can you figure out:

Which locker hid the ram? ______ Which locker-owner did the deed? ______________

Name

Skills Test

Use these entries from the telephone book's yellow pages to answer the questions below.

ANGELINO'S PIZZA
Authentic New York Style Pizza, Roasted Chicken, Calzone, Pasta
Televised Sports—Free Delivery
11 A.M.–1 A.M. 7 Days a Week
6666 Anton Parkway 668-9222

Chicago Style Deep-Dish Pizza
40 Varieties of Pizza
Take Out—Delivery—Dine In

692 Lakeside
862-0944

BRUNO'S PIZZA

PIZZA DEN
We Deliver
Pizza • Pasta • Salad Bar
4 locations

16 E. Main	772-1111
2770 Western	774-1909
1402 N. 5th	772-1414
Northside Plaza	772-6200

Voted Best Pizza in Town 1996

Open 7 Days noon–midnight

PAPA G'S PIZZA CO
Award-Winning Pizza You Bake at Home

11 A.M.–11 P.M. Daily

Long's Plaza	488-6111
20 N. Broadway	488-0777

Delicioso!
B

32. How many of these places deliver pizza? ______________________

33. How many of these places have more than one location? ______________________

34. How many describe the style of pizza they serve? ______________________

35. What does Angelino's have that no one else mentions (name 2 things)?

______________________ and ______________________

36. What is distinctive about PAPA G'S? ______________________

37. Which establishment is open the longest hours? ______________________

38. Which two places have won some honor? ______________________

Name ______________________

TEACHER'S FIELD TRIP BLUES

I am never taking this class on a field trip again! I mean it! Never! I have had it!

The trouble started, as it always does, with the bus ride to the aquarium. Jason somehow sneaked a bologna sandwich on the bus, even though I had collected all the lunches in my possession before we left school. We had been on the bus only 20 minutes when the sandwich ended up under Rosa Benson's bottom. The mustard was all over her white shorts, the bus seat, James's new jacket, and Jennifer's hair. I haven't figured out yet how it got in Jennifer's hair—she was 7 rows behind Rosa.

And this was just after Melanie sprayed hairspray on the bus driver and Louis threw up his breakfast.

I won't even try to describe the noise level on the bus, the damage to my ears, or the other bus disasters. I will say only that the chocolate milk in one fish tank, the wet clothes on 26 fourth-graders, the bad words yelled at the 2 nuns guiding a class from St. Mary's Kindergarten, the $20 bill Kim's mother was foolish enough to send along that is now in the belly of a shark, and the request from the aquarium guide that we refrain from visiting next year add up to more than I can take.

And while I'm complaining, I'll say that no helper I have ever taken along on a field trip is much help in controlling the chaos. Mrs. Vincent spent most of her time in the bathroom reapplying her makeup and hair after getting drenched in the dolphin show. And Mr. Hornsby said something like this every three minutes: "My children aren't allowed to be disrespectful." (His children were spraying drinking fountain water down the collars of primary students who were unfortunate enough to wander by) or . . . "Can't you do something to make these kids behave?"

"NO, I can't!" I said to myself, but not out loud. But what I can do is never, ever, set foot in a zoo, planetarium, airport, ice cream factory, museum, laboratory, or aquarium with anyone under 21—ever again.

39. Which of these events happened third?
    a. chocolate milk in the fish tank
    b. mustard all over Rosa
    c. Louis threw up
    d. Melanie sprayed hairspray
40. What is the meaning of *chaos* as used in paragraph #3? ____________________
41. What is the author's tone? ____________________
42. What is the piece's point of view? ____________________
43. Who sat 7 rows behind Rosa on the bus? ____________________
44. According to the written account, how many people got wet? ____________________

Match these literary devices with their descriptions

_____ 45. giving human attributes to a nonliving object

_____ 46. an implied comparison without *like* or *as*

_____ 47. extreme exaggeration

_____ 48. details that have concrete appeal to the senses

_____ 49. the main meaning of a written work

_____ 50. the attitude of the writer toward the subject

A-hyperbole
B-imagery
C-personification
D-irony
E-metaphor
F-simile
G-tone
H-theme

Total Score ______________ (2 pts for each question)

Name ______________________________

SKILLS TEST ANSWER KEY

1. food
2. A, C, D
3. Answers will vary.
4. D, E
5. B, E
6. D, E
7. paddle toward shore
8. the face, just ahead of the crest
9. as the wave picks up the board
10. nothing
11. she'll "wipe out"
12. c
13. 19 counting title
14. keep calm
15. "out in the cold"
16. getting mad, or going crazy
17. hit, or smashed
18. "over the hill"
19. c
20. lip color, eyeliner
21. any two: cancer, infections, diseases, eye damage
22. angry
23. Possible answer: Slices or cuts are made in the skin, and color is put into the cuts under the skin.
24. unclean
25. His locker is between Michelle's and Andrea's.
26. #117 and #119
27. c
28. #116, because the article said the lowest number locker was Tara's
29. search for the ram; interrogate students; open lockers
30. leaking out of; coming out of
31. 4 (EXTRA: The ram is in locker # 118. Matt is the culprit.)
32. 3
33. 2
34. 2
35. Two of these: chicken, calzone, televised sports, NY style pizza
36. You bake the pizza at home.
37. Angelino's
38. Pizza Den and Papa G's
39. b
40. confusion, wild time, a mess
41. angry, disgusted, or cynical
42. first person
43. Jennifer
44. 27 (26 4th graders plus Mrs. Vincent)
45. C
46. E
47. A
48. B
49. H
50. G

ANSWERS

page 18

A. 9	F. 5
B. 1	G. 2
C. 4	H. 10
D. 7	I. 3
E. 6	J. 8

page 19

1. the headache's; first person
2. head is the best place for an ache to reside
3. always a vacancy
   ears and teeth have less room
   ears have wax
   mouths have bad breath
   get to meet interesting people
4. aspirin
5. Answers will vary.
6. Answers will vary.

page 20

Answers may vary slightly.
poem lines . . .
1-2. C
3-4. A
5. B
6-7. C
8. F
9-12. C
13-16. D
17-21. E
22-23. F
24-32. Answers will vary.

page 21

1-15. Answers will vary.
16. 3 and 7

page 22

1. Joseph
2. 2
3. older
4. 4
5. She is a doctor.
6. Mike
7. 9
8. Father is an engineer.
9. Tess
10. Dap
11. no
12. no
13. 4
14. Dap lives next door to Tess.

page 23

Answers will vary.

pages 24–25

1069 B.C.— King Tut lives
A.D. 1200 — St. Francis of Assisi tames wolf
1564 — Shakespeare is born
1775 — Paul Revere rides
1800s — Johnny Appleseed plants orchards
1835 — Mark Twain is born
1860s — George Washington Carver invents ingenious stuff
1945 — Disney wins Oscars

page 26

1. Albert borrows his brother's baseball.
2. He goes to picnic and plays games and eats food.
3. He loans the ball to his friend Ralph.
4. He rides the bus home.
5. He gets off the bus whistling.
6. He sees his brother and friends waiting; feels sick.
7. He realized his brother and friends are waiting for the ball.

8-10. Answers will vary.

page 27

1. E-C	6. E-C
2. C-E	7. C-E
3. C-E	8. E-C
4. E-C	9. E-C
5. E-C	10. E-C

page 28

1. 4
2. Titles will vary.
3. a. the most beautiful state of all
   b. favorite playground of mainland Americans
   c. fascinating place to live
   d. delightful place to vacation

Explanations will vary.

page 29

1. O	8. F	15. O
2. F	9. F	16. F
3. O	10. O	17. O
4. F	11. O	18. O
5. F	12. O	19. O
6. O	13. O	20. F
7. O	14. O	21. O

page 30

1. stubbornness or stubborn pride
2. stubborn pride can lead to trouble or foolish actions
3. Answers will vary.

page 31

Answers on both sections will vary.

page 32

1. One who is too greedy may lose everything.
2. "The Fox and the Grapes"
3. "The Boy Who Cried 'Wolf!'"
4. "The Ants and the Grasshopper"
5. "The Lion and the Mouse"

page 33

A. He fell in a cistern.
B. A logging accident
C. His wife and children left him.
D. She was homeless, insane, kind-hearted, and always seemed cheerful.
E. Blacksmith
F. She rejected life in this world.
G. Many die when they are only halfway through life—in their youth or prime.

page 34

Answers will vary.

page 35

Answers will vary.

page 36

1. Answers will vary somewhat.
   a. anxious
   b. friendly, honest, realistic
2. # 2
3. # 1
4. # 2
5. # 1
6. child's point of view; (third person limited point of view)
7. niece's point of view (first person point of view)
8. a

page 37

1. Answers will vary.
2. cynical
3. Answers will vary.
4. Answers will vary.
5. Answers will vary somewhat.
6. b

page 38

1. accidentals—incidentals
2. Arabic—aerobic
3. extinguished—distinguished
4. unparalyzed—unparalleled
5. predicate—precedent
6. dreaded—breaded
7. tudors—tutors
8. emasculation—emancipation
9. historically—hysterically
10. presbyterians—pedestrians
11. mockeries—monarchies
12. irritate—irrigate

page 39

1. Killed is serious—four were killed, not one.
2. "To be prepared" is three words, not one.
3. A bachelor IS a single man.
4. Sequence means to put in a particular order.
5. Perfect is an absolute—it can't be more perfect than perfect.
6. Your ancestors precede you in death—they're already dead.
7. Permanent is forever.
8. If he's worth it, then he can't be paid too much.
9. If you have access, you can enter.
10. Infinite is without end—it can't be almost without end.
11. If it is spontaneous, it can't be planned.
12. Déjà vu means to happen again, so the sentence repeats itself.

page 40

1. 15 hours plus several hours on weekends
2. Answers will vary somewhat:
   Kids have a longer workday than adults.
   The amount of homework is stressful.
   The long hours are not healthy.
   Kids should do most of the learning in class.
   Kids have little time for social and family life.
3. 15 hours and 25 minutes
4. social time, family time, relaxation, health, fun, sleep
5. in addition

page 41

Answers may vary somewhat

1. 10
2. 5
3. prune juice, toothpaste, strawberries, cucumbers, lettuce
4. cow manure, chocolate chips, and paper bags
5. to show discouragement or hopelessness

pages 42-43

1. attractive bonuses; good monthly rates
2. KEEPFIT
3. teenfit@atfc.com
4. $9
5. 4 passes to water park; 10 guest passes
6. $48
7. dance club membership; water park passes; guest passes
8. $180

9-10. Answers will vary.

11. Join by March 1

page 44

1. Marty	6. Chad
2. Will	7. 116
3. Ben and Price	8. 10 dozen
4. Marty	9. Will, Peter, Chad
5. Peter and Price	10. Marty, Andrew

page 45

1. Central United States
2. S.E. United States
3. warm
4. N.W. United States
5. rain
6. They will likely drop.
7. Western mountains and Central East
8. S.E. United States

page 46

Titles will vary.

page 47

1. a surprise element
2. I. rhyme, metaphor, simile
   II. sensory imagery
3. I. thirsty person (first person)
   II. person in love (second person)

4-5. Answers will vary.

page 48

1-6. Answers will vary.

page 49

Descriptions will vary.
The following items have common stereotypes: 2, 3, 5, 8, 9

page 50

1. bias against the present justice system

2-3. Answers will vary.

4. Crime cannot be eradicated by laws and systems alone. Every person of good will must get involved.

5-7. Answers will vary.

page 51

1. wrath—great anger
   foe—enemy
   deceitful wiles—underhanded acts
   veiled—hidden
2. anger disappeared
3. anger grew
4. fruit—evil results
5. apple
6. Garden of Eden
7. Answers will vary.
8. He dies, poisoned by the fruit.
9. b

page 52

Answers will vary.

page 53

Answers may vary somewhat.

Poetry lines . . .

Line 1—1	11—2
2—1	12—2
3—2	13—2
4—1	14—4
5—4	15—1
6—4	16—1
7—4	17—1
8—4	18—4
9—2	19—1
10—2	

page 54

1. How to escape to the great outdoors
2. To interest the reader in outdoor activity
3. playful
4. There are several examples:
   Seasons' doors, Nature's lovely store, lady who paints, her shelves are filled
5. none (Line 15 uses the word "like," but not for a simile.)
6. there are several: craggy cracks, scraggly huskery stalks, starlight skies, slide back on shadows
7. craggy cracks
   some soap or snips of string
   best, most beautiful
   filled with fun
8. aa, bb, cc, dd, aa

page 55

A. 2, 7, 8, 9, 10, 11
B. 1, 2, 3, 5, 8, 9, 10, 11, 12, 15, 16
C. 4, 12, 13, 14
D. 2, 8, 9, 13, 16
E. Answers will vary.
F. Money is green, too.

page 56

There are 23 instances of figurative language.
Paragraph answers will vary.

page 57

1. personification
2. Matt
3. Gardens and fields are patches of a quilt.
4. Check students' individual pages.
   Paul is the football player.

page 58

Answers will vary.

WRITING

Skills Exercises

SKILLS CHECKLIST FOR WRITING

✔	SKILL	PAGE(S)
	Make precise word choices	72, 73
	Use effective words (specific, unusual, colorful, active, etc.)	72–75, 77
	Use active rather than inactive words	75, 76
	Choose words that produce strong visual images	76
	Avoid unnecessary or repetitive words, phrases, ideas, sentences	78
	Avoid overused words, phrases, and clichés	79
	Arrange words within sentences for clarity	80
	Arrange words within sentences for interesting sound	81
	Make strong connections between ideas or parts of the piece	82
	Create sentences and paragraphs that are fluid	82, 109
	Include elements that are surprising, unusual, or extraordinary	83
	Arrange sentences for proper sequence	84
	Create strong titles	85
	Create sentences with interesting rhythm	86, 87
	Create smashing beginnings	88, 89
	Create pieces that have strong beginnings, middles, and ends	88, 90, 91, 110, 111
	Create strong endings	90, 91
	Vary sentence length and structure	92, 93
	Choose words, phrases, and style to create a certain mood	94, 95
	Use dialogue effectively	96
	Adapt form, style, or content for a specific audience	97–99
	Include literary techniques to make writing effective	100, 101, 104
	Experiment with many different forms of writing	102, 103, 105–114
	Adapt form, style, or content for a specific purpose	104
	Use writing skills to write a report	105
	Show clear organization within a written piece	105–111
	Use writing skills to write a descriptive piece	106, 107
	Use writing skills to write an expository piece	108
	Use writing skills to write an imaginative narrative tale	109
	Create pieces that reveal and support the main idea well	110, 111
	Use writing skills to write a characterization	110, 111
	Infuse the piece with personal flavor (voice)	112, 113
	Use writing skills to write on topics of personal choice	112, 113
	Use writing skills to write a persuasive piece	114

MAKE YOUR MOVE!

Go, walk, run, jump, fly, move—these are fine English words, but they are very imprecise in that they do not describe exactly **how** a character or object relocates itself in space. Of course, the best word choice depends on who or what is moving and under what conditions.

Example: An elephant **lumbers** when he moves, while a mouse **scurries.**

For each suggestion below, choose a verb that means the same as one of the italicized words at the top of the page, but is more precise in describing how the object relocates itself in space. Avoid the obvious word. Use an answer only once. Try to make a perfect match of each noun and verb! (Use your thesaurus if necessary.) Then share your answers with one of your classmates. See how many verbs you wrote that no one else chose.

hot fudge ______________________

angry teenager ______________________

snake ______________________

hail ______________________

sky diver ______________________

pole vaulter ______________________

wild horse ______________________

wind ______________________

avalanche ______________________

snake ______________________

broom ______________________

leaf ______________________

ice skater ______________________

penguin ______________________

brass band ______________________

plump walrus ______________________

snowflakes ______________________

football player ______________________

stream ______________________

tired hikers ______________________

speeding bullet ______________________

canary ______________________

Olympic runner ______________________

dust ______________________

jet ______________________

army tank ______________________

kite ______________________

worm ______________________

comet ______________________

feeble man ______________________

ocean storm ______________________

falling dishes ______________________

toes ______________________

volcanic ash ______________________

syrup ______________________

surfboard ______________________

sleepy toddler ______________________

Name ____

PRECISE IS POWERFUL

I MET A REALLY NICE GUY WITH A GREAT PERSONALITY AND A FANTASTIC SMILE. HIS CLOTHES WERE INTERESTING AND HE HAD SOME WONDERFUL IDEAS ABOUT AWESOME PLACES TO GO ON OUTDOOR ADVENTURES.

Pretty trite words for such a find, don't you think? Hey, the reader would probably flip if this new acquaintance were described so precisely that he could be accurately pictured. Make him come alive! (You may change the gender if you wish, and use your thesaurus to find the most powerful, descriptive words possible . . . Make your reader want to meet this person!!)

I met a (an) ______________________ guy (girl) with a (an)____________________ personality

and a (an) ____________________ smile. Her (his) clothes were ________________________

and he (she) had _____________________________ (of) _______________________________

ideas about ___________________________________ places to go on outdoor adventures.

Now, captivate your reader with a description of your day with this new friend. Use only precise, powerful verbs and adjectives. Don't allow even one ordinary, overused word creep in!

Here's your opening sentence.

You'll never believe the ____ day we had!

____

____

____

____

____

____

____

____

Name ____

SENSE-ABLE WORD CHOICES

A writer's job is to affect the reader as strongly as possible. The more sad, happy, satisfied, angry, annoyed, explosive, excited, etc. the reader's reaction to the piece, the more successful the writing!

One effective way to evoke a strong response in a reader is to assault his or her senses with the most vivid images possible. The images may challenge any one or more of the reader's senses—touch, taste, smell, sight, or hearing. To practice making effective word choices, select the most precise word for each sentence from the parentheses in the sentences below.

PUTRID
RANCID
NOXIOUS
DISGUSTING
STOMACH-TURNING
REVOLTING
REPULSIVE
HORRIBLE
NAUSEATING

1. The engine (made an awful sound, hissed and sputtered its objections).
2. A (wonderful, spicy) holiday aroma filled the warm kitchen.
3. The garbage bin emitted a (horrible, putrid) odor.
4. His coat was (old and torn, worn and tattered).
5. Her fingernails on the glass (hurt, grated against) my ears.

Add at least eight additional vivid words to each list below.

TASTE	TOUCH	SMELL	SIGHT	SOUND
acrid	gritty	fragrant	luminous	murmur
peppery	rubbery	rancid	angular	excruciating

On a separate sheet of paper, write a short piece that creates an extraordinary, sensory experience. You must address at least three of the five senses by using the most effective words possible to evoke reader response.

Name

IT IS WRITTEN—I WROTE IT!

The title above gives examples of both the passive and the active voice. A verb is in **active voice** when its action is **performed by** its subject. A verb is in **passive voice** when the action is **performed on** the subject.

GRRRRRRRR

Example: **Active:** The car hit the tree.
Passive: The tree was hit by the car.

Passive voice puts the action of a sentence in a weak and awkward position. Active voice usually makes writing more forceful and dynamic. (High school and college teachers often give less credit to written work which consistently employs passive voice.)

The sentences below employ either active or passive verbs. Smile when you read each active sentence. Rewrite each passive sentence to make it active.

1. The teacher taught the lesson.

 ____

2. We were embarrassed by the bad joke.

 ____

3. My purse was stolen.

 ____

4. I recognized the thief!

 ____

5. The thief was put in jail.

 ____

6. I've lost my mind!

 ____

7. Have the grades been recorded?

 ____

8. The story has never been told.

 ____

9. Are those the eggs brought by the Easter bunny?

 ____

10. Is this the hat upon which an elephant sat?

 ____

Name ____

WINDS THAT SIGH & CLOUDS THAT CRY

A favorite, easy way to begin practicing the use of strong visual images is to **personify**—give human attributes and actions to—things, ideas, and qualities.

Write a human action next to each object listed below. Then expand your description by thinking about when, where, why, or how the action might happen.

I'M REALLY BURNED UP!

Example:

- The motor coughed, choked by the bitter cold. *(why)*
- The river nestled lazily into its sandy bed. *(how) (where)*
- The rosebush slowly spread its toes in the warming mud of spring and sighed happily. *(how) (where)*

The toaster ______________________

The sun ______________________

The crowd ______________________

Numbers ______________________

The diamond ______________________

Our porch light ______________________

The traffic ______________________

The fog ______________________

A shovel ______________________

The angry sea ______________________

Skyscrapers ______________________

The mirror ______________________

A stone ______________________

Raindrops ______________________

Her raincoat ______________________

My fork ______________________

The tree ______________________

His boots ______________________

The frost ______________________

Candles ______________________

A flute ______________________

A hole ______________________

Name ______________________

PUT THE EXTRA IN ORDINARY

It's like eating bread, butter, and beans with milk every meal of your life. Aren't you just bored to death with the everyday, humdrum, run-of-the-mill, **ordinary**? Then kick the habit. Get rid of worn-out words like *do, give, get, go, put, make,* and *take*.

Writing comes alive when you "ditch" these old standbys and access words that draw stronger mental pictures for your reader—making an ordinary experience **extraordinary**. There is power in words. You can take any character or object and change its whole persona by substituting just one strong verb.

Try these: change only the word in italics to effect a significant difference in the character.

1. The students *walked* out of the building.

   ____________________ (make them appear enthusiastic)

   ____________________ (make them angry)

   ____________________ (make them seem relaxed, carefree)

   ____________________ (make them seem introverted, withdrawn)

2. The horse *came* out of the barn.

   ____________________ (make the horse appear elegant)

   ____________________ (make the horse appear nervous)

3. The children *ran* toward the playground.

   ____________________ (make the children appear out of control)

   ____________________ (make the children appear playful)

Jackson hit the ball out of the park and went home.
GOOD GOING
KSAY
Jackson walloped the ball out of the park and bolted home!
FIZZ K
ELECTRIFYING!!

Name ____________________

SUBTRACTION ACTION

If you are a middle school student, you can probably think of several people in your experience who often overexplain things, using more words than you ever needed or wanted to hear. *Economy* is a word normally associated with money, but it is also a very important idea in communication. *Verbose* (look that up!) people appear to misunderstand something about listeners. They don't see that listeners pay more attention when the speaker or writer uses only the words really needed to relay a message clearly and forcefully. One of the most difficult things a writer has to do is to subtract words. "Extra" words are not necessarily incorrect; they just clutter and sometimes confuse the message.

Example:

Verbose - There were these two, young, frightened teenagers who were always saying how they were so afraid of dentists.

Better - The two teenagers were afraid of dentists. (Eleven words can be eliminated!)

See if you can eliminate the unnecessary words in the following sentences. (You may occasionally need to replace or reposition a word or two.)

1. It seems that the only reason that she refused his invitation to the dance was that she didn't have anything to wear. ______________________________

____

2. We couldn't hear the words to the song on account of the fact that the track was too loud.

____

3. The room was square in shape. ______________________________
4. If students cooperate together, they can outwit the teacher. ______________________________

____

5. The thing that was so bad was John's attitude. ______________________________

____

6. In my opinion, I think the assignment is unfair! ______________________________

____

7. He drew three round circles on his paper. ______________________________
8. Actually, I think the bald principal is kind of cute. ______________________________

____

9. Chad is a great player who really plays well. ______________________________
10. What I would really like is a new friend. ______________________________
11. My parents are overprotective; they watch and monitor and examine everything I do.

____

12. Waitress, what is today's soup du jour of the day? ______________________________

____

Name ______________________________

CLICHÉ: AVOID IT LIKE ~~THE PLAGUE~~ BAD BREATH

"Quick as a wink" is how fast you'd like to get your homework done. "A mind like a steel trap" is what you need to prepare for exams. "Faster than a speeding bullet" is what you hope your time will be on your next cross-country run.

These phrases do communicate because they are familiar—perhaps too familiar! They are trite, hackneyed, ordinary, overused, worn out, unoriginal, and utterly predictable. Therefore, they lose their punch. Good writers avoid them like . . . bad breath?

Use your imagination to create the strongest and most original substitutes possible as replacements for the clichés associated with these phrases.

1. Busy as ________________
2. Hard as ________________
3. Slow as ________________
4. Smart as ________________
5. Nervous as ________________
6. Light as ________________
7. Uncomfortable as ________________
8. Funny as ________________
9. Bald as ________________
10. Sweet as ________________

Make up some fresh, new phrases that can be substituted for these clichés.

11. Not worth the paper it's printed on ________________
12. Fit to be tied ________________
13. Raining cats and dogs ________________
14. Feeling down in the dumps ________________
15. Looked like the back side of bad weather ________________
16. They don't see eye-to-eye ________________
17. Head over heels in love ________________
18. Together through thick and thin ________________
19. Spreads like butter ________________
20. Feathered his nest ________________

Name ________________

ESCHEW OBFUSCATION

"Sitting in the dark,
the story was scary!"

The title of this activity is a tongue-in-cheek expression that means "avoid making anything difficult to understand!" It's a good motto for writers! "Sitting in the dark, the story was scary!" Have you ever seen a scary story sitting in the dark—all by itself? Poor little story! This sentence is silly, but not unusual. Careless writers cause all kinds of strange occurrences. See if you can repair the damage by rearranging each of the following sentences to more clearly show its intended meaning.

1. While cleaning the attic this morning, a mouse scared me.

   ____

2. Paddling quietly along in the canoe, the moon shone brightly.

   ____

3. I read about the bank robbers who were caught in the morning paper.

   ____

4. Having collapsed in a convulsion of laughter, the students were worried that the teacher would never regain consciousness.

   ____

5. To earn enough money for the prom, Mr. Blake gave Joey a job mowing his lawn.

   ____

6. The fans booed the football players in the stands.

   ____

7. While eating her cat food, Mom noticed that Fluffy had a burr in her paw.

   ____

8. As a child, my mother taught me many lessons.

   ____

9. There was a tiny cottage behind the junkyard that was very beautiful.

   ____

10. On the top shelf of my locker, I could not find my math book.

    ____

11. He sold ice cream sodas to the children with tiny umbrellas in them.

    ____

12. The eighth graders were punished after the fire alarm prank by the principal.

    ____

Name ____

A LITTLE RIDDLE THAT RHYMES IN THE MIDDLE

Clever title, huh? It sort of rolls off your tongue! **Sound** is one element that makes language so intriguing. One way to arrange the sounds of a language for easy listening is to create short poems that are filled with words that tickle your ears.

There's nothing quite so gooey
There's nothing quite so chewy
As a brown and gooey
Brown and chewy
Piece of caramel candy.

It sticks to your teeth
Above and beneath
Thick and glue-y
Brown and chewy
Soft and gooey
Caramel candy

— *a classroom collaboration*

The trick is to stick some silly sounds together intelligently!

In the poem and in the single sentence following the poem, underline the words that are especially fun and interesting to say and hear. Then choose from the words below some that you just like and use them to create a short poem or a group of playful sentences that will be fun to read aloud. (Of course you may use your own fun-to-say words, rather than those in the list.)

mush, crush, hush, brush, rush
little, fiddle, riddle, ka-diddle, kid'll, middle, piddle
fuzzy, fishy, funny, flirt, flitter, flutter, funky, flip
snooze, schmooze, ooze, goos, choose, chews, cruise, moos, news, bruise, zoos
sprinkle, wrinkle, crinkle, twinkle
spooks, gadzooks, dukes, kooks
toodle, doodle, kaboodle, strudel, poodle, noodle
scabby, crabby, flabby, blabby, gabby
bodacious, boggle, bogeyman, brusque, bouillabaisse, bubbles, Budapest, buggy
hyphen, gopher, Philadelphia, pharaoh, graph, paraphrase, telephone, phlox
position, missionary, fishing, slosh, Ishtar, mishmash, mush
parsimonious, sauerkraut, hypotenuse, tessellate

Note that words that are fun to say together usually share some common sounds at the beginning, end, or middle **or** they have a pleasing rhythm when read one after the other.

Name

THE MISSING LINKS

You've probably had a conversation with someone who suddenly changed the subject. You were left wondering what planet he or she was on. It's confusing and frustrating when a conversation jumps to a new subject without any transition or connection.

Writers sometimes have a bad habit of doing the same thing. But this problem is easily resolved by learning to use a few simple expressions that link or connect ideas. Here's how it works!

Each part of a piece of writing showcases a thought or idea. To connect those thoughts and ideas to one another and make sentences flow smoothly, you need to choose from your list of "links" (words or phrases that bridge together, or connect, one idea to the next one).

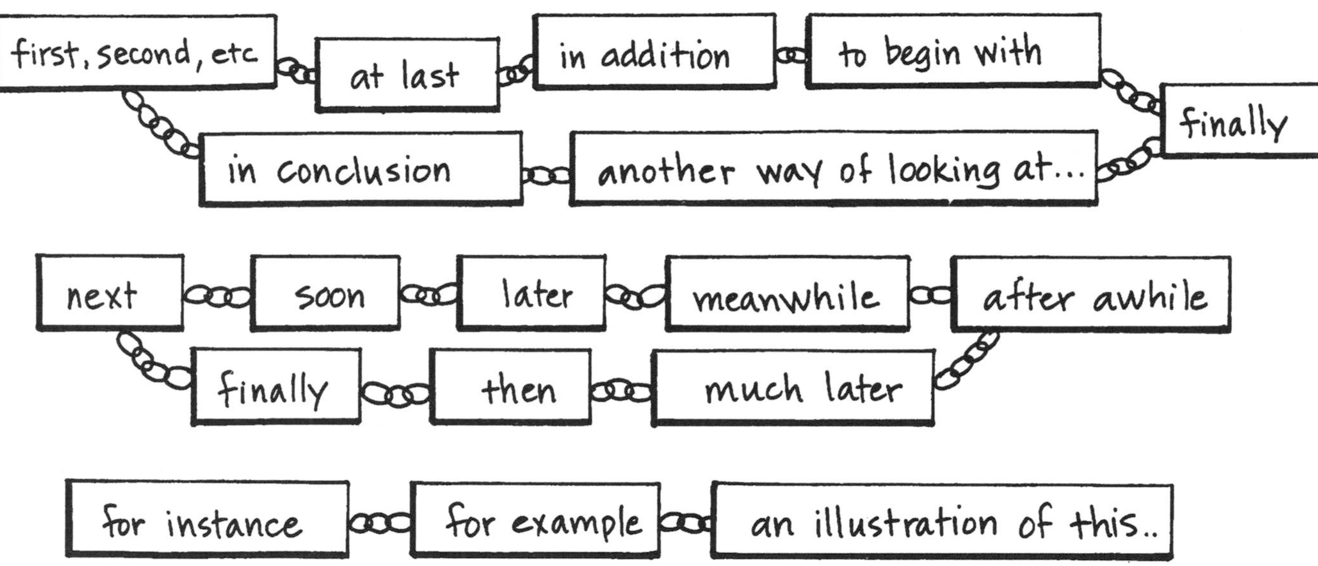
first, second, etc
at last
in addition
to begin with
finally
another way of looking at...
in conclusion
next
soon
later
meanwhile
after awhile
much later
then
finally
for instance
for example
an illustration of this..

Other connecting words:

therefore	however	instead	likewise
as a result	consequently	nevertheless	similarly
accordingly	on the other hand	because of this	in spite of this

Write a composition of about 300 words in which you focus on making your thoughts flow smoothly, clearly showing your reader the relationship between each sentence or paragraph and the one that follows. Choose a topic that explains **how, why,** or **in what order** something is done. This will give you practice using your store of connecting words.

Topics:

How to memorize 100 facts for a test
Why you should never fully believe an advertisement
How **not** to fail an exam
How not to win your parents' trust and confidence
How to talk your mom into letting you have a pet boa (tiger, iguana)
A day in the life of a middle school marvel—OR, you name it . . .

Name

GOTCHA!

Up a long, rickety staircase,
Behind a creaking, rusty-hinged door
In a dark and musty attic space,
Cramped by cast-off objects, strangled by cobwebs
And obscured by decades of dust,
BLOOD
Stained a rough hewn floor where, long ago,
A murder had taken place . . .
A murder for which
The villain had never paid his debt.
An amateur sleuth
And an aspiring coroner
Could detect
Only that the blood was human,
But of the mutilated body,
Only three legs
Were left intact —
Pity!

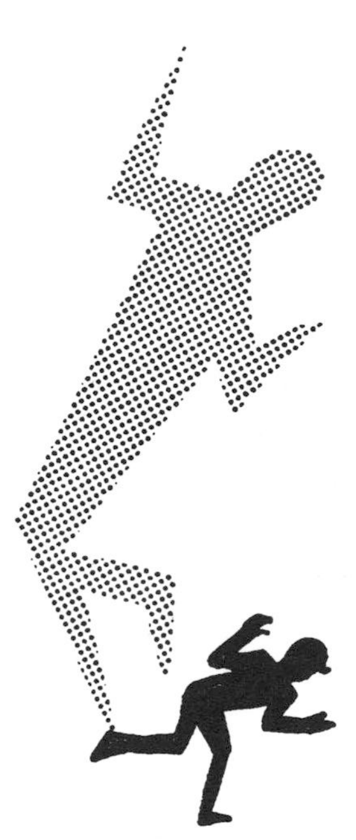

Who is the victim in this poem? What creature would contain human blood but have more than two legs? (See page 121 for the answer.)

What fun to be caught up in a story in which the writer "sets you up" to anticipate a certain sequence of events, and then surprises you with an unusual twist or catches you off guard with an unforeseen occurrence.

Use the space on the back of this page to write a short piece that contains some surprising element. Perhaps the list below will spark an idea, but you may, of course, generate your very own!

IDEAS:

An unseen speaker
An accident
An earthquake
A storm reveals something unusual
Caught!
An explosion (of any kind)
A secret revealed
A dream that wasn't a dream

Unexpected visitor
A reversal of roles
A beginning that is an end
The shadow
A noise in the night
Flash Flood!
The trunk in the attic
The wrong person in the right place

A locked door
What's missing?
A map to an unknown place
An unusual code
A computer virus
A stampede in the circus
The lost cave
Mysterious mushroom

Name

BRAINBUSTER BONANZA

Clever Christopher could make up the best brain busters in Boston, but no one could ever solve them because the details were told in such riotous sequence as to befuddle even the most intelligent puzzle freak.

Use the space below to rewrite the clues in proper sequence. As you write, do any editing you feel will improve the flow of the piece and make it easier to read. You may even delete unnecessary words or information. Then try to guess the solution to Christopher's brainbuster.

The man asked his housekeeper to forward his mail while he was gone. Was he doing the right thing, or was he being unfair? He called home to ask what had happened. The man apologized and promised to mail the key. A wealthy businessman from Boston left home on a three-month vacation trip. When he got home, he fired the housekeeper on the spot. Two weeks after he arrived at his vacation villa, he had received no mail. She explained that he had forgotten to leave the key to his mailbox. He was fortunate to have a very responsible housekeeper. Immediately thereafter, he went to the post office and did so. A month later, he still had received no mail, though the housekeeper had told him there was a considerable pile in the box.

(Answer: page 121)

Brainbuster Solution: ____________________

Name ____________________

COMIN' ON STRONG

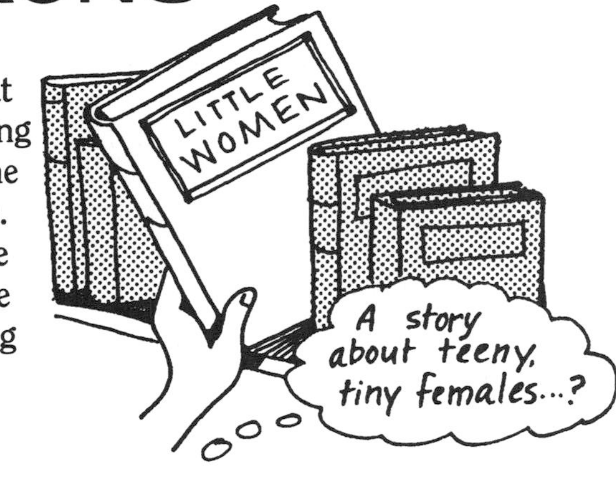
LITTLE WOMEN
A story about teeny, tiny females...?

When you are looking for something to read for enjoyment, what attracts you to a particular book or story? What is that "something special" that begs you, "Read me! Choose me!" Sometimes it's the subject, or the book cover, or an illustration. Often, it is the title. However, there are a multitude of classic stories that do not have particularly smashing titles. Some are listed below. For each title familiar to you, create what you would consider a more appealing title for that story. Then add to the list several other books you have read, and suggest a new title for each.

Charlotte's Web ______________________

The Adventures of Tom Sawyer ______________________

____

Robin Hood ______________________

A Christmas Carol ______________________

Mary Poppins ______________________

Pocahontas ______________________

The Yearling ______________________

The Story about Ping ______________________

Cinderella ______________________

Pinocchio ______________________

Romeo and Juliet ______________________

Hamlet ______________________

The Cay ______________________

Animal Farm ______________________

The Three Bears ______________________

The Black Pearl ______________________

Hoops ______________________

The Old Man and the Sea ______________________

____

Pilgrim's Progress ______________________

Johnny Tremain ______________________

The Wind in the Willows ______________________

____

Sounder ______________________

Treasure Island ______________________

West Side Story ______________________

Your Additions: ____

____

What is the title of your favorite book? ______________________

What is the best book title you can remember? ______________________

Name ____

MAKING WORDS SING

A. TUM TUM TUM TUM TUM TUM

B. TUM ta-ta , TUM ta-ta, Tum Tum Tum

Read these two lines aloud to yourself.
Now clap each syllable as your read; clap loudly on the tums, softly on the ta's.
Which has the most interesting rhythm?

If you chose line B, you already understand something very important about rhythm in literature. When the rhythm of a sentence is active and playful, it sweeps the reader along. It has a whole different motion than a line that just marches along to a straight beat.

Whenever you write a sentence, read it aloud to yourself so you can hear how it sounds. If it flows easily, like a song, it has good rhythm. Read these two charming poems by the same young author. Both are lovely sensory experiences. Each uses well-chosen, delightful words and ideas. Can you tell which has better rhythm—sings or flows more easily as it is read aloud?

Love is the color of lemon drops
Love smells something like cinnamon spice
Love feels like satin against your cheek
Love is a favorite song sung twice.

Friendship is rosy red
Friendship smells like cookies baking
Friendship sounds like jingle bells
Friendship is soft and comfortable.

The rhythm of the first poem flows more easily, partly because it is more playful and more regular. Its alliteration (cinnamon spice, song, & sung) and rhyme (spice & twice) also help to make it lively and fun to hear.

To practice writing words that sing, follow the instructions on page 87.

Use with page 87.

Name

MAKING WORDS SING, CONTINUED

Use with page 86.

Use this space to create some short poems of your own. Follow the model of the Love and Friendship poems on the first page, using the senses to "show" the qualities of each idea. Practice writing sentences that have lively rhythms. See if you can make them sing!

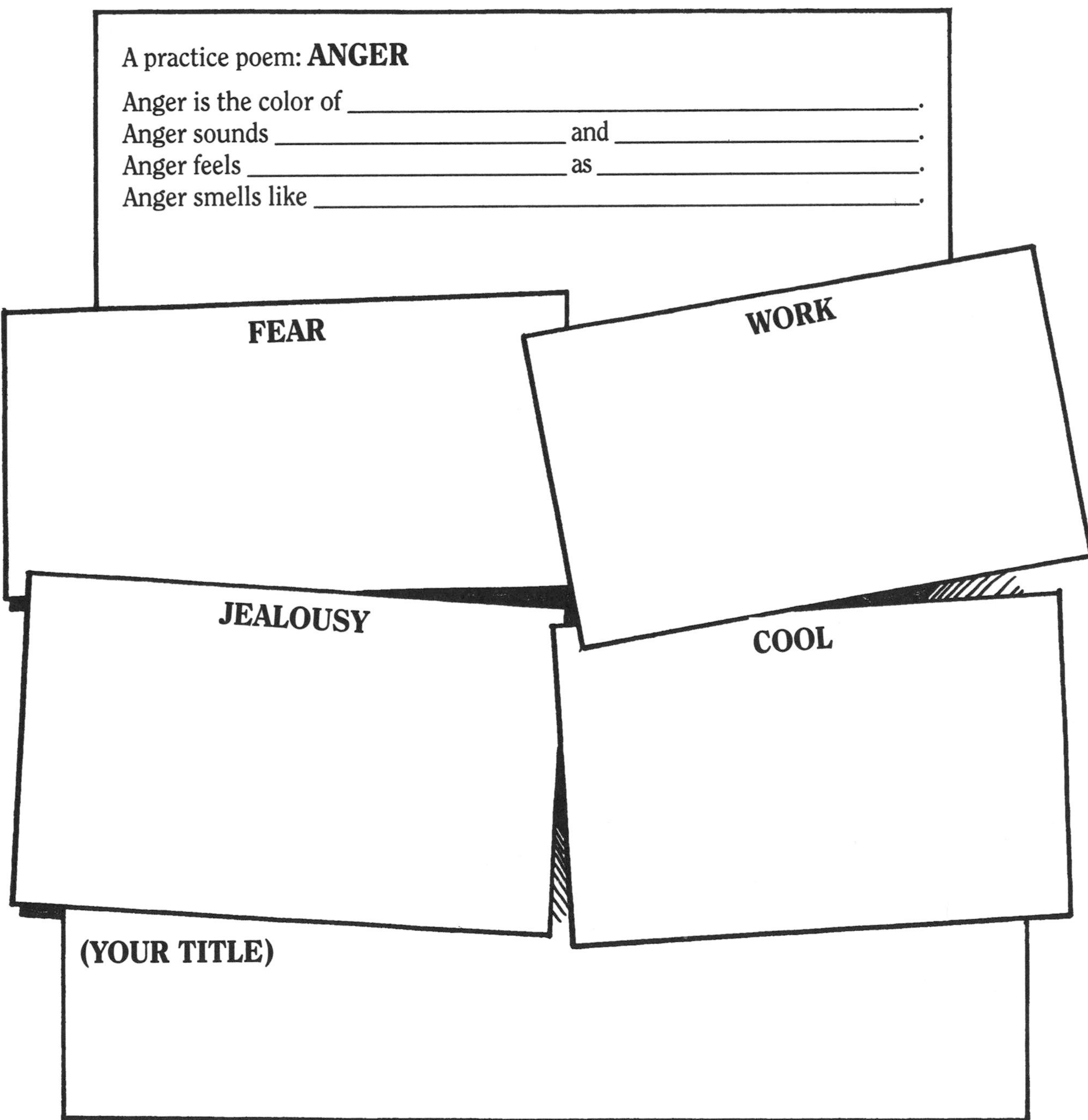
A practice poem: **ANGER**
Anger is the color of ____________________.
Anger sounds ____________ and ____________.
Anger feels ____________ as ____________.
Anger smells like ____________________.
FEAR
WORK
JEALOUSY
COOL
(YOUR TITLE)

Name ____________________

BODACIOUS BEGINNINGS

A. "Nothing . . . A big, hard, cold lump of nothing . . . was stuck in the pit of my stomach, and it wasn't going to go away."

OR

"Kris and I had a fight. It was one of those battles nobody wins."

BODACIOUS, MAN!

B. "Charity was a very unconventional angel."

OR

"Gadzooks!"
"Gadzooks??? What kind of language is that for an angel?"

The words you choose to begin a piece of writing are the readers' invitation to "come in." The words must be strong enough to cause the readers to believe it is worth their time to set aside whatever else they may wish to do in order to read. Writers often call these openings a "hook," because, hopefully, they hook the readers. Which of each pair of beginnings above best catches your attention and hooks you to want to read on? There is no right answer.

For at least five of the ten items below, create a smashing opening that you believe will command your readers' rapt attention. Then give each of your intended stories a compelling title.

1. the story of a storm ______________________
2. a warning about food poisoning ______________________
3. a report on safety inspections of elevators ______________________
4. a thriller about the capture of an international spy ______________________
5. a description of the best meal you ever ate ______________________
6. a news story of an alleged alien attack ______________________
7. a graduation speech ______________________
8. a soccer newsletter ______________________
9. a love letter ______________________
10. a memo to the school board about students' rights ______________________

Use with page 89.

Name ______________________

BODACIOUS BEGINNINGS, CONTINUED

Use with page 88.

Choose your favorite bodacious beginning. Write it on the first few lines. Then develop an intriguing body to follow your opening and close with a stunning ending. Add a compelling title.

Share your finished piece with your friends, parents, and classmates.

(Title)

Name

HAPPILY EVER AFTER

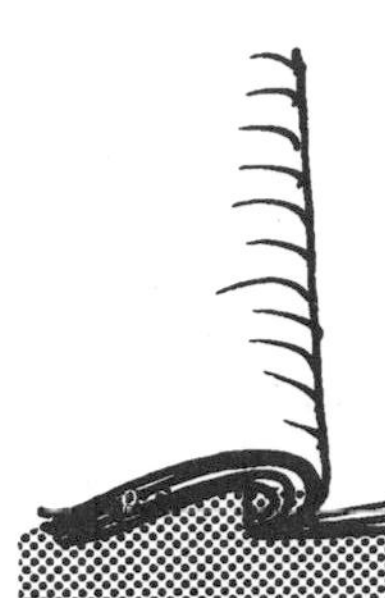

Hutch never knew for sure whose shadow he had seen projected on the window that stormy night. But the following spring, while mulching the rose beds beneath that window, his shovel unearthed a pipe—a graceful, ebony pipe bearing a carved Egyptian symbol.

Don't you just love an ending like that—the kind that strings you along almost to the last syllable? Or do you like happily-ever-after endings?

Imaginative endings are great fun to write. With a creative ending, you can:

. . . resolve a question, dilemma, or crisis completely

. . . leave the reader totally hanging

. . . leave the reader slightly mystified

. . . teach a lesson

. . . ask a question

. . . thoroughly surprise the reader with a striking turn-about

. . . use any other tactic you think will work

To write an ending, you first have to have an idea of what the piece might be about. That's where to start. Think about how to end:

. . . a report of a mysterious disappearance

. . . a vigorous protest against something you abhor

. . . a caution against a dangerous activity

. . . a wild adventure tale

. . . an unbelievable escapade into the future

. . . an apology for something you weren't all that sorry about

. . . a sad account of a disappointment or tragedy

Use with page 91.

Name

HAPPILY EVER AFTER, CONTINUED

Use with page 90.

Use the empty strip spaces to create some stunning new endings. Then cut the strips apart and distribute them to a few classmates. Ask each of them to invent a good story that leads to the ending on the strip you have given him or her. Invite them to create endings for a story or stories you will write. Then find a comfortable setting in which to enjoy the stories together.

Name

LINE PUZZLES

Sometimes a short, abrupt sentence can make the perfect statement. On other occasions, a longer, more complex sentence best expresses what you want to say. It is difficult to write a piece that has an appealing combination of sentence length and structure. To practice this skill, work the following exercise, "Line Puzzles."

On this page and the next are four groups of short, choppy sentences. Practice your skill at "line puzzling" by combining and rearranging the sentences in the groups to form a well-composed paragraph of various sentence lengths. Be sure it will engage the reader and "flow"—read smoothly. (Feel free to change the sequence, add connecting words, etc.). Use extra paper if you run out of space here.

QUIET
LACY DAISY IS
EXPERIENCING
DOWN TIME

I have a cat.
Her name is Lacy Daisy.
That's because she is unquestionably feminine.
She also likes long, leisurely siestas.
She sips, rather than laps milk.
She tilts her head saucily.
She expects to be pampered.
She's a tease.
I love her.

Storms are scary.
They announce themselves in different ways.
Tornadoes are so sudden.
You have little time to prepare.
You can't defend yourself.
You can know too far ahead of time about a storm.
Hurricanes come slowly.
Then you have to worry longer.
You can see rainstorms boiling up in the distance.
Then they roar in on a thunderbolt.
They can come slow or fast.
However a storm arrives, I get extremely nervous.
I wish they could be stopped somehow.
I'd like to make a law against them.
I'd stamp them "Canceled!"
I would click them off like a TV.
I can't control nature.
Nature is a lot like life.
You just have to let it happen.

Use with page 93.

Name

LINE PUZZLES, CONTINUED

Use with page 92.

Saturday was a bummer.
It was raining.
The telephone rang at 6:00 A.M.
No one was up.
It was a wrong number.
Drat!
The toilet wouldn't flush.
The top had been left off the garbage.
The dog dragged the trash all over the yard.
The paper delivery service hit the window.
It cracked.
My father swore.
My mother cried.
I forgot my piano lesson was changed—to Tuesday.
I rode my bike six blocks in the rain before I remembered.
That made me miss a phone call.
It was from a girl.
She'll probably never call again.
I ate cold pizza for lunch.
I got sick.
I went back to bed.

I broke up with my boyfriend today.
Well, that's not exactly true.
He broke up with me.
I didn't want this.
It wasn't my choice.
Jana told me that Brad told her.
Jesse told Brad that Mike was getting tired of me.
But Mike told Jesse not to tell anyone.
And Jesse told Brad not to tell that he told.
Brad told Jana he'd kill her if she told me.
But she did.
I asked Mike if it was true
I prayed he'd say, "No."
But he said, "Yes."
Well, he's a jerk anyway.

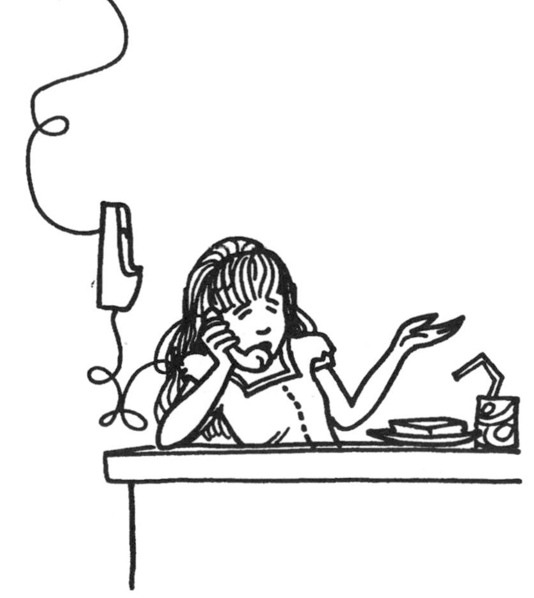

Name

MOOD MADNESS

Words are the tools a writer uses to "set the stage" for his or her story. The examples below illustrate how a writer sets the mood of a poem or drama in the opening lines. Notice how each author uses these lines to create an atmosphere which will influence his reader.

On the lines under each piece, see if you can identify its mood by writing a few precise words or phrases that describe the feel or atmosphere the author has created.

from *Plato's Apology*

"How you, O Athenians, have been affected by my accusers, I cannot tell; but I know that they almost make me forget who I was--so persuasively did they speak; and yet they have hardly uttered a word of truth..."

____

____

____

from
"On Returning to Dwell in the Country"

"Long I have loved to stroll among the hills and marshes
And take my pleasures among the woods and fields . . ." Tao Chien, ancient 4th Century Chinese poet

____

____

from Marlowe's
The Tragical History of the Life & Death of Dr. Faustus

"Now that the gloomy shadow of the night,
Longing to view Orion's drizzling look,
Leaps from the Antarctic world into the sky
And dims the heavens with her pitchy breath,
Faustus, begin thine incantations
And try if devils will obey thy hest . . ."

____

____

Use with page 95.

Name ______________________________

MOOD MADNESS, CONTINUED

Use with page 94.

Pretend you are planning to create stories on the topics below.

Write opening lines that determine the mood needed to "set the stage" for each of your new works. Just for fun, write an intriguing title for each one that is guaranteed to grab a reader's attention.

A WILD TALL TALE:

A MYSTERY:

A JUNGLE ADVENTURE STORY:

A LONG, NARRATIVE POEM ABOUT VIKINGS:

Name

"HOW TERRIBLY TRAGIC," SOBBED THE READER

BINGO! This is exactly how a writer wants his or her reader to respond to a sad story. One of the saddest stories of all time is the love story of Pyramus and Thisbe. It is retold below, but the portion which appears in italics is fairly dull and awkward. Make it come alive by rewriting just this part in dialogue form. Your dialogue must be true to the story, but you should make the conversation as fascinating and suspenseful as possible. Be sure to use proper punctuation and paragraph breaks so that the story flows easily and the reader can clearly tell who is speaking. Otherwise, he or she won't be sobbing at the end! (Use a separate piece of paper.)

Long ago, there were two young lovers who lived next door to one another. Sadly, an exceedingly thick wall divided the two properties, and they were forbidden by their parents to see one another. However, as is most often the case, true love "finds a way," and the lovers talked in secret by communicating through a small chink in the great wall. One night, as the two lovers met in the shadows, they made a daring plan.

Pyramus told Thisbe that he could no longer live without the freedom to see her. Thisbe said that she was also longing to be with Pyramus—see him and talk to him without fear of being discovered. Pyramus replied that he had thought of a way that they could meet. Thisbe was anxious to hear his plan. Pyramus explained that, on the next holy day, each would get permission from his or her parents to visit the chapel in a nearby park in order to say prayers. He said that, near the chapel, was a lovely tree with thick, white blossoms. Thisbe should meet him there, just as the chapel bells struck three o'clock. Thisbe agreed excitedly. She dreamed aloud about how they would then run off together and be married and live happily ever after.

Tragically, Thisbe went to the chapel early. As she arrived, she was met by a lion in her path. Frightened, she ran to hide behind the chapel to wait for Pyramus. In her flight, she lost her veil which was picked up by the lion who had just finished a bloody dinner. As Pyramus approached at the three o'clock bell, he observed the lion tearing at the now bloody veil. Of course, he assumed that the lion's dinner had been his precious Thisbe. Distraught with guilt that he had brought his lover to such a violent death, he took a knife from his belt and stabbed himself. As he lay dying, Thisbe peered out from her hiding place. She ran to Pyramus, but only in time to hear his last words of devotion for her. Finally united with her lover, she could not let him go alone. She took the knife from his hands and stabbed herself in the heart. The two lay together under the lovely tree whose white blossoms turned red as they drew the lovers' blood from the earth. The tree stands as a memorial to them, even to this day!

PYRAMUS,
OH, PYRAMUS!

Name

ALPHABETICS

Young children are intrigued with the sounds of a language. The repetitive, playful sounds of the alphabet can become very effective tools to help them learn how to use their language. Simple rhymes such as these are joyous for them to say.

B GOES BUMP
AND I CAN JUMP!

P is for punchin'
Mmmm is for munchin'
C is for crunchin'

See if you can make up an alphabet-based rhyme to go with each of the flash cards below. Decorate them, cut them apart, and try them out on your favorite kindergartner or preschooler. Then go on to the more sophisticated alphabet activity on page 98.

C	F
S	M

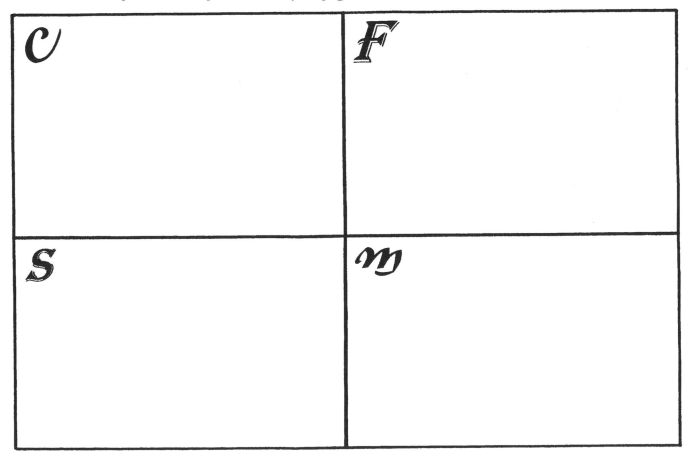

Sparkling ideas: How about . . . an animal alphabet, Christmas or other holiday alphabet, baseball or sports alphabet, music alphabet, an edible alphabet, a literary alphabet, a history alphabet . . .

Name

MORE ALPHABETICS

On page 97, you wrote some alphabet rhymes for little kids. Now change your audience focus and test your skill at a more sophisticated form of "alphabetics" by creating a poem like the one below. This poem will showcase your nomination for "Most Fascinating Letter of the English Alphabet."

Use the poem below as a model, but don't be confined by approach or form. You can write whatever kind of a poem you wish. Just make sure that it makes a **big deal** out of that letter of the alphabet. Use the space on the following page, page 99.

ALPHABETICALLY SPEAKING

B was born with a bang!
It's Bewitching
Brainy
and Beautiful!
B has a Billion in the Bank
And Believes in the Bible.
It has seen a Bazooka
in the Bayou
And a Bawdy Bartender
on a Balcony.
B Buzzes, Bops, Bites and Blabbers.
And it Beguiles,
Bedazzles and Bewilders.
It's been both a Bachelor and a Bigamist.
B is always on its Best Behavior,
Except when it Blunders
Into Bootlegging.

– Marguerite & Leon, Grade 5

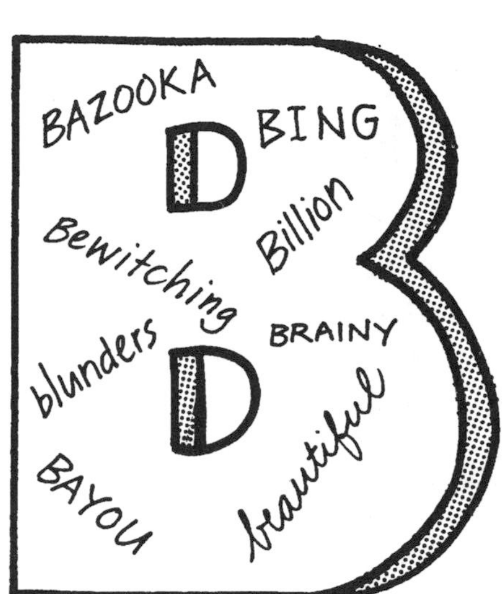
BAZOOKA
BING
Bewitching
Billion
BRAINY
blunders
beautiful
BAYOU

SHAN'T SURVIVE SANS SSSSSSSS

Vote for S
It starts off some of the super-est stuff
Seven—the most perfect number
Scrumptious and sumptuous
Shush and slosh and smithereens.
You need it to snooze or sneeze or smooch.
S is great in the middle, too.
Without it you don't have kisses or wishes,
whispers or tessellations
And what a great ending! S my favorites:
mess and bless, wish and kiss (again!)
Stop and sign up for SSSSSSSSSSS!

– Tamara, Grade 6

Use with page 99.

Name

ALPHABETICS, CONTINUED

Use with page 98.

This is a place for you to advertise one letter. Show it off. Impress everyone with how great it is. You might start by spending some time with your dictionary. Build a list of words (on a piece of scrap paper) that begin with this letter. That will give you good ideas and get you started with your poem.

I nominate the letter ________ as THE ALPHABET'S MOST FASCINATING LETTER, and here's why:

Name

TELL - TALE ART
(Poe - king Fun at the Famous)

Poking fun at familiar or famous writers and their writing is a sure way to get a reader's attention. If the reader agrees, he or she will cheer; if he or she is offended, he or she will grimace in disgust —either way, your writing has been effective!!

Parody (a spoof or play on words or ideas) is a favorite literary tool for poking fun. It can be used as a joke or meant to be satirical or ironic.

Example:

Silly – (Original) "A bird in the hand is worth two in the bush."
(Parody) "A bird in the hand is likely to soil the hand."

Serious – (Original) "Children should be seen & not heard."
(Parody) "Children should not be seen as a herd."

I. Try writing a parody or two, using familiar poems, rhymes or sayings as your models. Read your parodies aloud to friends or classmates and enjoy their responses!

Suggestions for a first try:

"Jack Be Nimble," "Jack & Jill," "Little Boy Blue," "Mary, Mary, Quite Contrary," "Roses Are Red," "Twinkle, Twinkle Little Star," "Time flies when you're having fun," "Don't count your chickens until they hatch" . . .

II. Now, on the next page, write a parody on a poem or piece that is a bit longer—perhaps one of your favorites from Wordsworth, Frost, Sandburg, Rossetti, Longfellow, Silverstein, Browning, or Shakespeare.

Use with page 101.

Name

Use with page 100.

TELL - TALE ART, CONTINUED

____
(your title)

A parody on ____________________ with apologies to ____________________
(title of original work) (author)

Name

FUN WITH MULTIFARIOUS FORMS

A writer's message may be delivered to a reader in **multifarious** (look it up) forms! One simple idea can be written as a slogan, a song, a poster, a story, a chant, a speech, a letter, or a rhyme. Identify a wish or dream you have, and express your idea in as many different forms of writing as possible. On this page you will find an example idea and a variety of forms of writing you might use to express it to a reader.

IDEA—I wish I had a horse!

A PLAY

A horse! My kingdom for a horse!*

* Wm. Shakespeare's "Richard III"

A WANT AD

Wanted: Equine beast of excellent quality. Royal lineage preferred over brawn or speed. Contact I. Thackeray at Brighton Eaves, Cornwall.

A POEM

Oh, how I wish I had a horse,
A beast of elegant stature, of course –
Not the drudge of a farmer's land
Or a racer trained by a jockey's hand,
But a steed who is spirited, fearless and free,
A powerful creature of majesty!
But should my magical equine dream
Melt like a dollop of sweet ice cream
In the heat of harsh reality,
I'll have any beast of fair quality!

A TONGUE TWISTER

My speedy steed supersedes the speed of a velocipede!

A LETTER

Captain of the Horse Guard
Her Majesty's Royal Stables
Kensington Palace
London

31 W Brighton Eaves
Cornwall
9 October

Dear Sir,
I am writing to inquire whether you might be acquainted with a horse of elegant stature who may have proved a bit spirited for the rigorous formal duties of the horse guard and is therefore available for purchase. If so, please respond to the above address. Anxiously and humbly awaiting your kind response.

Your fellow equestrian,
Ian Thackeray

Use with page 103.

Name

FUN WITH MULTIFARIOUS FORMS, CONTINUED

Use with page 102.

Express a dream or wish of your own in three or four of these multifarious forms: limerick, chant, cartoon, couplet, haiku, mystery, fantasy, recipe, me-poem, contract, jingle, menu, news story, advertisement, résumé, announcement, ode, bumper sticker, photo essay, song, tribute, gossip column, speech, play, banner, conversation, or tall tale.

Name

INSPIRATION: IMITATION

Imitation is said to be the sincerest form of flattery. It is also an excellent vehicle for having some good fun.

A poem that Clement C. Moore wrote for his three young daughters to capture their anticipation of the Christmas Eve visit of St. Nicholas is one of the most imitated pieces in literature. It has inspired hundreds of humorous, copycat derivatives. “The Night Before Christmas” is one of those poems that makes imitation easy and enjoyable because it is written with rhythm and rhyme that is appealing and playful. It sings! It's almost as if it has a little self-propelling motor. It “comes alive,” even when read by a poor reader.

Try your skill at using at least part of Moore's poetic idea to create a new narrative tale for the purpose of explaining the anticipation of a coming event or reflecting on a past event. Choose from the several suggestions below to get your tale started—or invent your own scenario. (You don't have to make it rhyme, but imitating Moore's style and form will move it along and make it fun to hear.)

Twas the night (day, hour, moment, month, etc.) before (after) (finals, homecoming, dinner, date nite, soccer, the hurricane, report cards) when all through the (house, school, camp, town, etc.) . . .

'Twas the __________ before __________

'Twas the week before finals
And all through the school
Not a student was happy—
Each felt like a fool!

So they picked up their pencils
And opened their books
And started to study
With miserable looks!

Name

ABORT REPORT BOREDOM

The word *report* immediately sends a signal to the brain that says, "YAWN!" The dictionary definition of the word is even more of a yawn: *A detailed, formal, factual account or summation, the purpose of which is to inform.*

But a report doesn't have to be boring! If it is written well, a report can uncharacteristically make the reader's ears perk up, eyes bug out, or whole body dance. Well, okay . . . at the least, it should be written in a manner that makes the information easily readable and understandable for the reader. If it can be entertaining, that's a plus!!

Guidelines to Help You Write Dynamic Reports

1. Choose and limit your subject:
   Enough material must be available to make a report worthwhile, but not so much that you can't cover the big ideas in a few pages.
2. Locate source materials:
   Keep looking until you have found information that is fascinating to you. If you're bored, you will have difficulty making it interesting for your reader. (Don't forget that people can be resources.)
3. Take notes:
   Record only the details that are most important and have intense reader appeal.
4. Make a brief outline or plan for your report:
   - An opening (including a strong thesis or topic statement) that grabs the reader's attention
   - A body of riveting, reader-friendly supporting information
   - A strong conclusion that makes the reader glad he read your work
5. Write a smashing, memorable account that flows easily and keeps your reader begging for more, beginning to end. You can do it!!

Suggested Topics:

How to Really Ace a Test
The Language of Dolphins
Pet Peeves of Middle School Teachers
Poisons that Lurk in Your House
Sleepwalking
How Lead Gets Inside a Pencil
Ventriloquism
Tarantulas—Tame or Terrifying?
. . . or a topic of your own choosing

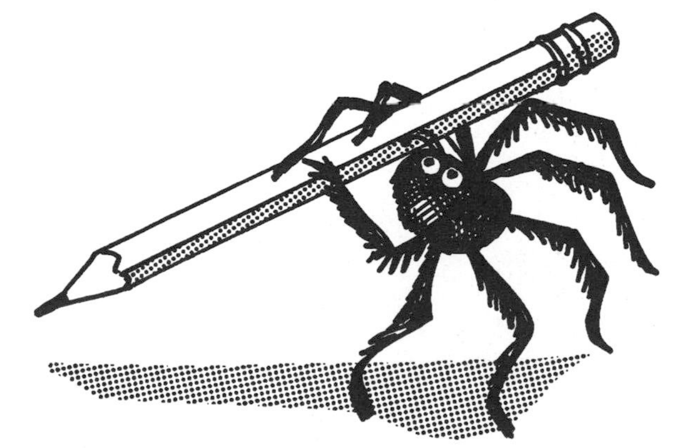

Name

SENSE-SATION!

SurroundSound® is an advanced audio technique that envelopes the listener with sound from all sides. You may have heard it in a movie theater.
A powerfully written description creates the same kind of sensation for the reader; it doesn't just tell you about something, but rather, makes you see it, feel it, experience it.

Read Taylor Siegrist's description of fear. See if you agree that he has skillfully put the reader into a situation which makes him or her experience this emotion, rather than just read about it.

FEAR

The moon settles behind a thick mass of swirling clouds. You take a fleeting, desperate glance behind you and descend along the steep path into the portentously poised valley. An enormous, tangled maw of black forest gradually opens before you, and wisps of darkness clutch at your beating heart.

Phantom specters glide through the night, reaching into your soul with their scrawny, dead fingers. Ghosts dance in your mind's eye, their cold images sending chills down your spine into the core of your being. The night burgeons into a living, writhing entity which strives to strangle you in inescapable terror. The silence is interrupted only by your pulse, echoing against the valley's dark sentinels.

Thoughts of escape race in your head, then explode into hazed visages of grim torture and grizzly death. Alone, terrified, you fall to the ground, hoping for comfort in the earth's embrace. Unfortunately no solace can hide you from the pale rider in the night.

Is your heart beating a little faster than when you began reading? Perhaps you are shaking uncontrollably or your hair is standing erect on your head.
If so, Taylor's piece is effective.

Choose one of the emotions listed on the next page (page 107), or identify another of your own.
Use this to write a descriptive piece that causes the reader to feel that emotion intensely. Some suggestions are given to help you get started.

Use with page 107.

Name

SENSE-SATION, CONTINUED

Use with page 106.

In the space below, write a piece that describes one of these emotions (or another one you choose). Make your description powerful enough to cause the reader to FEEL the emotion, too:

joy, anxiety, loneliness, anger, anticipation, grief, surprise, longing, jealousy, disappointment, ecstasy, relief, dread, guilt, pride

Name

ROGUES' EXPOSÉ

Expository writing? Sounds terribly stuffy and academic, doesn't it? But look at the root of the word *expository—expose.* Aha! That provides a different perspective. Writing that exposes makes the unseen seen—takes its covers off and shows the reader what's underneath. Now that sounds much more intriguing!

A written piece of this sort is sometimes called—guess what—an exposé; *exposé* is defined as *an exposure of something discreditable.* (The dictionary's second meaning is much less exciting—*an exposition of facts.*)

Below is a list of some of the most famous convicted criminals, rogues, and scalawags of all times. Choose a name to research. See if you can locate a body of information about this person or group of persons that will pique the interest of readers your age. Then write an expository piece that tells the highlights of the story (What made him/her/them turn to crime? What made them so "successful?" What flaw or circumstance caused their downfall or demise?). Begin writing about your chosen rogue at the bottom of this page. Use the back of the paper for more room.

?

John Wilkes Booth
Sirhan Sirhan
Bruno Richard Hauptmann
Bonnie & Clyde
William & Emily Harris (Hearst kidnapping)
Al Capone

Gotti or Gambini families
Baby-Face Nelson
Benedict Arnold
Lizzie Borden
de Medici Family
Genghis Khan
Frank and Jesse James

____

____

____

____

____

____

Name ____________________________________

IMAGINE THAT . . .

Imagine that . . .

. . . you can't shake a shadow that is following you everywhere

. . . your best friend has just told you the world's hardest-to-keep secret

. . . something embarrassing happens as you are giving a speech before a large audience—e.g. your pants split or your skirt drops to your ankles

. . . you are nightly abducted from your room by a group of friendly aliens who return you by dawn

. . . you are chosen to sing the national anthem at a ball game, and you can't remember the words

. . . you have discovered half a wriggling worm in the hamburger from which you have just swallowed your first monstrous bite

. . . you can become invisible

. . . and so on and so on and so on . . .

Use the space below and the back of this page to create an imaginary narrative that will hold your audience at rapt attention. Your story does not have to be long, but its sentences must be dynamic and fluent. Give your readers a thrill!

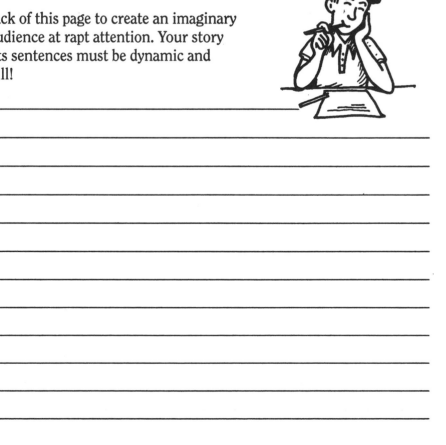

Name

PERFECTION DETECTION

How would you describe each of the six characters listed below?

Under each title, make a list of qualities or attributes you associate with that kind of person. Then choose your favorite and use the outline on the following page to plan a characterization (description of that person's character). Do not merely repeat the words and phrases you have listed. Create precise word pictures that will show the reader that person's character through his or her speech and behavior.

> *Example:*
> **NOT** - Ben makes an ideal friend because he is unselfish.
>
> **RATHER** - "What would you like to do?" Ben always asks me, before he expresses his preference. He once loaned me his car to go to a job interview while he walked to the store in the rain to buy groceries for his mother.

An ideal friend
An absolute bore
An honor student
A+
A high school hero/heroine
A lovable pest
A memorable teacher/coach

Use with page 111.

Name

PERFECTION DETECTION, continued

Use with page 110.

A PLAN FOR WRITING A CHARACTERIZATION

I. A captivating title to command the reader's attention:

II. A masterful opening statement that will invite the reader to want to know my person:

III. Several follow-up sentences that introduce the major character traits I see in this person:

IV. A very strong body (one or more paragraphs) that will include these examples of behavior to support statements made in my opening paragraph:

V. Ideas I will use in a concluding paragraph that will summarize the character I have presented and make my reader glad to have read this piece:

Name

SUPERSNOOP

Aha!

Your mission, supersnoop, is to choose a fictional or real character about whom information will be easy to track down. Pose as this person and create a journal of 8–10 entries, chronicling experiences, events, thoughts, and ideas related to his or her life. Use the space provided on the next page (page 113).

The entries may be sequential (dated in chronological order) or random. When a reader has read all the entries, he or she should be able to identify the "owner" of the journal.

This can be a challenging and entertaining activity—especially if you do your job as a "supersnoop," finding interesting and juicy information to include in your journal! Everything you write must be true to the reputation and personality of the character you are impersonating. You may have to do a bit of research to get the "good stuff!"

Remember that a journal may include all kinds of written material: very personal entries; thoughts and opinions on people and things; mini-essays related to politics, philosophy, social issues, literature, religion, moral issues, etc.; poetry; drawings or sketches; lists; notes or reminders to oneself, etc.

You can be anyone from Cruella DeVil to Winston Churchill, Mother Theresa, Hamlet, Michael Jordan, Chelsea Clinton, your English teacher, or the Pope. However, it is very important that you write in the voice and style you think that person would use—see and say things as you believe he or she would see and say them. (Of course, be sure that what he or she says is fascinating to read!)

Note: Trade journals with a friend and try to guess each other's identity.

The Diary of Queen Anne Boleyn
Tudor Castle, 1539
I almost lost my head the other day in an argument with the King. I said 'Don't talk with your mouth full, dear." And he
The Super-Journal of SUPERMAN
Monday: The boys upstairs think that I'm starting to look a little out-of-date.
Tuesday: Help! They've hired a 'personal dresser' to fit me up with a new power suit! Talk about a new image!!!
Fluffy THE CAT – HIS VERY OWN JOURNAL
2-2-97 – The Boss says that the mouse situation at the White House is out of control! My official assignment is to track, capture, and escort these rodent intruders off the premises!

Use with page 113.

Name

SUPERSNOOP, CONTINUED

Use with page 112.

Name

QUOTATION QUANDARY

"A little knowledge is a dangerous thing." Really?

"The only thing we have to fear is fear itself." Do you agree?

"Early to bed, early to rise / Makes a man healthy, wealthy and wise." Why would that be true?

Have you ever wondered how time-honored quotations like these have come to be famous—and generally accepted as truth? Some were originally the words of famous people, but that is not necessarily what made them endure through the generations of time.
Quotations like these grow out of the discernment, enlightenment, and good horse sense offered by people of all eras of history, all culture, all ages, and all levels of education. Together they have become a kind of folk wisdom that offers guidance for everyday life. They keep finding their way into commonplace conversation, and we take them for granted—often giving little thought to their meaning. But should we believe them? Do they represent truth? What do you think?

Write a short, informal essay that takes a position of agreement or disagreement with one of the above quotations. Use a combination of your finest writing and persuasive skills to convince the reader to "buy" your bias or point of view!

BIFF'S USED CARS
WOW, DO I HAVE A DEAL FOR YOU

Name

WRITING
ASSESSMENT AND ANSWER KEYS

WRITING
SKILLS TEST

Each correct answer in Part I is worth 1 point. Answers to Part II are worth 10 points each. Total possible score: 100 points.

PART I

For items 1–5, choose the word that is the most precise one for the sentence. Each question is worth 1 point.

1. Three cold, wet six-year-olds ____________ along home, wearily pulling their sleds after a long day of sledding in the woods.
   a. scampered
   b. slithered
   c. trudged
   d. ambled

2. With cheeks full of crumbs from our pantry, the _____ mouse scuttled behind the stove.
   a. plump
   b. chunky
   c. stout
   d. burly

3. Her friends were ______________ by Sara's terrifying tale of falling into the sewer.
   a. provoked
   b. captivated
   c. attracted
   d. inspired

4. "Absolutely not!" __________ Mother when we told her we were going to shave the cat.
   a. shrieked
   b. drawled
   c. muttered
   d. advised

5. I wasn't prepared at all for the science test, so I went into the classroom feeling pretty ______________________________ .
   a. alarmed
   b. shy
   c. haunted
   d. apprehensive

6–9. Choose the word or phrase that is most effective for the sentence. Each question is worth 1 point.

6. The principal gave the students a(n) ____________________________ after she discovered the band uniforms flying from the flag pole.
   a. oration
   b. admonishment
   c. talk
   d. speech

7. Tom ________________________________ his friend after the game and went off with some girls he'd just met.
   a. released
   b. left
   c. abandoned
   d. walked away from

8. We started a campaign to _______________ drugs in our school.
   a. drop
   b. dismiss
   c. omit
   d. abolish

9. Tamara looked _______________________ in her black velvet prom dress.
   a. nice
   b. exquisite
   c. pretty
   d. beautiful

Name ____

For items 10–20, there may be more than one answer on some questions. Write all correct answers.

10. Which example (examples) has (have) active voice? ______________
    a. Her heart was broken.
    b. She had a broken heart.
    c. Her boyfriend broke her heart.

11. Which example (examples) has (have) active voice? ______________
    a. The alligator grabbed my foot.
    b. My foot is in the alligator's mouth.
    c. I put my foot in the alligator's mouth (by mistake).

12. Which example (examples) has (have) active voice? ______________
    a. Who dropped the bag of jelly beans?
    b. Why are the jelly beans rolling down the hall toward the science lab?
    c. Is it true that the jelly beans are all over the school?

13. Which sentence(s) contain(s) personification?

    ____
    a. The damp fog reached its fingers into my coat.
    b. Summer has snuck up on us so quickly.
    c. Samantha is singing in her sleep.

14. Which sentence(s) contain(s) a metaphor?

    ____
    a. Lightning cracks with popcorn quickness.
    b. Jessica's popcorn is saturated with salt.
    c. This popcorn is as old as the Constitution.

15. Which sentence contains a simile?

    ____
    a. My popcorn tastes like sawdust.
    b. The hissing popcorn maker is calling us to the kitchen.
    c. Popcorn is expensive at the movie theater.

16. Which words are unnecessary in this sentence? ______________
    This old man who was kind of like older than my grandpa went skydiving together with my brother.

17. Which sentence(s) contain(s) alliteration?

    ____
    a. Don't you dare drop doughnuts down the downstairs drain.
    b. Grimy, slimy, wiggly, squiggly things are coming out of my salad.
    c. Crash! Bang! Slam! What is going on down there?

18. Which sentence(s) do(es) NOT include a metaphor? ______________
    a. My English teacher is as sour as a lemon today.
    b. The numbers on my clock glow eerily green in the dark night.
    c. My hair grows faster than you do your homework.

19. Which sentence(s) evoke(s) a strong visual image? ______________
    a. Traffic lights make me wildly impatient.
    b. The traffic light winked its yellow eye at me.
    c. This traffic light has the longest yellow in the city.

20. Which sentence(s) do(es) NOT evoke a strong visual image? ______________
    a. I shuddered as the darkest corner of the attic beckoned me to come explore.
    b. Your gum chewing sounds like cows walking through mud.
    c. How did you get that purple-green golf ball–sized lump above your eye?

Name ______________________________

PART II

Below are eight different writing tasks. For each one, follow the directions given at the beginning of the task. Each task is worth 10 points.

TASK 1 Each underlined word is an overused word or phrase. Replace each one with something more interesting and fresh—a word or phrase that is more effective or appealing to the reader.

This is a tale of trouble—unhappy, big trouble. It began when I walked into a dark corner behind the old shed. Right away, I knew I should have moved out of there quicker than a wink.

TASK 2 Rearrange the words in these sentences to make the sentences more clear.

1. Scott whistled to his dog driving his motorcycle. ______________________

   ____
2. Riding a bike in the morning, the sun was getting hot on my back. ______________________

   ____
3. My sister liked to tell her favorite jokes when we had the preacher's family for dinner. ______________________

   ____

TASK 3 Write a sentence that has interesting sounds and rhythms. Use some of these words, if you'd like to. You can add others, or you can use all your own words.

flitter	thrice	bubbles	gadzooks
flutter	African	buggy	mush
cruise	generation	gopher	shush
news	obligation	loafer	hush
bruise	conflagration	information	sloshes
ounce	mitigation	kooks	galoshes
dice	boggle	nukes	

____

____

TASK 4 Remove the excess words in these sentences by crossing them out.

1. There were these three kids who were friends who came up with a plan to totally eat a whole cow.
2. Abby made a geometric design in math class that had four shapes that were squares, seven three-sided triangles, and six round circles.

TASK 5 Use these short sentences to form a short paragraph. Combine the sentences in interesting ways so that you create a paragraph which has variety in sentence length and structure.

It started suddenly.
Before we knew it, things were out of control.
Tom sneezed.
Matt fell backwards.
Matt knocked Jon over.
Jon's bike fell.
His bike crashed into Dave's horse.
The horse bolted.
The garage door was in the way.
Were we in trouble!

____

____

____

____

TASK 6 Write a strong beginning for one of these sample topics.

An accident
A visit from a very strange stranger
An unplanned trip into the past
An unplanned trip into the future
Being in the wrong place at the wrong time
The test you forgot about
A topic of your choice

____

____

____

____

Name ______________________

TASK 7 Write a strong ending for one of these sample topics.

The most embarrassing moment of your life
A locked place
The trouble you may or may not have gotten out of
A person you wish you'd never met
A place you're glad you went
A place you never wanted to go
A piece of information you stumbled across
A topic of your choice

TASK 8 Rewrite this brief story using dialogue.

She ran to the police station and tried to explain that the car had gone into the bakery through the window. She said that several people on the sidewalk hollered at the driver to stop, but it didn't help. She told the police sergeant that the bakers were screaming for help and that there were pastries and frosting everywhere and people grabbing baked goods. She also told him that kids were cheering and saying that free doughnuts were rolling down the street. She insisted that there was chaos and that someone needed to come quickly. The policeman responded by asking if she would please state her name, address, and social security number.

SCORE: Total Points ________________ out of a possible 100 points

Name

WRITING

SKILLS TEST ANSWER KEY

PART I

Students may choose answers for questions 1–20 that vary slightly from the answers given below, as word choices and sentence interpretation are subjective acts. Give student credit for any reasonable answer.

1. c
2. a
3. b
4. a
5. d
6. b
7. c
8. d
9. b
10. b, c
11. a, c
12. a, b
13. a, b
14. a
15. a
16. (answers will vary): old, kind of like, together
17. a
18. a, b, c
19. b
20. b

PART II

Answers will vary considerably on these eight writing tasks. There are no right and wrong answers. Give students up to 10 points for each task, judged on:

a) how thoroughly they completed the task
b) if they followed the directions
c) if they succeeded in accomplishing what was asked of them

ANSWERS

For most of the activities in these pages, the answers will vary. Check to see that students have completed the tasks with reasonable responses that fit the requirements of the tasks, that they have taken the directions seriously, and that they have given effort to completing the exercise as explained. Answers are listed below for the pages that have specific answers.

page 75

Answers may vary somewhat.

1. OK
2. The bad joke embarrassed us.
3. Someone stole my purse.
4. OK
5. They put the thief in jail. OR, The thief went to jail.
6. OK
7. Have you recorded the grades?
8. No one has ever told the story.
9. Did the Easter Bunny bring those eggs?
10. Did an elephant sit on this hat?

page 78

Answers may vary somewhat.

1. The reason she refused his invitation to the dance was that she had nothing to wear.
2. We couldn't hear the words to the song because the track was too loud.
3. The room was square.
4. If students cooperate, they can outwit the teacher.
5. John's attitude was bad.
6. In my opinion, the assignment is unfair. Or, I think the assignment is unfair.
7. He drew three circles on his paper.
8. I think the bald principal is kind of cute.
9. Chad is a great player. Or, Chad really plays well.
10. I would like a new friend.
11. My parents monitor everything I do.
12. Waitress, what is today's soup?

page 80

Answers will vary somewhat. These are some possibilities.

1. While I was cleaning the attic this morning, a mouse scared me.
2. As we were paddling quietly along in the canoe, the moon shone brightly.
3. In the morning paper, I read about the bank robbers who were caught.
4. The students were worried that the teacher, having collapsed in a convulsion of laughter, would never regain consciousness.
5. So that Joey could earn money for the prom, Mr. Blake gave him a job mowing his lawn.
6. The fans in the stands booed the football players.
7. While Fluffy was eating her cat food, Mom noticed that she had a burr in her paw.
8. When I was a child, my mother taught me many lessons.
9. Behind the junkyard, there was a tiny cottage that was very beautiful.
10. I could not find my math book on the top shelf of my locker.
11. He sold ice cream sodas with tiny umbrellas in them to the children.
12. The eighth graders were punished by the principal after the fire alarm prank.

page 83

"Gotcha!": The victim is a mosquito.

page 84

The housekeeper could not open the mailbox because the key was in the box since he sent it through the mail.

page 94

Answers will vary slightly.
Some possible answers:

1. formal, defensive, accusatory, imploring
2. leisurely, languid, relaxed, free
3. dark, foreboding, ominous

SPELLING
Skills Exercises

JUST
SPELL
it

SKILLS CHECKLIST FOR SPELLING

✔	SKILL	PAGE(S)
	Spell commonly misspelled words	124, 125, 130, 141, 142, 144–148, 155–160, 162–164
	Identify words that are spelled incorrectly	124, 126, 136, 145–147, 152, 153, 157, 162–164
	Correct spelling in a variety of situations	124, 126, 136, 145–147, 152, 153, 157, 159, 162–164
	Spell words that contain particularly tricky letters	126, 127, 129, 130, 140, 155–160
	Recognize and use a variety of spelling rules	126–128, 130–140
	Recognize and spell words that follow unusual rules	127
	Recognize and spell words that follow patterns	127, 129, 131, 134–139
	Spell words that break the rules	128
	Spell words that contain silent letters	130
	Spell words with prefixes	132
	Use prefixes to spell words correctly	132
	Use knowledge of roots to spell words correctly	133
	Spell words with special endings	134–137
	Use suffixes and endings to spell words correctly	134–139
	Spell words with tricky endings	138–139
	Spell and distinguish among words that look alike	141, 142, 145
	Spell and distinguish among words that sound alike	141, 142, 145
	Spell and distinguish among confusing words	141, 142, 145
	Spell words that fall into a variety of categories	141–143, 145, 147–154, 161
	Spell words of foreign origin	143
	Spell difficult words	144, 148
	Spell unusual words	144, 148
	Spell small words	147
	Spell big words	148
	Spell proper nouns that are commonly used	149

TROUBLE-MAKERS

These are some of the most commonly misspelled words in the English language—some of those words that are always causing trouble for spellers. Two spellers have each written the same twenty-five words below. Each word is spelled correctly on one list and misspelled on the other. Examine both lists. Cross out the MISSPELLINGS. Notice how they're misspelled. These are errors spellers frequently make in these particular words. Don't let these trouble-makers trip **you** up any more!

MEDLAND MIDDLE SCH.
V.
ASHFORD MIDDLE SCH.

MY WORDS ARE SPELLED CORRECTLY, AND YOURS ARE NOT!

1.	**business**	**1.**	**buisness**
2.	**defence**	**2.**	**defense**
3.	**receive**	**3.**	**recieve**
4.	**citizen**	**4.**	**citazen**
5.	**chocolate**	**5.**	**chocalate**
6.	**February**	**6.**	**Febuary**
7.	**lisence**	**7.**	**license**
8.	**potato**	**8.**	**potatoe**
9.	**fortunate**	**9.**	**fortunite**
10.	**enuf**	**10.**	**enough**
11.	**ocur**	**11.**	**occur**
12.	**Wensday**	**12.**	**Wednesday**
13.	**cheif**	**13.**	**chief**
14.	**exercize**	**14.**	**exercise**
15.	**summersalt**	**15.**	**somersault**
16.	**separate**	**16.**	**seperate**
17.	**cinammon**	**17.**	**cinnamon**
18.	**privilege**	**18.**	**privalege**
19.	**dinasour**	**19.**	**dinosaur**
20.	**restaurant**	**20.**	**resturant**
21.	**answer**	**21.**	**anser**
22.	**abcense**	**22.**	**absence**
23.	**benefit**	**23.**	**benifit**
24.	**advertize**	**24.**	**advertise**
25.	**suprise**	**25.**	**surprize**

ANNUAL
SPELL-OFF

AU CONTRAIRE! I'M RIGHT AND YOU'RE WRONG!

Who has the most words spelled correctly? ______________________

Name ______________________

WORDS THAT PUZZLE

Here are fifteen of those words that constantly puzzle spellers. One set of numbered puzzle pieces gives you the beginnings of these tricky words. Another set of pieces gives you a clue for a word. After reading each clue, finish spelling the word correctly. On the matching puzzle piece, finish spelling the word correctly.

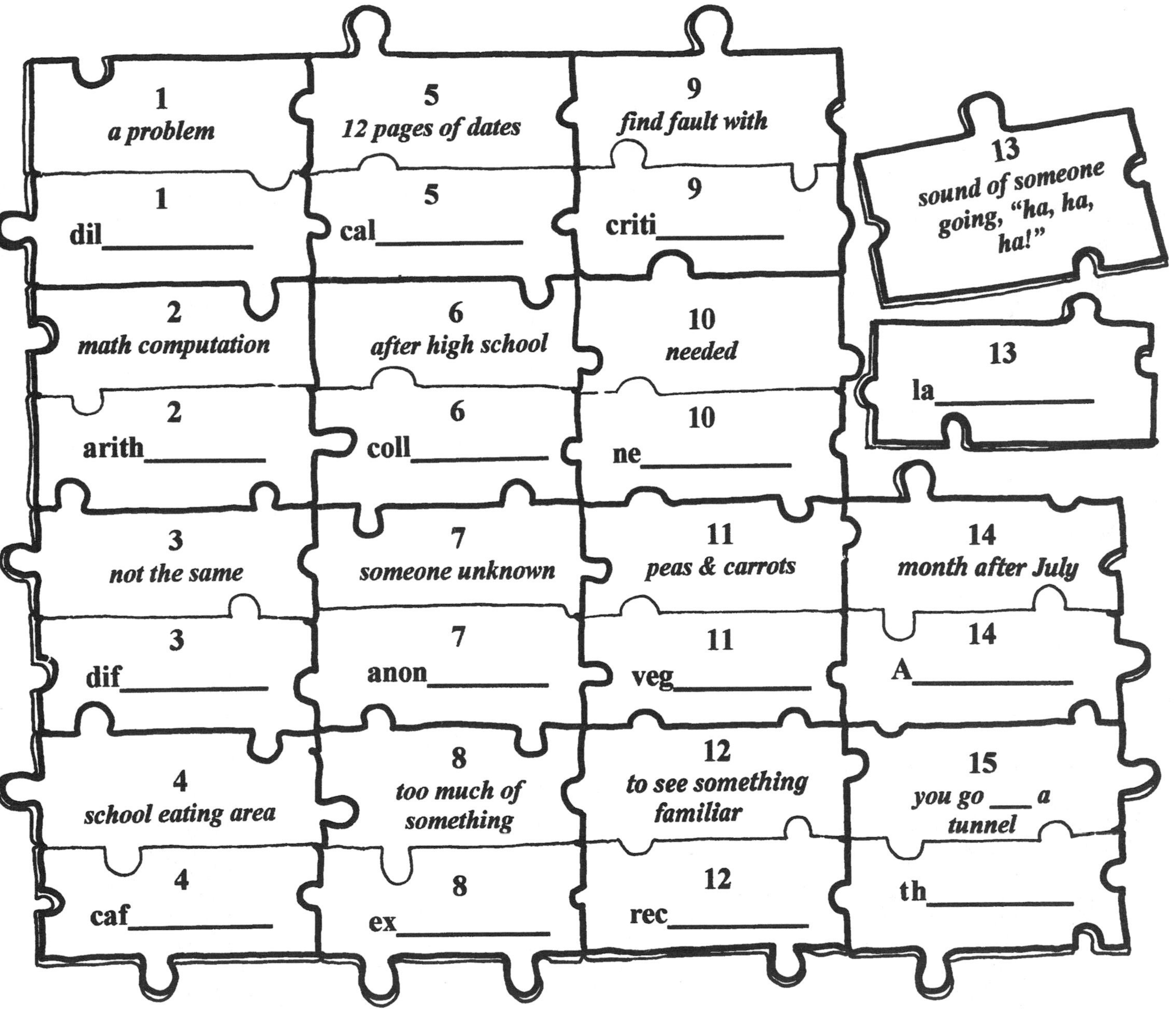

1
a problem
1
dil________
5
12 pages of dates
5
cal________
9
find fault with
9
criti________
13
sound of someone going, "ha, ha, ha!"
13
la________
2
math computation
2
arith________
6
after high school
6
coll________
10
needed
10
ne________
3
not the same
3
dif________
7
someone unknown
7
anon________
11
peas & carrots
11
veg________
14
month after July
14
A________
4
school eating area
4
caf________
8
too much of something
8
ex________
12
to see something familiar
12
rec________
15
you go ___ a tunnel
th________

Name

SEEING DOUBLE

Daniel thinks he's seeing double when he sees all the double letters in the words below. Do they belong? Are the right letters doubled? Is he seeing double, or are these letters supposed to be doubled? Decide if each word should have a double letter and if the letter doubled is correct. If a word is **not** correct, rewrite it correctly. (Some mistakes do not involve double letters.)

MAYBE I NEED NEW GLASSES!
tt
nn
PP
pp
mm
oo

1. butterscotch ______
2. caterpillar ______
3. bennefit ______
4. zipper ______
5. accountant ______
6. annimal ______
7. dessert ______
8. ommitted ______
9. embarass ______
10. misspell ______
11. quizzacal ______
12. chauffeur ______
13. bizarre ______
14. basaar ______
15. cerreal ______
16. mousse ______
17. ammonnia ______
18. travelling ______
19. comma ______
20. paralell ______
21. mammal ______
22. horrid ______
23. ballott ______
24. barracudda ______
25. ballcony ______
26. boycott ______
27. annual ______
28. rudder ______
29. carrot ______
30. memmory ______
31. cellophane ______
32. oppossum ______
33. hipoppottamus ______
34. staccatto ______
35. Tenessee ______
36. penniless ______
37. cenntennial ______
38. anniversary ______
39. proffessor ______
40. cellebrate ______

Name ______

A DEVIOUS DUO

Here are two letters that are hazardous to spellers when they get together. You've heard the rule:

LET ME SEE NOW, HOW DOES THAT RULE GO?

I before E
Except after C
Or when sounding like A
As in "neighbor" or "weigh"

E
ie
EI
i

Usually follow this rule—but not always. Practice using the rule on the words below. Write a word with **I** and **E** in it to match each clue. Then do the activity on page 128, where you'll practice breaking some rules.

1. fr________________t	1. kind of a train
2. sl ________________h	2. Santa owns one
3. n ______________hood	3. place to live
4. mis ________________f	4. naughtiness
5. ach ________________e	5. to accomplish
6. r__________________n	6. king does this
7. con ______________ce	7. tells you right from wrong
8. con ______________ted	8. stuck-up
9. quo ________________t	9. answer to division
10. p__________________e	10. eat a ________ of cake or pizza
11. soc ________________y	11. huge group of people
12. eff________________nt	12. opposite of sloppy and wasteful
13. gr _________________f	13. sadness
14. sc ________________ce	14. subject with a lab
15. _________________ght	15. after seven
16. w__________________t	16. number on a scale
17. defi_______________nt	17. lacking
18. con_______________nt	18. easy and accessible
19. hy________________ne	19. personal cleanliness
20. shr ________________k	20. piercing scream

Name

RULE BREAKERS

Sometimes words break the rules, and you just have to remember which ones are the rule breakers. Get to know these rule breakers below. First read the three rules. Decide if each word below breaks one of these rules. On the line after the word, write the number of the rule it breaks. Then practice the word by writing it again.

RULE A: When a word ends in a silent **e** and has one consonant following a vowel before that silent **e,** do not drop the silent **e** when adding a suffix that begins with a consonant.

RULE B: Most plurals are formed by adding **s, es,** changing **y** to **i** and adding **es,** or changing **f** to **v** and adding **es.**

RULE C: I comes before **e,** except after **c** (or when sounded like **A,** as in **neighbor** or **weigh**).

1. women________________
2. foreign________________
3. deer ________________
4. sovereign________________
5. alumni________________
6. neither________________
7. geese ________________
8. truly________________
9. heir ________________
10. mice________________
11. sheik ________________
12. weird ________________
13. financier ________________
14. height ________________
15. either________________
16. cacti________________
17. ninth ________________
18. leisure ________________
19. sheep________________
20. teeth ________________
21. counterfeit ________________
22. argument ________________
23. children________________
24. their________________
25. seize________________

26. Go back and look at the underlined letters in the 25 words. They spell a message. What is it?

____

____

____

Name ________________________

THE OUTRAGEOUS O

Lots of words have **O**s inside them. **O**s make words fun, interesting to look at, and wonderful to say. They also make words tricky to spell. These clues hint at words with at least two **O**s in them. But where do the **O**s go? Use the clue to decide what the word is. Then write the word with the right number of **O**s in the right places!

1. (a slogan)	2. (opposite of remembered)	3. (moth hatches from one)	4. (smell)	5. (opposite of rare)	6. (tropical storm)
M ________	F ________	C ________	O ________	C ________	M ________
7. (picture)	8. (study of poisonous stuff)	9. (guaranteed; won't fail)	10. (trail behind)	11. (insignia)	12. (skin design)
PH ________	T ________	F ________	F ________	L ________	T ________

Olive Ordered Oranges One October.

13. (to view from above)	14. (ducklike bird)	15. (train engine)	16. (whistlelike instrument)	17. (speaker)	18. (one-lens eyeglass)
O ________	L ________	L ________	K ________	O ________	M ________
19. (holey, like a sponge)	20. (African magic)	21. (stinging arachnid)	22. (foe)	23. (no longer a freshman)	24. (boring)
P ________	V ________	S ________	O ________	S ________	M ________

Name ________________________________

THE SILENT TREATMENT

Some letters hang around in words and make themselves seen, but they can't be heard. They don't add any sound to the word at all. Each of these titles for stories, articles, or essays has one or more words with silent letters. Look at them carefully. Then complete each title by writing in a word with the silent treatment.

1. Life in the ______________ of the Inner City
2. Rising ______________ Takes Over Bakery
3. Rat ________ Power Lines
4. Why You Should Give ______________ to Pigeons
5. Children Laugh at ______________ (Rhymes with Zoo)
6. Police Find Money ______________ in Newspaper
7. Circuit Court ______________ Rules Golden Gate ______________ Safe
8. Congress Asks; President ______________, "NO!"
9. Governor ______________, Effective Immediately
10. King Arthur's Favorite ______________ Steals Famous Silver ______________
11. Bear Eats Red ______________ from Mayor's Bush
12. Diners Suffer From ______________ Poisoning
13. Butcher Bakes Carving ______________ into Wedding Cake
14. Tests Show Third Graders Are Smart, Not ______________
15. Children ______________ Allegiance to the Flag
16. The Hunter Who ______________ the Grizzly for Six Weeks
17. Policeman Drops Shiny ______________ Down City Drainpipe
18. The Sheep Who Birthed Thirty-Three ______________
19. Always ______________ before You Enter
20. King ______________ for Eighty Years

OOOFF
MAYBE I SHOULD HAVE TAKEN THE LITTLE ONE.

Name ______________________________

"F" IN DISGUISE

The sound that F makes is not always made by F. Sometimes it's made by impostors—phony Fs! Usually the impostor is Double Agent PHRANKIE PHRENCH or Double Agent RALGH RATLOUGH. Both of these agents pose as other sounds in other words.

Each of these words can be finished correctly by one of these impostors. Tell which one by filling in **ph** or **gh** to complete each word.

1. ____ONY
2. SI____ON
3. GRA____ING
4. ENOU____
5. SYM____ONY
6. ROU____
7. ____ONICS
8. LAU____TER
9. EM____ASIS
10. TOU____
11. ____OBIA
12. ____YSICAL
13. COU____
14. STEREO____ONIC
15. TRIUM____ANT
16. XYLO____ONE
17. TROU____
18. ____ILOSO____Y

Name

TO BEGIN WITH . . .

Thousands of words begin with a handful of little beginning word parts called prefixes. If you know how to recognize these and spell them, you'll have a good beginning on the road to spelling success. When you know about prefixes, you can take a word apart and the spelling will be much easier.

In this assignment, you know the beginnings. You just have to track down the rest of the words and spell them right! Follow the clues. Match each clue to a prefix and finish the word.

biblio__________

in__________

dis__________

tri__________

ad__________

extra__________

ultra__________

anti__________

CLUES

1. doctor's orders
2. leave out
3. do the essay again
4. alikeness in form
5. leave
6. break down into parts
7. change to another language
8. tiny piece inside a computer
9. make last longer
10. not able to be seen
11. go ahead of
12. written list of books
13. beyond ordinary
14. exceptional sound
15. not approve
16. cycle with three wheels
17. against war
18. not tied

un__________

ex__________

re__________

con__________

de__________

sub__________

trans__________

micro__________

pro__________

pre__________

Name ____________________

AT THE ROOT OF IT

You may not think of words as living things with roots. But roots are places from which words grow—sort of like plants. Words have roots as the "center" of their structure, and often other parts, such as prefixes, endings, and suffixes, are added on. Another important thing about a root is that it supplies the basic meaning of the word.

These words are missing their roots. The meaning of each **root** is given; see if you can fill in the missing root to hold the word together. Spell the roots correctly!

FERTILIZE
GERMINATE
HORTICULTURE
POLLINATE
CULTIVATE
SEEDLINGS

1. ____________ ify (truthfulness)
2. ____________ tude (high)
3. em ____________ y (feelings)
4. ____________ ible (touch)
5. ____________ ifist (peace)
6. ____________ able (hard)
7. ____________ rarian (book)
8. ____________ ility (move)
9. ____________ ulation (people)
10. sus ____________ (hang)
11. ____________ ure (break)
12. trans ____________ (carry)
13. ____________ ant (sleep)
14. ____________ biography (self)
15. ____________ tion (make or do)
16. ____________ nal (day)
17. ____________ inous (light)
18. ____________ logy (star)
19. ____________ iculous (laugh)
20. bio ____________ y (write)

Name ____

SPELLING "ANT"-ICS

Ants are everywhere! So are words with **ants** in them. Every clue below tells about an **ant** word (a word that ends with an "ant"). See if you can get all twenty. Write the whole word, and spell it correctly—make sure the **ant** is at the end.

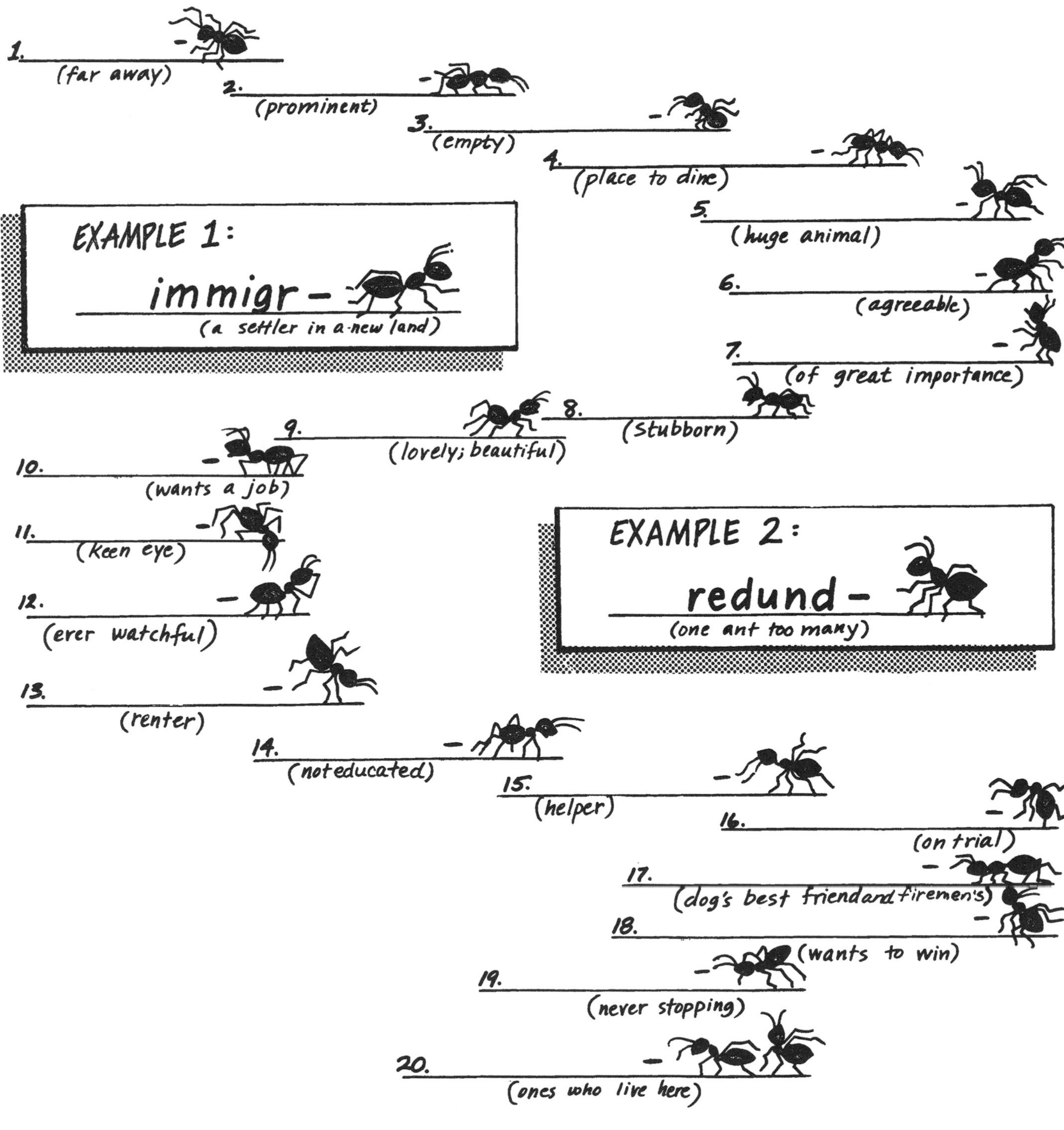

1. (far away)
2. (prominent)
3. (empty)
4. (place to dine)
5. (huge animal)
EXAMPLE 1:
immigr-
(a settler in a new land)
6. (agreeable)
7. (of great importance)
8. (stubborn)
9. (lovely; beautiful)
10. (wants a job)
11. (keen eye)
EXAMPLE 2:
redund-
(one ant too many)
12. (ever watchful)
13. (renter)
14. (noteducated)
15. (helper)
16. (on trial)
17. (dog's best friend and firemen's)
18. (wants to win)
19. (never stopping)
20. (ones who live here)

Name

EDIBLE ENDINGS

EAT and ATE keep turning up in lots of words. Maybe it's because, as language developed, people were always thinking about their favorite pastime—eating. These two endings finish off many good words—like dessert finishes off a good meal. The trouble is, people often get them mixed up. Every one of these words can be completed with **eat** or **ate**. Finish each one with the correct ending.

EAT

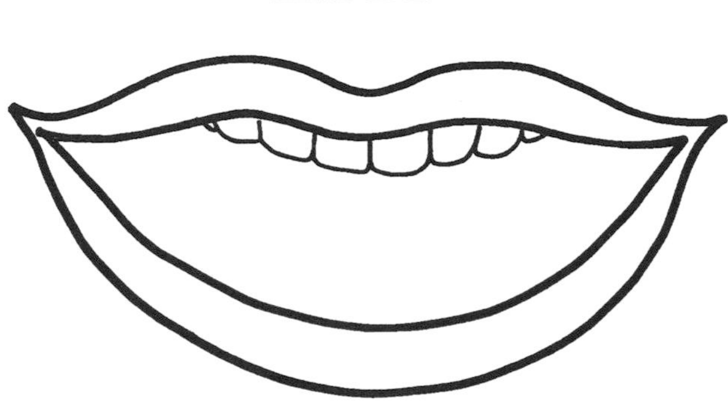

ATE

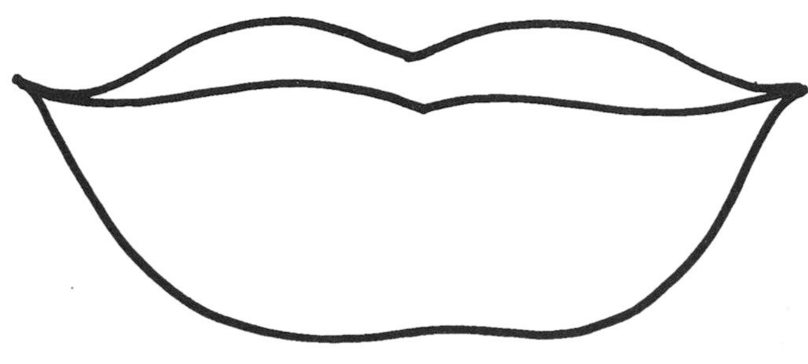

1. imit ____________
2. candid ____________
3. educ____________
4. ch____________
5. celebr____________
6. chocol ____________
7. retr ____________
8. gradu____________
9. rep ____________
10. wh ____________
11. rot ____________
12. irrig____________
13. thr ____________
14. separ ____________
15. incub ____________
16. oper ____________
17. loc ____________
18. sw ____________
19. devast ____________
20. estim ____________
21. hesit____________
22. hibern ____________
23. bl ____________
24. duplic ____________
25. decor ____________
26. def ____________

Name ____________________________

A MESS IN THE END

AL, **EL**, and **LE** just get mixed up all the time by spellers. And it's happened again. Some of these words are spelled correctly. Others have an **EL** where an **AL** or **LE** should be or an **AL** where an **EL** or an **LE** should be or an **LE** where an **AL** or an **EL** should be! Whew! What a mess! Please straighten it out. If the word is correct, give it a star. If it has the wrong ending, cross it out and write the correct one.

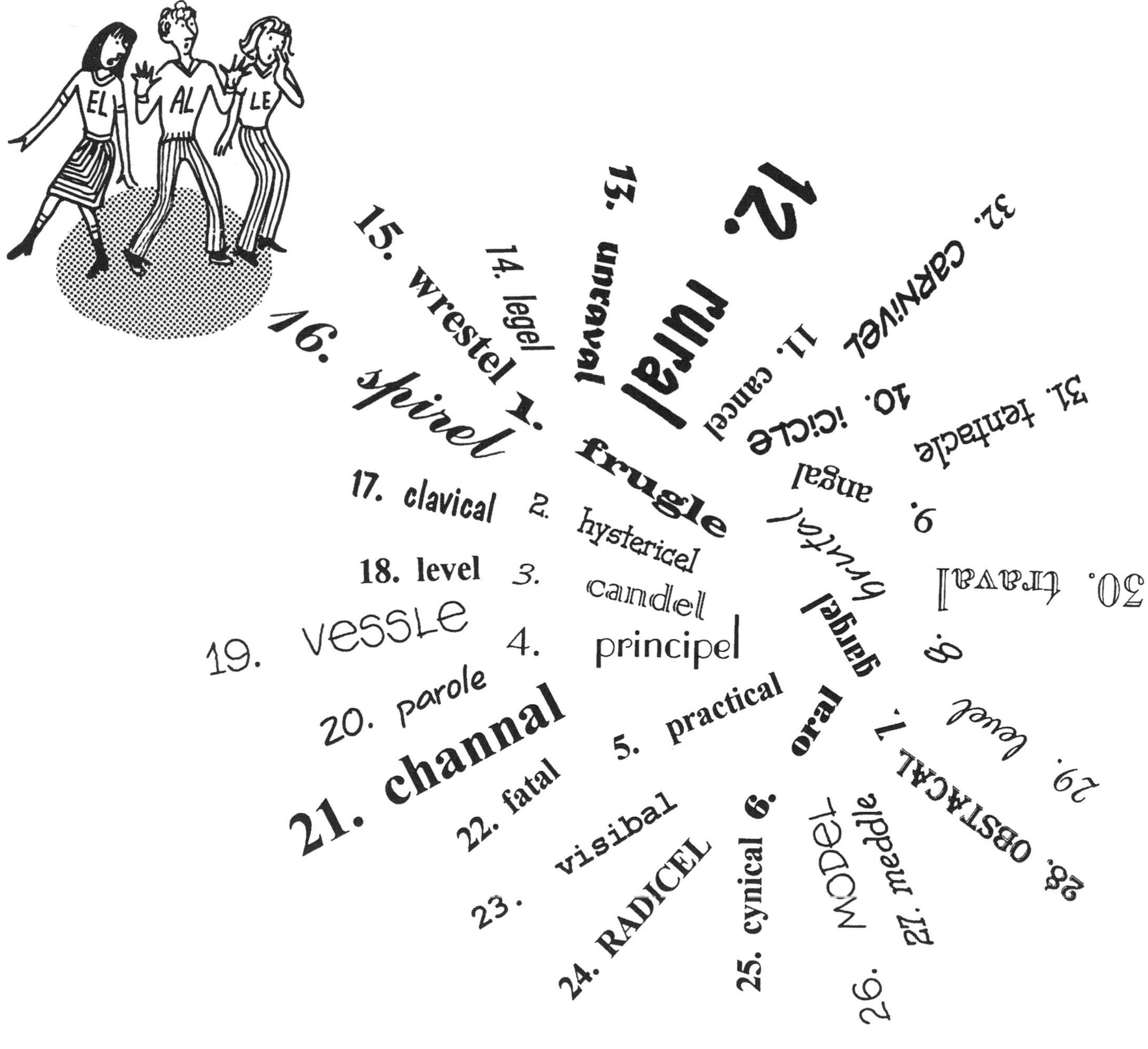
EL
AL
LE
1. frugle
2. hystericel
3. candel
4. principel
5. practical
6. oral
7. gargal
8. brutal
9. angal
10. icicle
11. cancel
12. rural
13. unravel
14. legel
15. wrestel
16. spirel
17. clavical
18. level
19. VESSLE
20. parole
21. channal
22. fatal
23. visibal
24. RADICEL
25. cynical
26. MODEL
27. meddle
28. OBSTACAL
29. level
30. travel
31. tentacle
32. CARNIVEL

Name

WATCH YOUR TAIL!

A huge number of spelling errors happen because the spellers aren't watching their tails (the tails of their words, that is). Endings really can trip you up. Here are nine different three-letter endings. Which one is the right one for each word?

Look at each word beginning below. Decide which "tail" is the right one for it, and write it (with its correct ending) in the place where it belongs. (See "tails" in the drawing below.)

1. apolog ____________________
2. host ____________________
3. infant ____________________
4. fugit ____________________
5. varn ____________________
6. telev ____________________
7. optim ____________________
8. self ____________________
9. child ____________________
10. negat ____________________
11. punit ____________________
12. pessim ____________________
13. juven ____________________
14. fool ____________________
15. pol ____________________
16. abol ____________________
17. expens ____________________
18. critic ____________________
19. exerc ____________________
20. defens ____________________
21. cynic ____________________
22. styl ____________________
23. optim ____________________
24. burglar ____________________
25. opportun ____________________
26. initial ____________________
27. favor ____________________
28. dent ____________________
29. flor ____________________

IMAGINE THE MOUSE....
IZE · ISH · ISE · ISM · IVE · ITE · ILE · IST ·

Name ____________________

TRICKY ENDINGS

How do you spell **confusion?** . . . Is it **confution? confucion? confucian?** And how do you spell **genius?** . . . **genus? genious? geneous?** It doesn't take a spelling genius to clear up the confusion. It just takes some practice with the tricky endings that confuse spellers. Practice spelling words that end with these:

ion tion sion cian tune us ious eous ius uous

Look at the words in the columns below. Finish each word with the correct ending chosen from the corresponding cards. Then write the number of the word on the correct card with its matching ending.

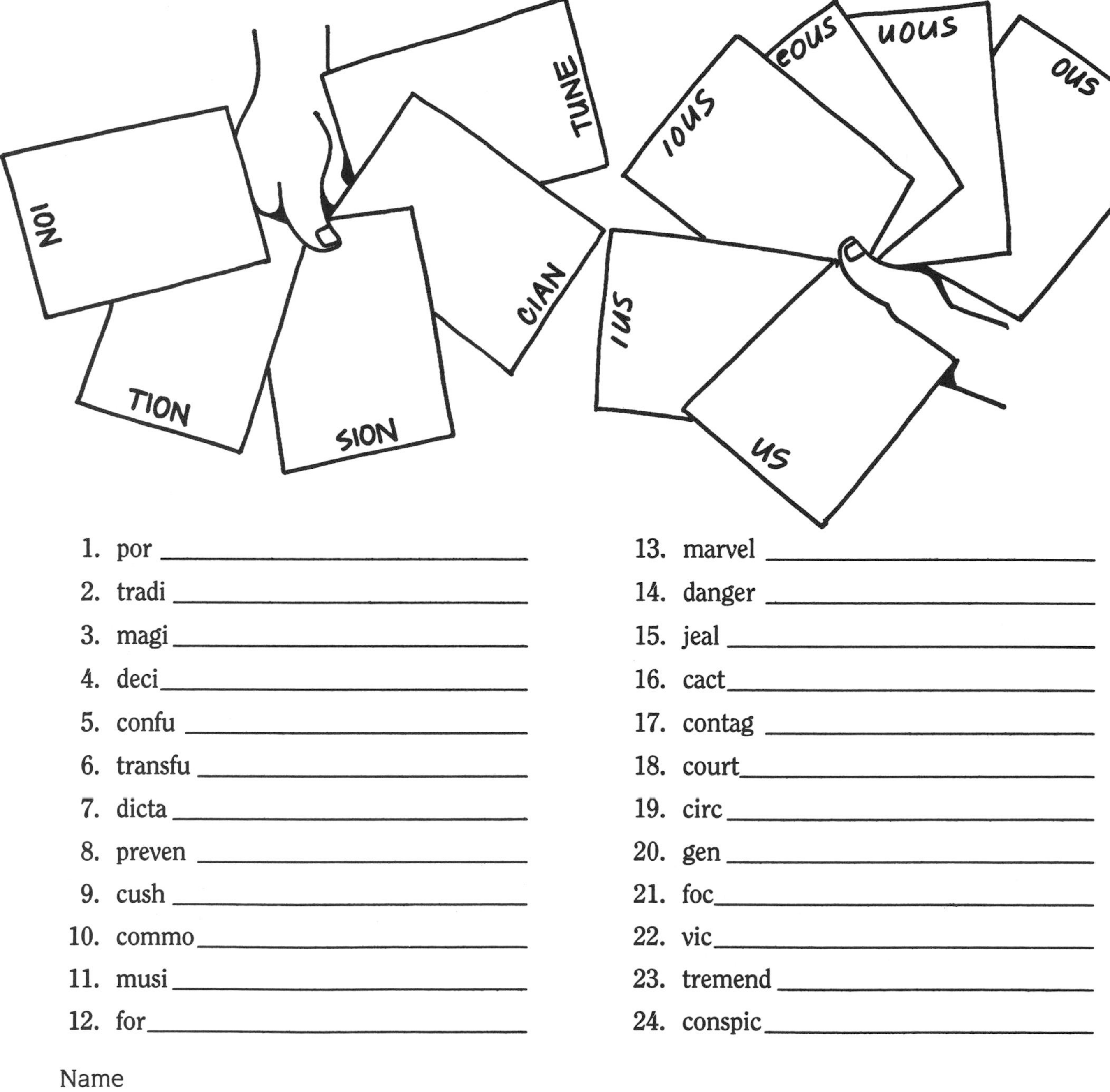
ION
TION
SION
CIAN
TUNE
IOUS
EOUS
UOUS
OUS
IUS
US

1. por ____________________
2. tradi ____________________
3. magi ____________________
4. deci ____________________
5. confu ____________________
6. transfu ____________________
7. dicta ____________________
8. preven ____________________
9. cush ____________________
10. commo ____________________
11. musi ____________________
12. for ____________________
13. marvel ____________________
14. danger ____________________
15. jeal ____________________
16. cact ____________________
17. contag ____________________
18. court ____________________
19. circ ____________________
20. gen ____________________
21. foc ____________________
22. vic ____________________
23. tremend ____________________
24. conspic ____________________

Name ____________________

MORE TRICKY ENDINGS

Do you know **ible** from **able** and **ence** from **ance?** To be an accurate speller, you'd better know which words require which endings. Here are some more words to practice. Finish the words in the columns below with the correct ending chosen from the cards. Then write the number of each word on the card where it belongs.

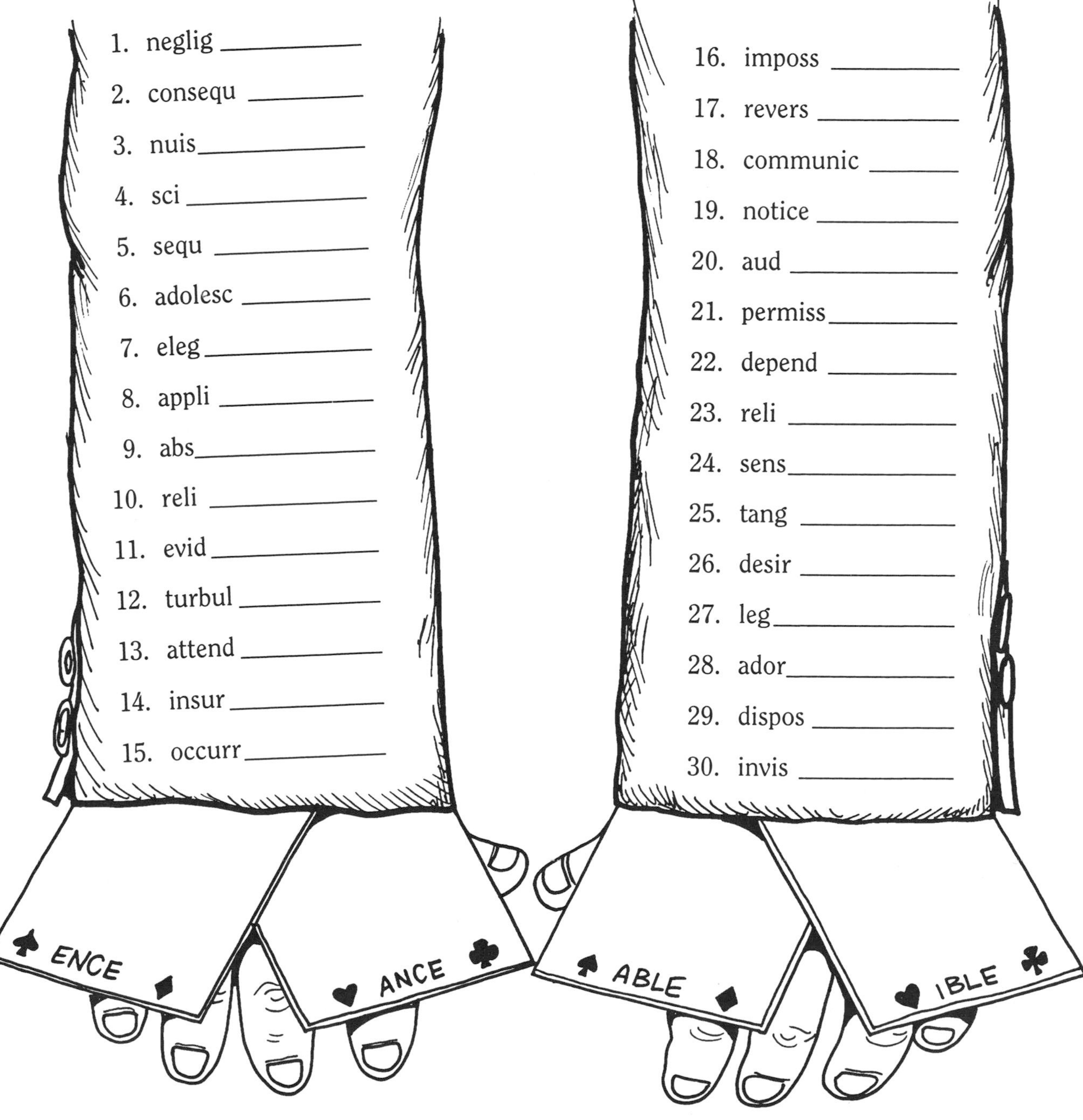
1. neglig ________
2. consequ ________
3. nuis________
4. sci ________
5. sequ ________
6. adolesc ________
7. eleg________
8. appli ________
9. abs________
10. reli ________
11. evid________
12. turbul ________
13. attend ________
14. insur ________
15. occurr________
16. imposs ________
17. revers ________
18. communic ________
19. notice ________
20. aud ________
21. permiss________
22. depend ________
23. reli ________
24. sens________
25. tang ________
26. desir ________
27. leg________
28. ador________
29. dispos ________
30. invis ________
ENCE
ANCE
ABLE
IBLE

Name

TROUBLE IN THE MIDDLE

GROAN... WHY DID I EAT THOSE VOWELS?

Do you ever get lost in the middle of a word? You know how it starts, you know how it ends, but somewhere in the middle things fall apart? It seems that the beginnings and endings of words get all the attention! But what's in the middle is pretty crucial to correct spelling.

Get better at middles by practicing these words that have tricky vowel combinations inside them. The middles are firmly in place this time. Figure out the rest of the word that surrounds these CORRECT middles.

1. great pain ___ ___ ___ ui ___ ___
2. great confusion ___ ___ ao ___
3. dangerous ___ ___ ea ___ ___ ___ ___ ___ ___ ___
4. a fake ___ ___ au ___
5. very poor person ___ au ___ ___ ___
6. no rain for a long time ___ ___ ou ___ ___ ___
7. a large cat ___ ou ___ ___ ___
8. place to find synonyms ___ ___ ___ ___ au ___ ___ ___
9. a prejudice ___ ia ___
10. loud, noisy ___ oi ___ ___ ___ ___ ___ ___ ___
11. color that hides an animal ___ ___ ___ ou ___ ___ ___ ___ ___
12. believable ___ ___ au ___ ___ ___ ___ ___
13. impressive speaker ___ ___ ___ ___ ue ___ ___
14. fish home ___ ___ ua ___ ___ ___ ___
15. spicy hotdog ___ au ___ ___ ___ ___
16. facial hair ___ ea ___ ___
17. big cat with spots ___ eo ___ ___ ___ ___
18. white, cabbage-tasting vegetable ___ au ___ ___ ___ ___ ___ ___ ___ ___
19. epidemic sickness ___ ___ ___ ___ ue ___ ___ ___
20. opposed to ___ ___ ai ___ ___ ___
21. idea ___ ___ ou ___ ___ ___
22. fake identity ___ ___ ___ ___ ui ___ ___

Name ______________________________

LOOK-ALIKES & SOUND-ALIKES

Which is underage . . . a **minor** or a **miner?** On a dark night in a dark alley . . . are you likely to be **scared** or **sacred?** Who runs the school . . . the **principal** or the **principle?** Is Washington D.C. the Unites States' **capital** or **capitol?** And do you and your friends look for adventure **altogether** or **all together?** Words that look or sound exactly alike or similar are the cause of many spelling errors. Here's a chance to get some of them straightened out. Choose the correct word from the box to fit in each space.

No MINORS ALLOWED

1. Jaycee is 15. She doesn't work in a mine. She is a ____________.
2. On a dark night in a dark alley, you'll probably be feeling __________ and thinking that your life is very __________ to you.
3. The bold, ambitious knight from King Arthur's court had one favorite steel ____________, which he left to his favorite ______________ after he died.
4. The school ____________ reported 22 ____________ of food-throwing in the cafeteria last month. She noted that the _____________ of these episodes had doubled since September. As a result, she declared that _______________ would no longer be served at the end of school lunches.
5. If a bike doesn't have a _______________, it will be extremely hard to ______________ up the hill to the high school.
6. If a ________________ in your classroom dove off a 50-foot ______________ into the ocean, would you be likely to do the same?
7. On my vacation, I ______________ in a glider, rode a camel across a _____________, and helped a ________________ pan for gold.
8. Magda decided that, for her visit to the ______________ city of her state and the ______________ building, she would dye her _________________ blue, the color of her state bird.
9. _______________, I have collected seven different varieties of scorpions (all dead, of course!).
10. When my sister becomes president, as I know she will, I'll write her a letter of congratulations on the __________________ she designed for me when she was in kindergarten.

soared	stationary	principal	stationery
pier	all together	scared	incidence
sacred	desert	pedal	capitol
peer	sword	hair	miner
capital	incidents	peddle	altogether
minor	dessert	principle	heir

Name ____

MORE LIKELY ALIKE

Should you seize the daze . . . or seas the days? Is a lyre untruthful . . . or a carrot valuable? Do colonels get kernels stuck in their teeth . . . or is it kernels that give military orders? Here are some more of those words that look alike, sound alike, or are so similar that they trip you up on spelling. Write a question or sentence that uses each group of words.

1	2	3
carat daze taught	colonels kernels pray	hymn council lyre

1. ______________________________
2. ______________________________
3. ______________________________

4	5	6
suite carrot witch scent	which liar accept sense	except scents prey seize

4. ______________________________
5. ______________________________
6. ______________________________

7	8	9
addition sent days	sweet counsel taut	him edition seas

7. ______________________________
8. ______________________________
9. ______________________________

Name ______________________________

BORROWED WORDS

Thousands of English words that we use daily are borrowed from other languages. They add a rich flavor to our language. Here are just a few of the words that found their way to us across seas and borders.

algebra (Arabic)
antique (French)
blitz (German)
bourgeois (French)
buoy (Dutch)
chauffeur (French)
chemistry (Arabic)
elite (French)
emerald (French)
freight (Dutch)
guru (Indian)

gorilla (African)
kindergarten (German)
lasso (Spanish)
macaroni (Italian)
magazine (Arabic)
molasses (Portuguese)
mosquito (Spanish)
mandarin (Chinese)
mustang (Spanish)
pajama (Indian)
paradise (Persian)

piano (Italian)
sarong (India)
sauerkraut (German)
shampoo (Indian)
tambourine (Arabic)
tourniquet (French)
tsar (Russian)
tycoon (Japanese)
vanilla (Spanish)
veto (Latin)
yacht (Dutch)
zombie (African)

French
GERMAN
Italian
African
RUSSIAN
Japanese
Indian
English
DUTCH
SPANISH

Find a word (or words) above that matches each meaning. Write the word on the line, and make sure you spell it correctly.

1. precious gemstone __________
2. biting insect __________
3. Italian food __________
4. school for young children __________
5. things that float __________
6. school subjects __________
7. old and valuable __________
8. something to read __________
9. German food __________
10. an ultimate environment __________
11. animals __________
12. clothing __________
13. say "no" to __________
14. music makers __________

Name __________

WILD, WEIRD, & WACKY WORDS

Some words are just plain weird—or outrageous—or unusual. It might be because of the way they look, or sound, or are spelled. It might be because of their meanings. And, of course, different people have different opinions about what makes a word weird.

Here are some unusual words. Say each one to yourself, because they sound interesting. Write each one, spelling it correctly. Then find out what 10 of them mean (all, if you want).

BIZARRE etiquette & supercilious OGRES WITH lorgnettes:

PETIT-FOURS ?
HUMPH
WE ONLY EAT STURGEON PATÉ,
OR, LADY-FINGERS

etiquette ____________________

bizarre ____________________

ogre ____________________

kazoo ____________________

morgue ____________________

lozenge ____________________

catastrophe ____________________

niche ____________________

incisors ____________________

rogue ____________________

cipher ____________________

tongue ____________________

hyperbole ____________________

elixir ____________________

blasé ____________________

facsimile ____________________

etcetera ____________________

dungeon ____________________

pathos ____________________

menagerie ____________________

bamboozle ____________________

anachronism ____________________

sousaphone ____________________

petit fours ____________________

sturgeon ____________________

paté ____________________

jodhpurs ____________________

supercilious ____________________

onomatopoeia ____________________

lorgnette ____________________

Name ____

WORDS THAT CONFUSE

AND
I'M
LATE,
TOO!

I always loose my notes when I get ready for a test, accept for math, because I warp my lunch in those and always have them near. My mother gives me unending advise about how to get thorough this problem, but, I insure you, it's a useless excise. It'll be major croupe if I ever get excepted into any collage.

I. This writer is confused—help him! Rewrite his paragraph (above) and replace the wrong words with the correctly spelled words he meant to use.

____

____

____

____

II. Next, help him with his spelling assignment. Locate each word that is incorrect. Cross it out and replace it with the correctly spelled word he should have chosen.

1. If I could just get trough this week, I can get though anything! ________________
2. I wonder weather the whether will get any better. ________________ ________________
3. The district attorney decided to persecute the clown for failing to make people laugh. ________________
4. My mother never knows witch buttons to push on the remote control for the VCR. ________________
5. I certainly could use a guardian angle today (particularly one who knows geometry). ________________
6. My English teacher says I have a serious lack of comas in my essay. ________________
7. My older brother is always threatening to afflict pain on me if I don't get off the telephone. ________________
8. Jeanie inferred to Michelle that she was going to the prom with Joe. ________________
9. You got one hundred on your science test? That's inedible! ________________
10. As you can see by how outgoing I am, I'm definitely an introvert. ________________

Name ________________________________

HOW TO TURN A FLEA INTO A LEAF

It isn't really all that hard to turn a **flea** into a **leaf**! Just rearrange the letters in the **flea**, and you get a **leaf**. Once you know how to spell many words correctly, you can have fun with them by moving the letters around to get new words. Each of these sentences below is a bit of a puzzle for you. Fill in each blank by making a new (correctly spelled) word from the letters in the CAPITALIZED word.

THE FARE, I FEAR, IS TOO STEEP FOR ME.
TRAVEL TO THE ALPS

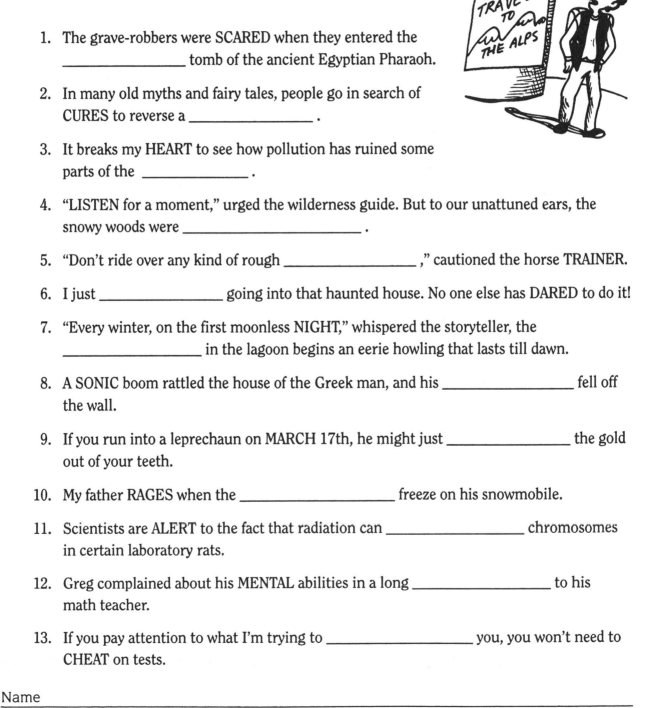

1. The grave-robbers were SCARED when they entered the _______________ tomb of the ancient Egyptian Pharaoh.
2. In many old myths and fairy tales, people go in search of CURES to reverse a _______________ .
3. It breaks my HEART to see how pollution has ruined some parts of the _____________ .
4. "LISTEN for a moment," urged the wilderness guide. But to our unattuned ears, the snowy woods were ______________________ .
5. "Don't ride over any kind of rough ________________," cautioned the horse TRAINER.
6. I just _______________ going into that haunted house. No one else has DARED to do it!
7. "Every winter, on the first moonless NIGHT," whispered the storyteller, the _________________ in the lagoon begins an eerie howling that lasts till dawn.
8. A SONIC boom rattled the house of the Greek man, and his ________________ fell off the wall.
9. If you run into a leprechaun on MARCH 17th, he might just ______________ the gold out of your teeth.
10. My father RAGES when the ___________________ freeze on his snowmobile.
11. Scientists are ALERT to the fact that radiation can _________________ chromosomes in certain laboratory rats.
12. Greg complained about his MENTAL abilities in a long ________________ to his math teacher.
13. If you pay attention to what I'm trying to __________________ you, you won't need to CHEAT on tests.

Name

SMALL PROBLEMS

Problems can come in small packages. Many of the most commonly misspelled words are little ones. Some small words trouble people all their lives! Get a handle on these small words now, so they won't turn into big spelling problems for you later on. Here are fifty-one small words that you use all the time. This guy has spelled all but two of them incorrectly. Identify the two correct words, and spell the others correctly for him.

1. abowt
2. abov
3. acke
4. aftter
5. alilke
6. allmost
7. allready
8. allways
9. arne't
10. atach
11. ahful
12. balence
13. bottel
14. brige
15. bary
16. sertin
17. cheif
18. choise
19. coler
20. dary
21. doller
22. dout
23. ege
24. enuf
25. field
26. fourty
27. gost
28. gues
29. hopeing
30. iland
31. juise
32. nock
33. lauf
34. lenth
35. lovly
36. obay
37. ofen
38. peple
39. peice
40. probaly
41. recieve
42. raize
43. safty
44. sence
45. stomack
46. Tusday
47. twoard
48. usful
49. vary
50. wen
51. whoze

Name

THESE ARE A MOUTHFUL

Don't be intimidated by big words—even if they fill up your mouth when you try to say them. Sometimes big words are even easier to spell than small words. Just break them down into small parts and spell them one piece at a time.

Practice spelling these mouthful words by asking someone else to say them to you, slowly, in syllables. Write them until you have them under your control! (By the way, if you don't know what some of these mean—find out! Never write a word that you don't understand.)

inconspicuous
ventriloquism
arteriosclerosis
impeachment
obstreperous
ORTHODONTICS
PLAGIARISM
reminiscence
hippopotamus
CORROBORATE
polysyllable
picturesque
juxtaposition
requisition
ambidextrous
XENOPHOBIA
philanthropic
acrophobia
PECULIARITY
PHARMACEUTICAL
unambiguous
toxicology
braggadocio
transmutation
PARENTHETICAL
simultaneously
catastrophic
SARSAPARILLA
PHOSPHORESCENCE
HIEROGLYPHICS
philanthropic
PARLIAMENTARIAN
syllogism
magnanimous

Name

NAMES TO KNOW

There are thousands of them! People! Places! Events! Organizations! Things! Whenever a proper name is used, it's called a **proper noun.** These are all capitalized. This directory lists several proper nouns. They are all words you should know how to spell. The problem is, the words are missing. Fill them in (using the clues to the right), and spell them correctly. You will probably need a dictionary to help you out.

1. A ______________________ city in New Mexico
2. A ______________________ coldest continent
3. A ______________________ month after July
4. B ______________________ capital of Idaho
5. B ______________________ writing for the blind
6. C ______________________ world-selling soda pop
7. C ______________________ explored America, 1492
8. C ______________________ south of Massachusetts
9. D ______________________ document that set off the Revolutionary War
10. D ______________________ U.S. political party
11. D ______________________ capital of Iowa
12. D ______________________ U.S. capital
13. E ______________________ country east of Algeria
14. E ______________________ U.S. President before Nixon
15. F ______________________ month after January
16. H ______________________ city—site of atomic bomb
17. H ______________________ country east of Austria
18. L ______________________ U.S. President in Civil War
19. L ______________________ largest city in California
20. M ______________________ north of Connecticut
21. M ______________________ state north of Wisconsin
22. M ______________________ sea south of France
23. N ______________________ city—site of atomic bomb
24. P ______________________ world's largest ocean
25. P ______________________ cuts across isthmus in Central America
26. P ______________________ government body in England
27. P ______________________ newcomers to America
28. R ______________________ river between U.S. & Mexico
29. R ______________________ U.S. political party
30. R ______________________ country west of Ukraine
31. S ______________________ site of Golden Gate Bridge
32. S ______________________ stands above NY harbor
33. T ______________________ capital of Florida
34. T ______________________ 33° S of equator
35. T ______________________ day after Monday
36. T ______________________ king of dinosaurs
37. V ______________________ capital of British Columbia
38. V ______________________ country south of Paraguay
39. W ______________________ day after Tuesday
40. Z ______________________ country in center of Africa

Name ______________________

AARDVARKS & EMUS

Use the clues to lead you to the correct animal names. Write them down and spell them correctly, and you will be able to answer the question below. Write the letter that matches each number in the correct space at the bottom to solve the puzzle.

1. a long, narrow tropical fish with protruding jaws ___ ___ ___ ___ ___(1) ___ ___ ___ ___(8)
2. a big cat with spots ___ ___(10) ___ ___ ___ ___ ___
3. a big, black, fast-running cat ___ ___(3) ___ ___ ___ ___ ___
4. ivory tusks and big feet ___ ___ ___ ___ ___ ___ ___(7) ___
5. long neck, but makes no sound ___ ___ ___ ___ ___(2) ___(11) ___
6. danger in the swamp ___ ___ ___(16) ___ ___ ___ ___ ___ ___
7. howls at the moon ___ ___ ___(6) ___ ___ ___
8. feeds on dead animals ___ ___ ___ ___ ___ ___ ___
9. eats wood in your house ___ ___ ___ ___(9) ___ ___ ___
10. huge, tough-skinned animal with one horn ___ ___ ___ ___ ___(16) ___ ___ ___ ___ ___
11. now extinct ___ ___ ___ ___ ___ ___(14) ___ ___
12. changes colors ___(5) ___ ___ ___ ___ ___ ___ ___ ___
13. large, wide-mouthed African mammal ___ ___ ___ ___ ___ ___ ___(17) ___ ___ ___ ___ ___
14. an ape with shaggy, reddish-brown coat and no tail ___ ___ ___ ___ ___ ___ ___ ___ ___(4)
15. plays dead; hangs upside-down ___ ___ ___(12) ___ ___ ___ ___
16. large, hairy, tropical spider ___ ___ ___ ___ ___ ___ ___ ___ ___
17. stinging arachnid ___ ___ ___ ___(13) ___ ___ ___ ___
18. carries packs in steep terrain ___ ___ ___ ___ ___
19. animal with stripes ___(15) ___ ___ ___ ___

I'M LOOKING FOR THE MENAGERIE. (WHATEVER THAT IS)

What is a menagerie?

___(1) ___(2) ___(3) ___(4) ___(5) ___(6) ___(7) ___(8) ___(9) ___(10)

___(11) ___(12) ___(13) ___(14) ___(15) ___(16) ___(17)

Name ________________________________

WORDS ON THE JOB

This puzzle is full of words that go to work every day—names of workers in different jobs and professions. See if you can find at least twenty. (There are 34.) Write these, spelled correctly, in the space below the puzzle.

D F I N A N C I E R B A N K E R X C F

A T T O R N E Y S S E R T C A N V O I

N T U R P M I S C D R A U G E F I L R

C V U T P T K L R E T N E P R A C W E

E L B H E G H M O R E B M U L P I A F

R E C O R G H A R O G D A R E H N I I

C L O D R D I H M A N A G E R A A T G

O L M O N B E P R O F E S S O R H E H

O M I N I S T E R I L U Y S S M C R T

K X C T O K J D B N O O S S A A E C E

F Y T I S A V B U S I N G E R C M M R

P H Y S I C I S T C M O P I P I S D S

R O K T C T C M C H U I N P S S O B U

O P H T H O K A H L S C U L P T O R R

T O O K C R O Y E M I S S T E R I H G

A N K C H O P O R I C K L K J U D G E

N O E L E C T R I C I A N S A S H E O

E O P Y F H E C B E A U T I C I A N N

S L O R E H C A E T N U R S E P H G O

TRUST ME, HONEY. YOU'RE GOING TO LOOK GREAT IN COURT TOMORROW!
ATTORNEY

Name

WORDS ON THE MOVE

One of the wonderful things about words is that you can use them to tell about **doing** so many things. Active words are very interesting and colorful to use, so you need to know how to spell them. Here are a few active words to practice spelling. All these words name some kind of action. And, oh, by the way, you'll have to unscramble them to get them spelled right.

1. gligew ____________
2. fliroc ____________
3. plogal ____________
4. leprop ____________
5. noubec ____________
6. plrow ____________
7. gargest ____________
8. pramsec ____________
9. duele ____________
10. naermeuv ____________
11. blowbe ____________
12. revish ____________
13. clutufate ____________
14. trotae ____________
15. blmic ____________
16. dhurel ____________
17. rursyc ____________
18. klast ____________
19. dlutner ____________
20. naperc ____________
21. lwarc ____________
22. leef ____________
23. surupe ____________
24. dawdel ____________
25. ptoms ____________

Name ____________

FEAST ON THESE

Don't get these words wrong, or it might spoil their flavor. Write the correct words in the "Gourmet Delights" section. Find the incorrect words, and write them correctly in the "Delectable Entrees" section.

GOURMET DELIGHTS COOK BOOK

carmel caulaflour

CANTALOPE biscets

soufflé CUSTERD

barbeq chicken cinnamon

chilly apacado

cucumber brocoli

COCOA tortilla sunday lettuse

moka casserole éclair croisant CHOCOLATE

omalet

tempura ketchup

Spaghetti sourkraut

lasana BURRITO

PRETZLE

DELECTABLE ENTREES COOK BOOK

Name

CHARACTERISTICALLY SPEAKING

Do you like to be around **obstreperous** people? Or do you prefer a **fastidious** friend? (You might need to look these words up to answer the questions!) The word-parts below can form words which describe characteristics of people. Put them together to correctly spell thirty characteristics. Choose one of the endings for each beginning. Some endings will be used more than once. Decide whether each word describes a characteristic you would like in a friend. Next to each one, write **yes** or **no**.

TIOUS ER

ORN IOUS LY ANT

LESS AL IVE IC ILE

ING SOME ED Y

ABLE IAR OUS ITE

1.	fastid	11.	sur	21.	witt
2.	defi	12.	touch	22.	letharg
3.	abras	13.	agree	23.	imaginat
4.	pol	14.	errat	24.	clev
5.	creat	15.	pecul	25.	entertain
6.	cau	16.	stubb	26.	bor
7.	negat	17.	grouch	27.	jeal
8.	critic	18.	host	28.	bigot
9.	adventur	19.	vigor	29.	toler
10.	reclus	20.	rest	30.	secret

PEOPLE CAN REALLY BE CHARACTERS

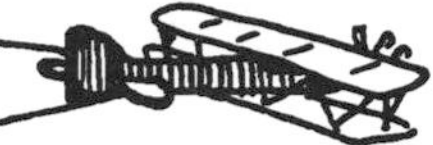

Name

A LETTER OF QUALITY

Quaint, quick, quizzical, and quite quirky! **Q** lends a unique sparkle to a word, whether it's found at the beginning, middle, or near the end. In many word games, **Q** gets more points than most other letters.

Give the correct spelling of a **Q** word that fits each description below. (The first letter of each word is given.)

AFTER A REQUEST FROM THE CLASS QUIDNUNC,* I'VE QUADRUPLED OUR QUOTA OF QUIZZES!

SPELLING QUIZ TODAY
B

* a "know-it-all"

1. get to know a ________________
2. often f ________________
3. a review of an artistic work c ________________
4. another chapter to the story s ________________
5. an exclusive group c ________________
6. find "not guilty" a ________________
7. great spread of food b ________________
8. sufficient quantity a ________________
9. to take over c ________________
10. deposits that collect on teeth p ________________
11. unusual u ________________
12. results of actions c ________________
13. failing to uphold obligations d ________________
14. argument q ________________
15. hideous g ________________
16. no light passes through o ________________
17. varnish l ________________
18. pretend m ________________

Name ________________________________

FROM SACRED TO SASSAFRAS

S starts off superb words such as sassafras, superior, soufflé, and smithereens. **S** words are some of the most common words in the English language. Practice spelling these commonly used **S** words that sometimes stump spellers. Do this by writing ten sentences—each having at least four of these **S** words in them. Make sure you spell the words correctly. You might try to write a sentence which has ALL **S** words.

SACRED

stew
sedative
shears
shriek
shrewd
situation
sinister
stagger
suspicious
solemn
scared
sacred
shush
stalk
stationery
surround
soprano
stethoscope
surgeon
sturgeon
syrup
significant
striped
squander
summit
secretive
severe
sneer

solo
synonym
surplus
soufflé
strudel
somersault
soccer
sacred
secretary
stallion
shoulder
soothe
sherbet
sauerkraut
subsequent
sympathy
splendid
security
smooth
spontaneous
supersonic
surfboard
section
scowl
surplus
suburban
survival
stereophonic

SASSAFRAS

Name

THE TROUBLE WITH W

The trouble with **W** is that so many words which start with it sound alike. Which . . . witch . . . whether . . . weather . . . wither . . . wherever . . . when . . . where . . . wherefore . . . .why . . . what . . . and so on. You really have to know the differences between your **W** words to spell them correctly. Correct any **W** words that are spelled wrong in these sentences. Just cross out the words, and write the correct spelling above them.

1. Reched wether always seems to welcum us whin we arrive in the wildernes for our weakly campout.

2. "Stop wining!," I wisper to my sister, as I waver and woble, struggling to carry her wait.

W-WET
WILD AND WACKY
WEATHER THIS WEEKEND

3. Whover took my rench? Are there any witneses to this theft wich must have just happened?

4. We wernt writting words of whisdom that day wile we wandered along the path in that wierd school writting activity. Actually we wernt wholy paying attention.

5. I'm woried about the weezing cough my sister Winnie has had ever since we swam by the wirlpool.

6. Rinkled clothes, wiked jokes, and waistful habits may lead adults to think you are withhout whisdom or good sense.

7. Her great whit is her best wepon against her whithering shyness.

8. I'm not sure weather or not you can help us make wreeths, as that is the worstest wreeth I ever saw.

9. Ware did you get that wreched pair of pants hanging around your waste? Whos are those wierd things? They make you look as if you way an extra fifty pounds.

10. Hopefully, widespred advertising will bring a large group of wimin to the meeting on Wensday.

Name

X-CEPTIONAL WORDS

You might think of "X-rated" when you hear about **X**. But actually, most words with **X** in them are NOT **X**-rated! Just interesting. And sometimes **X**-ceptional. Below are the meanings of some words that have the letter **X** in them. Write each word—being careful to get the **X** in the right place and, of course, to spell the whole word correctly.

1. e **X** ____________ (a species that is no longer living)
2. a **X** ____________ (Earth rotates on it)
3. e **X** ____________ (stretch the truth)
4. e **X** ____________ (look at carefully)
5. o ____________ **X** (strictly adhere to rules)
6. c ____________ **X** (complicated)
7. e **X** ____________ (very expensive)
8. e **X** ____________ (excused from the rules)
9. e **X** ____________ (stir up, incite)
10. e **X** ____________ (breathe out)
11. e **X** ____________ (reason for not doing something)
12. e **X** ____________ (dig up)
13. r ____________ **X** (instinctive reaction)
14. e **X** ____________ (pull out)
15. ma **X** ____________ (not minimum)
16. e **X** ____________ (too much)
17. c ________ **X** _____ (condition of skin)
18. e **X** ____________ d (disgusted)

Xavier expounds on his exotic excursion to Xixabangma, Africa:
eXCEPTIONAL !!!
XIXABANGMA OR BUST
eXEMPLARY,
eXQUISITE,
eXTREMLY...
eXCITING!
(eXHAUSTING)

Name

Y NOT?

Sometimes it's hard to remember just whether or not a word has a Y. Sometimes it's hard to remember exactly where to put the Y. Why not practice these common Y words, so you won't wonder? The words are scrambled, but there's a clue to help you figure out what they are. Unscramble them and write them correctly.

1. yocnev — carry something somewhere ____________
2. amytnno — a word that's opposite ____________
3. connay — a river flows through it ____________
4. cybilec — something to ride ____________
5. nymonys — word meaning the same ____________
6. yenv — jealousy ____________
7. thym — fictional story ____________
8. fedy — stand up to or oppose ____________
9. thymrh — musical beat ____________
10. omunnysua — no name given ____________
11. mehyr — poetry does it ____________
12. stymmsop — tells if you're sick ____________
13. pycano — an overhead cover ____________
14. phesisyhot — scientific theory ____________
15. arassipyl — inability to move ____________
16. fytimys — to puzzle ____________
17. phayta — no energy ____________
18. whcey — exercises your jaw ____________

Name ____________

Z LAST WORD

Which words have it? **Z** gets thrown into words where it doesn't belong. Sometimes we hear a **Z** sound, but the spelling is an **S**. And when **Z** really is there—are there one or two? Complete the puzzle below using correctly spelled words that have **Z** in them. In all cases, the **Z** is not at the beginning of the word.

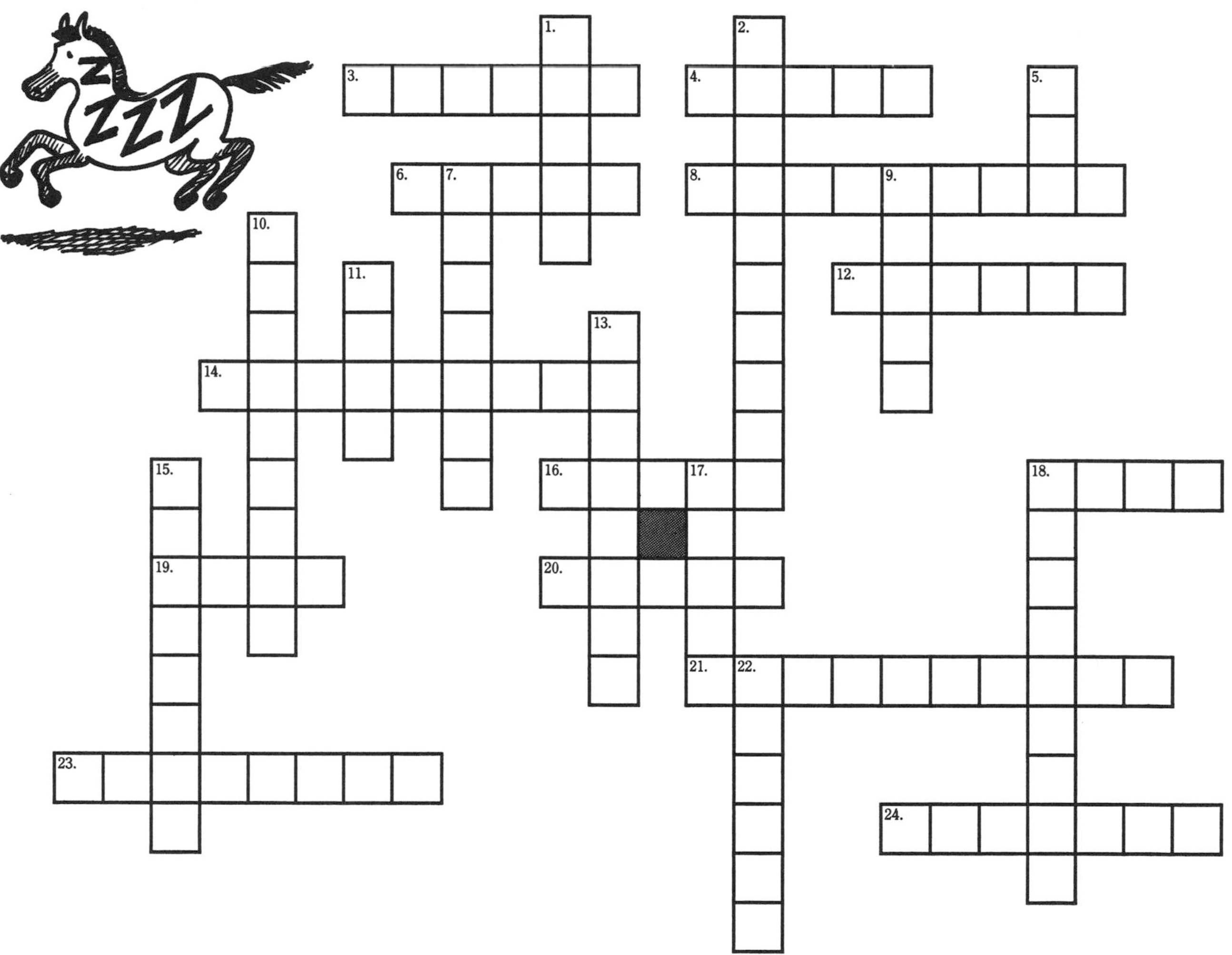

Down

1. a fashion fad
2. to put in danger
5. a cutting tool
7. to become aware of
9. layer of the atmosphere
10. picture it in your mind
11. to demolish
13. blinding snowstorm
15. to put into words
17. sharp-edged tool
18. mesmerize
22. skin eruptions

Across

3. a danger
4. to take by force
6. a reward
8. to say you're sorry
12. to convert into ions
14. questioning
16. south seas blue
18. smog
19. snug
20. Indian corn
21. a lovers' meeting
23. indolence
24. carcass-eater

Name

LAUGHABLE WORDS

Spelling, of course, is no laughing matter. But there are words about laughing and words to make you laugh. Actually, *laugh* is kind of a funny word to begin with. It isn't spelled the way it sounds. And it's not the sound that comes out when you do laugh. This makes it a little tricky to spell. Other words about laughing are sometimes spelling hazards too. Each of these twenty-four words has something to do with laughter. Enough letters are given to help you figure out what the words are and to help you spell them correctly.

1. la ___ ___ ___
2. la ___ ___ ___ ___ ble
3. la ___ ___ ___ ___ er
4. amu ___ ___ ___ ___ nt
5. co ___ ___ my
6. com ___ ___ ___ an
7. co ___ ___ c
8. ___ ___ gg ___ e
9. ch ___ ___ ___ le
10. m ___ ___ th
11. h ___ ___ ar ___ ___ ___ s
12. j ___ ___ ___

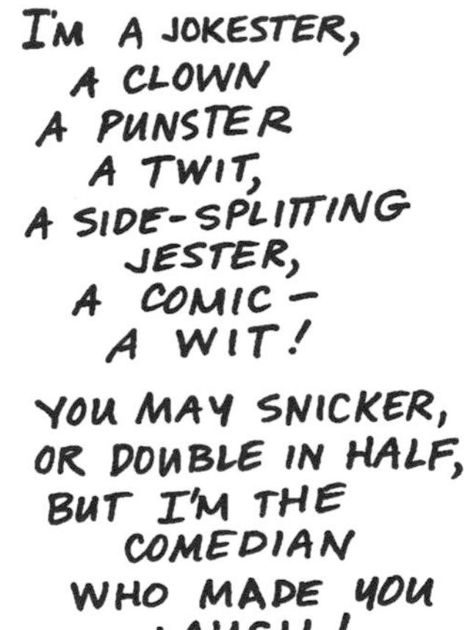
I'M A JOKESTER,
A CLOWN
A PUNSTER
A TWIT,
A SIDE-SPLITTING
JESTER,
A COMIC –
A WIT!
YOU MAY SNICKER,
OR DOUBLE IN HALF,
BUT I'M THE
COMEDIAN
WHO MADE YOU
LAUGH!

13. h ___ ___ or ___ ___ s
14. h ___ ___ ___ r
15. m ___ rr ___ ___ ___ nt
16. w ___ tt ___
17. am ___ ___ ing
18. w ___ ___ ___ cr ___ ___ ___
19. mis ___ ___ ___ ___ f
20. b ___ ff ___ ___ n
21. r ___ ___ ___ cule
22. pr ___ ___ ___ ster
23. lud ___ ___ ___ ___ ___ ___
24. am ___ ___ e

Name

EMPHATICALLY SPEAKING!

Oh, no! These emphatic statements are all plagued with spelling errors. Fix them! Quickly! Cross out the errors, and write the correctly spelled words underneath.

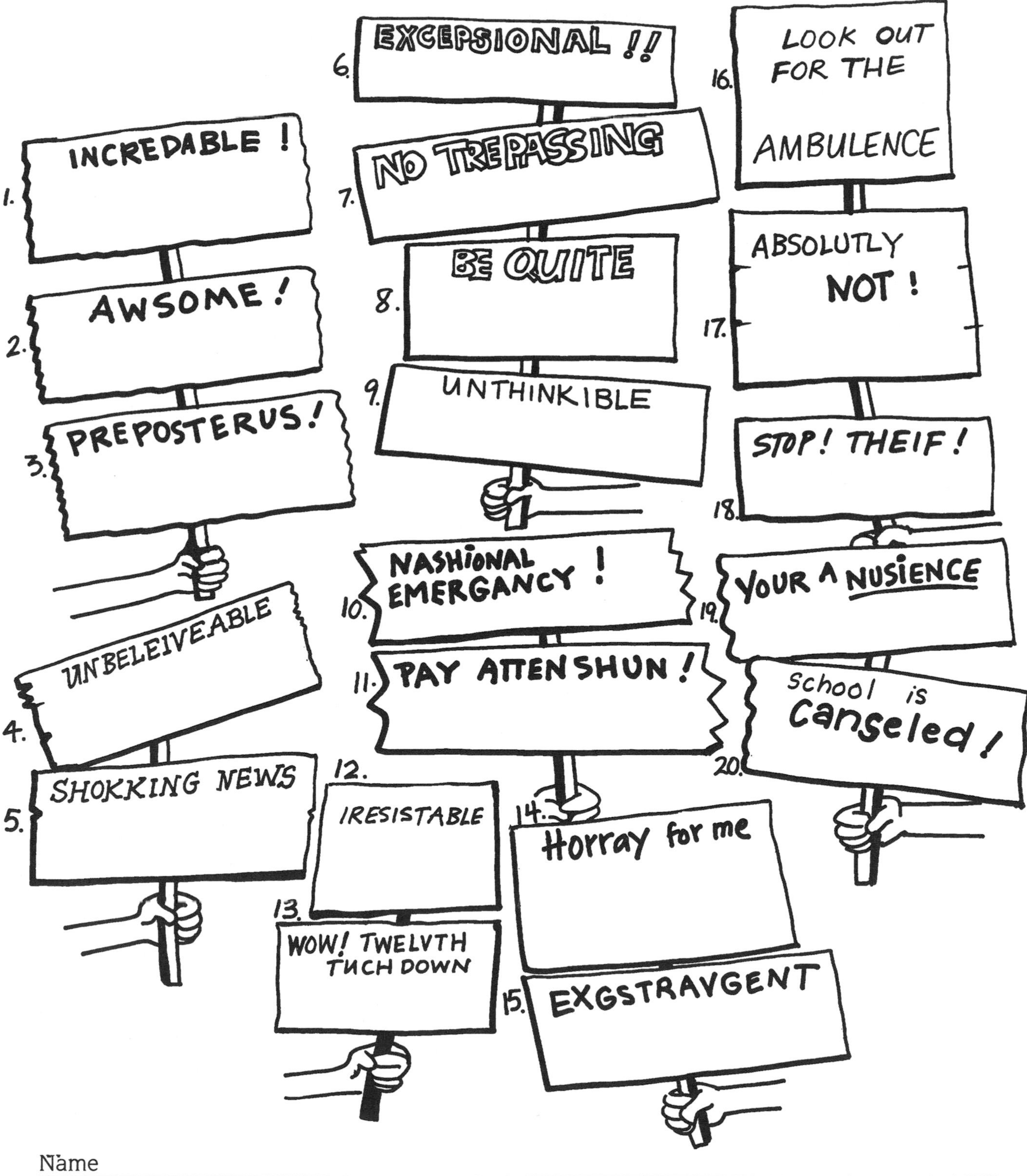

1. INCREDABLE !
2. AWSOME!
3. PREPOSTERUS!
4. UNBELEIVEABLE
5. SHOKKING NEWS
6. EXCEPSIONAL !!
7. NO TREPASSING
8. BE QUITE
9. UNTHINKIBLE
10. NASHIONAL EMERGANCY !
11. PAY ATTENSHUN !
12. IRESISTABLE
13. WOW! TWELVTH TUCH DOWN
14. Horray for me
15. EXGSTRAVGENT
16. LOOK OUT FOR THE AMBULENCE
17. ABSOLUTLY NOT !
18. STOP! THEIF!
19. YOUR A NUSIENCE
20. School is Canseled !

Name

HELP NEEDED!

You may not be able to help the situation described in the letter. But you can help with the spelling. Correct each misspelled word in Serena's letter by writing it above the wrong word.

Febuary 6

Dear Abby,

I'm sorry you missed the show. Finally I have time to tell you abot it.

It was an akward trick for a gorrilla, I admit, to clim onto a trapeeze balincing an arkatect and an artachoke on oppisite arms. Fortunatly, we hired a talanted gorrilla. This may seen wierd—not your obveous cercus preformence. But you have to admit, it was a unick idea. And certen peple flocked to perchase expenseve tickets.

The gorrilla was a tame and calm one, with no obveous tendancies toward vilence. He had practised this trick many times, even preforming it at a bankquet before a group of famos polatitians.

As the curtin went up and the show began, I was greatful that everything was going smoothely. And then—there was the mosquitoe that somhow got onto the gorrilla's tonge. Are freindly pet turned feirce. In less than a minit, he swung down to the net, turned a huge sommersalt, and devored the archatect—hole, as an unbeleving croud of spectaters, including me, wached in horor.

Sorry you missed it.

Your friend,
Serena

SPECIAL EDITION
TRAGEDY AT BIG-TOP
APE EATS FELLOW

Name

SPELLING
ASSESSMENT AND ANSWER KEYS

SPELLING SKILLS TEST

Each correct answer is worth 1 point. Total possible score: 100 points.

For questions 1-10, choose ***ie*** *or* ***ei*** *to correctly spell each word.*

1. ch_______f
2. n ___ghbor
3. for______gn
4. n______ther
5. w_______gh
6. ach ____ve
7. rec______ve
8. quot ____nt
9. w_______rd
10. s _______ze

For questions 11-28, choose the ending that correctly completes each word.

11. apolog_________(ise, ize, ice)
12. prom _________(ise, ice, is)
13. host_________(ige, age, ege)
14. marvel ______(us, ous, eous)
15. telev ___________(ise, ize, ice)
16. tradi ______(tion, sion, cian)
17. danger ______(us, ous, eous)
18. contag ____(eous, ous, ious)
19. evid______(ance, ense, ence)
20. sens ______(ible, able, eable)
21. vac___________(ant, ent, int)
22. cand___________(al, el, le, il)
23. fat_____________(el, al, le, il)
24. signific_______(ent, ant, int)
25. wrest ___________(el, al, le)
26. revers_____(ible, able, eable)
27. decor _________(eat, ate, at)
28. icic_____________(il, al, el, le)

For questions 29-38, if a word has one or more silent letters, write the letters. If a word has no silent letters, write NO.

____________ 29. empathy
____________ 30. gnu
____________ 31. judge
____________ 32. answer
____________ 33. memory
____________ 34. resignation
____________ 35. sword
____________ 36. stalk
____________ 37. pride
____________ 38. benefit

For questions 39-43, add a prefix to make a word that fits the meaning given.

_____ 39. approved (not approved)
_____ 40. ordinary (beyond ordinary)
_____ 41. regular (not regular)
_____ 42. state (between states)
_____ 43. germ (against germs)

For questions 44-48, add a root to make a word that fits the meaning given.

_____ 44. ility (ability to move)
_____ 45. ible (able to be touched)
_____ 46. ify (to show to be truthful)
_____ 47. ant (to be in a state of sleep)
_____ 48. inous (to be full of light)

For questions 49-58, choose the correct word to complete the sentence. Write the word on the line.

49. ______________________
The (principal, principle) manages the school.

50. ______________________
A concrete wall is a (stationary, stationery) object.

51. ______________________
Three frightening (incidence, incidents) happened to me today.

52. ______________________
We visited the (capital, capitol) building of our state.

53. ______________________
Everything's okay (accept, except) my two broken legs.

54. ______________________
Your rude behavior doesn't (effect, affect) me in the least.

55. ______________________
I've got some good (advise, advice) for you about romance.

56. ______________________
I'll tell you, (weather, whether) or not you want to hear.

57. ______________________
Do you know what obtuse (angles, angels) are?

58. ______________________
I did a (through, though, thorough) job of cleaning my room.

Name ____

For questions 59-69, correct the spelling of these misspelled words. Write each word on the line.

_____ 59. Lincon
_____ 60. doller
_____ 61. twoard
_____ 62. Conneticut
_____ 63. oppossum
_____ 64. pharmicist
_____ 65. manuver
_____ 66. choclate
_____ 67. Republacan
_____ 68. Pilgrums
_____ 69. peculier

For questions 70-78, write the correct spelling on the line.

_____ 70. butiful, beautuful, beautiful
_____ 71. busness, business, buisness
_____ 72. receive, recieve, receave
_____ 73. baloon, ballon, balloon
_____ 74. separate, seperate, sepurate
_____ 75. enough, enuogh, enuf
_____ 76. occurred, occured, ocurred
_____ 77. advertisement, advertizement, advertisment
_____ 78. benifit, benefit, benafit

For questions 79-85, correct the spelling of these misspelled words. Write the word on the line.

_____ 79. exsitement
_____ 80. suspisious
_____ 81. apologise
_____ 82. exeption
_____ 83. amuzement
_____ 84. exagerate
_____ 85. suprize

For questions 86-90, rewrite each misspelled word correctly.

86. Was there inadaquat food at the Big Eater's banquite? _____

_____

87. Did Colombus realy descover Amerika?

_____

_____

88. How long did it take the libarians to travel from San Fransisco to Los Angelas?

_____

_____

89. The docter won't give you an excuze from skool if you don't have eny symtoms of ilness.

_____

_____

_____

90. Is an antomim oppisit from a synanym?

_____

_____

For questions 91-100, choose the correct spelling for each word. Write it on the line.

_____ 91. resturant, restaurant, reasturant
_____ 92. celender, calander, calendar
_____ 93. embarrass, embarass, embarras
_____ 94. hippopotamas, hippopotomas, hippopotamus
_____ 95. lisence, lisense, license
_____ 96. necessary, nesessary, necesary
_____ 97. laborotory, labratory, laboratory
_____ 98. noticeable, noticible, noticable
_____ 99. dinasaur, dinosaur, dinosoar
_____ 100. paralel, parralel, parallel

SCORE: Total Points _____ out of a possible 100 points

Name _____

SPELLING

SKILLS TEST ANSWER KEY

1. ie (chief)
2. ei (neighbor)
3. ei (foreign)
4. ei (neither)
5. ei (weigh)
6. ie (achieve)
7. ei (receive)
8. ie (quotient)
9. ei (weird)
10. ei (seize)
11. ize (apologize)
12. ise (promise)
13. age (hostage)
14. ous (marvelous)
15. ise (televise)
16. tion (tradition)
17. ous (dangerous)
18. ious (contagious)
19. ence (evidence)
20. ible (sensible)
21. ant (vacant)
22. le (candle)
23. al (fatal)
24. ant (significant)
25. le (wrestle)
26. ible (reversible)
27. ate (decorate)
28. le (icicle)
29. no
30. g
31. d
32. w
33. no
34. no
35. w
36. l
37. e
38. no
39. dis (disapproved)
40. extra (extraordinary)
41. ir (irregular)
42. inter (interstate)
43. anti (antigerm)
44. mob (mobility)
45. tang (tangible)
46. ver (verify)
47. dorm (dormant)
48. lum (luminous)
49. principal
50. stationary
51. incidents
52. capitol
53. except
54. affect
55. advice
56. whether
57. angles
58. thorough
59. Lincoln
60. dollar
61. toward
62. Connecticut
63. opossum
64. pharmacist
65. maneuver
66. chocolate
67. Republican
68. Pilgrims
69. peculiar
70. beautiful
71. business
72. receive
73. balloon
74. separate
75. enough
76. occurred
77. advertisement
78. benefit
79. excitement
80. suspicious
81. apologize
82. exception
83. amusement
84. exaggerate
85. surprise
86. inadequate; banquet
87. Columbus; really; discover; America
88. librarians; San Francisco; Los Angeles
89. doctor; excuse; school; any; symptoms; illness
90. antonym; opposite; synonym
91. restaurant
92. calendar
93. embarrass
94. hippopotamus
95. license
96. necessary
97. laboratory
98. noticeable
99. dinosaur
100. parallel

ANSWERS

page 124

List 1
Incorrect
2, 7, 10, 11, 12, 13, 14, 15, 17, 19, 22, 24, 25

List 2
Incorrect
1, 3, 4, 5, 6, 8, 9, 16, 18, 20, 21, 23

page 125

1. dilemma
2. arithmetic
3. different
4. cafeteria
5. calendar
6. college
7. anonymous
8. excess
9. criticize
10. necessary
11. vegetables
12. recognize
13. laughter
14. August
15. through

page 126

1. okay
2. okay
3. benefit
4. okay
5. okay
6. animal
7. okay
8. omitted
9. embarrass
10. okay
11. quizzical
12. okay
13. okay
14. bazaar
15. cereal
16. okay
17. ammonia
18. traveling
19. okay
20. parallel
21. okay
22. okay
23. ballot
24. barracuda
25. balcony
26. okay
27. okay
28. okay
29. okay
30. memory
31. okay
32. opossum
33. hippopotamus
34. staccato
35. Tennessee
36. okay
37. centennial
38. okay
39. professor
40. celebrate

page 127

1. freight
2. sleigh
3. neighborhood
4. mischief
5. achieve
6. reign
7. conscience
8. conceited
9. quotient
10. piece
11. society
12. efficient
13. grief
14. science
15. eight
16. weight
17. deficient
18. convenient
19. hygiene
20. shriek

page 128

1. B
2. C
3. B
4. C
5. B
6. C
7. B
8. A
9. C
10. B
11. C
12. C
13. C
14. C
15. C
16. B
17. A
18. C
19. B
20. B
21. C
22. A
23. B
24. C
25. C
26. We don't stick with these rules.

page 129

1. motto
2. forgot
3. cocoon
4. odor
5. common
6. monsoon
7. photograph
8. toxicology
9. foolproof
10. follow
11. logo
12. tattoo
13. overlook
14. loon
15. locomotive
16. kazoo
17. orator
18. monocle
19. porous
20. voodoo
21. scorpion
22. opponent
23. sophomore
24. monotonous

page 130

Below are some suggested answers. Consider any answer that makes sense and contains a silent letter.

1. Ghetto
2. Dough
3. Gnaws
4. Crumbs
5. Gnu
6. Wrapped
7. Judge; Bridge
8. Answers
9. Resigns
10. Knight; Sword
11. Raspberries
12. Ptomaine
13. Knife
14. Dumb
15. Pledge
16. Stalked
17. Badge
18. Lambs
19. Knock
20. Reigns

page 131

1. ph
2. ph
3. ph
4. gh
5. ph
6. gh
7. ph
8. gh
9. ph
10. gh
11. ph
12. ph
13. gh
14. ph
15. ph
16. ph
17. gh
18. ph; ph

page 132

1. prescription
2. exclude
3. rewrite
4. conform
5. depart
6. subdivide
7. translate
8. microchip
9. prolong
10. invisible
11. advance
12. bibliography
13. extraordinary
14. ultrasonic
15. disapprove
16. tricycle
17. antiwar
18. untied

page 133

1. verify
2. altitude
3. empathy
4. tangible
5. pacifist
6. durable
7. librarian
8. mobility
9. population
10. suspend
11. fracture
12. transfer
13. dormant
14. autobiography
15. action
16. journal
17. luminous
18. astrology
19. ridiculous
20. biography

page 134

1. distant
2. important
3. vacant
4. restaurant
5. elephant

6. pleasant
7. significant
8. defiant
9. elegant
10. applicant
11. observant
12. vigilant
13. occupant
14. ignorant
15. assistant
16. defendant
17. hydrant
18. contestant
19. constant
20. inhabitants

page 135

1. ate
2. ate
3. ate
4. eat
5. ate
6. ate
7. eat
8. ate
9. eat
10. eat
11. ate
12. ate
13. eat
14. ate
15. ate
16. ate
17. ate
18. eat
19. ate
20. ate
21. ate
22. ate
23. eat
24. ate
25. ate
26. eat

page 136

1. frugal
2. hysterical
3. candle
4. principal or principle
5. ok
6. ok
7. gargle
8. ok
9. angel or angle
10. ok
11. ok
12. ok
13. unravel
14. legal
15. wrestle
16. spiral
17. clavicle
18. ok
19. vessel
20. ok
21. channel
22. ok
23. visible
24. radical
25. ok
26. ok
27. ok
28. obstacle
29. ok
30. travel
31. ok
32. carnival

page 137

1. ize
2. ile
3. ile
4. ive
5. ish
6. ise
7. ism or ize
8. ish
9. ish
10. ive
11. ive
12. ist or ism
13. ile
14. ish
15. ite or ish
16. ish
17. ive
18. ism or ize
19. ise
20. ive
21. ism
22. ist
23. ist
24. ize
25. ist, ism, or ize
26. ize
27. ite
28. ist
29. ist

page 138

1. tion
2. tion
3. cian
4. sion
5. sion
6. sion
7. tion
8. tion
9. ion
10. tion
11. cian
12. tune
13. ous
14. ous
15. ous
16. us
17. ious
18. eous
19. us
20. ius
21. us
22. ious
23. ous
24. uous

page 139

1. ence
2. ence
3. ance
4. ence
5. ence
6. ence
7. ance
8. ance
9. ence
10. ance
11. ence
12. ence
13. ance
14. ance
15. ence
16. ible
17. ible
18. able
19. able
20. ible
21. ible
22. able
23. able
24. ible
25. ible
26. able
27. ible
28. able
29. able
30. ible

page 140

1. anguish
2. chaos
3. treacherous
4. fraud
5. pauper
6. drought
7. cougar
8. thesaurus
9. bias
10. boisterous
11. camouflage
12. plausible
13. eloquent
14. aquarium
15. sausage
16. beard
17. leopard
18. cauliflower
19. influenza
20. against
21. thought
22. disguise

page 141

1. minor
2. scared; sacred
3. sword; heir
4. principal; incidents; incidence; dessert
5. pedal; pedal
6. peer; pier
7. soared; desert; miner
8. capital; capitol; hair
9. Altogether
10. stationery

page 142

Answers will vary.

page 143

1. emerald
2. mosquito
3. macaroni
4. kindergarten
5. yacht; buoy
6. algebra; chemistry
7. antique
8. magazine
9. sauerkraut
10. paradise
11. gorilla; mosquito; mustang
12. sarong
13. veto
14. piano; tambourine

page 144

Answers will vary.

page 145

I always lose my notes when I get ready for a test, except for math, because I wrap my lunch in those and always have them near. My mother gives me unending advice about how to get through this problem, but, I assure you, it's a useless exercise. It'll be major coup if I ever get accepted into any college.

1. through; through
2. whether; weather
3. prosecute
4. which
5. angel
6. commas
7. inflict
8. implied
9. incredible
10. extrovert

page 146

1. sacred
2. curse
3. earth
4. silent
5. terrain
6. dread
7. thing
8. icons
9. charm
10. gears
11. alter
12. lament
13. teach

page 147

1. about
2. above
3. ache
4. after
5. alike
6. almost
7. already
8. always
9. aren't
10. attach
11. awful
12. balance
13. bottle
14. bridge
15. bury
16. certain
17. chief
18. choice
19. collar
20. dairy
21. dollar
22. doubt
23. edge
24. enough
25. **correct**
26. forty
27. ghost
28. guess
29. hoping
30. island
31. juice
32. knock
33. laugh
34. length
35. lovely
36. obey
37. often
38. people
39. piece
40. probably
41. receive
42. raise
43. safety
44. sense
45. stomach
46. Tuesday
47. toward
48. useful
49. **correct**
50. when
51. whose

page 148

Check to see that words are spelled correctly.

page 149

1. Albuquerque
2. Antarctica
3. August
4. Boise
5. Braille
6. Coca Cola®
7. Columbus
8. Connecticut
9. Declaration of Independence
10. Democrat
11. Des Moines
12. District of Columbia
13. Egypt
14. Eisenhower
15. February
16. Hiroshima
17. Hungary
18. Lincoln
19. Los Angeles
20. Massachusetts
21. Minnesota
22. Mediterranean
23. Nagasaki
24. Pacific
25. Panama Canal
26. Parliament
27. Pilgrims
28. Rio Grande
29. Republican
30. Romania
31. San Francisco
32. Statue of Liberty
33. Tallahassee
34. Tropic of Capricorn
35. Tuesday
36. Tyrannosaurus Rex
37. Vancouver
38. Venezuela
39. Wednesday
40. Zaire

page 150

1. barracuda
2. leopard
3. panther
4. elephant
5. giraffe
6. crocodile
7. coyote
8. vulture
9. termite
10. rhinoceros
11. dinosaur
12. chameleon
13. hippopotamus
14. orangutan
15. opossum
16. tarantula
17. scorpion
18. llama
19. zebra

Answer: a fancy name for a zoo

page 151

actor
actress
attorney
banker
beautician
butcher
carpenter
chef
comic
cook
dancer
electrician
financier
firefighter
grocer
judge
lifeguard
manager
mayor
mechanic
minister
musician
nurse
opthamologist
orthodontist
pharmacist
physicist
plumber
professor
senator
sculptor
singer
surgeon
teacher
waiter

page 152

1. wiggle
2. frolic
3. gallop
4. propel
5. bounce
6. prowl
7. stagger
8. scamper
9. elude
10. maneuver
11. wobble
12. shiver
13. fluctuate
14. rotate
15. climb
16. hurdle
17. scurry
18. stalk
19. trundle
20. prance
21. crawl
22. flee
23. pursue
24. waddle
25. stomp

page 153

CORRECT ("Delights")
soufflé
éclair
tortilla
spaghetti
cocoa
tempura
cucumber
casserole
ketchup
chocolate
cinnamon

INCORRECT ("Entrees")
cantaloupe
cauliflower
chili
broccoli
caramel
sundae
biscuits
custard
mocha
lettuce
barbecue chicken
croissant
pretzel
avocado
omelette or omelet
sauerkraut
lasagna

page 154

1. ious
2. ant
3. ive
4. ite
5. ive
6. tious
7. ive
8. al
9. ous
10. ive
11. ly
12. y
13. able
14. ic
15. iar
16. orn
17. y
18. ile
19. ous
20. less
21. y
22. ic
23. ive
24. er
25. ing
26. ing
27. ous
28. ed
29. ant
30. ive

page 155

1. acquaint
2. frequent
3. critique
4. sequel
5. clique
6. acquit
7. banquet
8. adequate
9. conquer
10. plaque
11. unique
12. consequences
13. delinquent
14. quarrel
15. grotesque
16. opaque
17. lacquer
18. masquerade

page 156

Answers will vary.

page 157

1. Wretched weather always seems to welcome us when we arrive in the wilderness for our weekly campout.
2. "Stop whining!" I whisper to my sister, as I waver and wobble, struggling to carry her weight.
3. Whoever took my wrench? Are there any witnesses to this theft which must have just happened?
4. We weren't writing words of wisdom that day while we wandered along the path in that weird school writing activity. Actually we weren't wholly paying attention.
5. I'm worried about the wheezing cough my sister Winnie has had ever since we swam by the whirlpool.
6. Wrinkled clothes, wicked jokes, and wasteful habits may lead adults to think you are without wisdom or good sense.
7. Her great wit is her best weapon against her withering shyness.
8. I'm not sure whether or not you can help us make wreaths, as that is the worst wreath I ever saw.
9. Where did you get that wretched pair of pants hanging around your waist? Whose are those weird things? They make you look as if you weigh an extra fifty pounds.
10. Hopefully, widespread advertising will bring a large group of women here to the meeting on Wednesday.

page 158

1. extinct
2. axis
3. exaggerate
4. examine
5. orthodox
6. complex
7. extravagant
8. exception
9. excite
10. exhale
11. excuse
12. excavate
13. reflex
14. extract
15. maximum
16. excess
17. complexion
18. exasperated

page 159

1. convey
2. antonym
3. canyon
4. bicycle
5. synonym
6. envy
7. myth
8. defy
9. rhythm
10. anonymous
11. rhyme
12. symptoms
13. canopy
14. hypothesis
15. paralysis
16. mystify
17. apathy
18. chewy

page 160

Across

- 3. hazard
- 4. seize
- 6. prize
- 8. apologize
- 12. ionize
- 14. quizzical
- 16. azure
- 18. haze
- 19. cozy
- 20. maize
- 21. rendezvous
- 23. laziness
- 24. buzzard

Down

- 1. craze
- 2. jeopardize
- 5. adz
- 7. realize
- 9. ozone
- 10. visualize
- 11. raze
- 13. blizzard
- 15. vocalize
- 17. razor
- 18. hypnotize
- 22. eczema

page 161

1. laugh
2. laughable
3. laughter
4. amusement
5. comedy
6. comedian
7. comic
8. giggle
9. chuckle
10. mirth
11. hilarious
12. joke or jest
13. humorous
14. humor
15. merriment
16. witty
17. amusing
18. wisecrack
19. mischief
20. buffoon
21. ridicule
22. prankster
23. ludicrous
24. amuse

page 162

1. Incredible!
2. Awesome!
3. Preposterous!
4. Unbelievable
5. Shocking news
6. Exceptional!
7. No trespassing
8. Be quiet
9. Unthinkable
10. National Emergency!
11. Pay attention!
12. Irresistible!
13. Wow! Twelfth touchdown!
14. Hooray for me
15. Extravagant
16. Look out for the ambulance
17. Absolutely not!
18. Stop! Thief!
19. You're a nuisance
20. School is canceled!

page 163

February 6

Dear Abby,

I'm sorry you missed the show. Finally I have time to tell you about it.

It was an awkward trick for a gorilla, I admit, to climb onto a trapeze balancing an architect and an artichoke on opposite arms. Fortunately, we hired a talented gorilla. This may seem weird—not your obvious circus performance. But you have to admit, it was a unique idea. And certain people flocked to purchase expensive tickets.

The gorilla was a tame and calm one, with no obvious tendencies toward violence. He had practiced this trick many times, even performing it at a banquet before a group of famous politicians.

As the curtain went up and the show began, I was grateful that everything was going smoothly. And then—there was the mosquito that somehow got onto the gorilla's tongue. Our friendly pet turned fierce. In less than a minute, he swung down to the net, turned a huge somersault, and devoured the architect—whole, as an unbelieving crowd of spectators, including me, watched in horror.

Sorry you missed it.

Your friend,

Serena

WORDS & VOCABULARY

Skills Exercises

ENTRANCE
LAND OF THRILLS AMUSEMENT PARK
featuring: THE AVALANCHE!

SKILLS CHECKLIST FOR WORDS & VOCABULARY

✔	SKILL	PAGE(S)
	Learn and use new words	174–177
	Understand how context gives clues to a word's meaning	178, 179
	Use context clues to determine meanings of words	178, 179
	Distinguish between denotation and connotation	180, 181
	Use connotation to determine the best word for a purpose	180, 181
	Recognize and use synonyms	182–184
	Recognize and use antonyms	185, 186
	Recognize and use homonyms and homophones	187, 188
	Recognize and use homographs	189
	Identify and use multiple meanings of a word	190, 191
	Identify the meanings of common prefixes	192, 193, 196, 197
	Recognize prefixes to determine word meanings	192, 193, 196, 197
	Identify the meanings of common suffixes	194–197
	Recognize suffixes to determine word meanings	194–197
	Identify the meanings of common root words	196, 197
	Recognize root words to determine word meanings	196, 197
	Recognize, use, and form compound words	198, 199
	Distinguish between words that are often confused with one another	200, 201
	Distinguish between words that look or sound similar	200, 201
	Identify and use figurative language	202, 203
	Explore the history and origins of words	204, 205
	Use correct words to complete analogies	206, 207
	Classify words according to certain characteristics	208
	Identify words that are associated with one another	208

WOULD YOU? COULD YOU?

Use your dictionary to find the meaning of each word in bold type so that you can answer the questions. Then, on the back of this page, explain why you answered each one the way you did.

1. Would you take a **nonagenarian** on a rollercoaster called "The Heart Stopper"? ___________
2. Would you **flaunt** your **peccadillos** in front of your friends? ___________
3. Could you leave your **uvula** at home when you go to the amusement park? ___________
4. Would you invite a **misanthrope** to go with you to a surprise party? ___________
5. Could you give a piggyback ride to a **corpulent connoisseur**? ___________
6. Would you be honored to receive an **encomium** from the President? ___________
7. Could you take **fauna** along on a raft trip down a river? ___________
8. Would you want to share your favorite pizza with a **gourmand**? ___________
9. Could you ride a skateboard on a **provost**? ___________
10. Would you try to escape from a **maelstrom**? ___________
11. Could you get a good rest next to a **restive** dog? ___________
12. Would you like to snack on a plateful of **bibelot**? ___________
13. Could you sing a lullaby to a **matriarch** in a **lyceum**? ___________
14. Would you ask a **gammon** to dance? ___________
15. Could you eat a **holograph** for lunch? ___________
16. Would you take a **savant** to Africa on a safari? ___________
17. Could you put ketchup on a **cliché**? ___________
18. Would you swim in a **morass**? ___________
19. Could you feed a melon to a **felon**? ___________
20. Would you laugh at a **quip**? ___________
21. Could you **mesmerize** a panther? ___________
22. Would you pet a **carnivore**? ___________
23. Could you paint a **pirouette**? ___________
24. Would you **boycott** a **brawl**? ___________
25. Could you **confer** with an ape? ___________
26. Would you butter a **jetty**? ___________
27. Could you barbecue a **query**? ___________

Name ___________

DON'T TRY THIS AT HOME!

Each of these warnings is good advice.

First, use your dictionary to find out what the words in bold type mean. Then tell why it would NOT be a good idea to do each of these things.

IS THAT AN ABUTMENT DOWN THERE?

1. Don't bungee jump into an **abutment**. Why not?

2. Don't drink **brackish** water. Why not?

3. Don't try to sleep in **bedlam**. Why not?

4. Don't **jostle** a hippopotamus. Why not?

5. Don't go swimming in a **quagmire**. Why not?

6. Don't try to **hoodwink** a **pugilist**. Why not?

7. Don't be **vociferous** in a library. Why not?

8. Don't paddle a boat into a **maelstrom**. Why not?

9. Don't become a **sycophant** to a **hoodlum**. Why not?

10. Don't **procure** the services of a **pilferer**. Why not?

11. Don't run a marathon if you're **enervated**. Why not?

12. Don't **thwart** a lion's attempt to eat lunch. Why not?

13. Don't **jeer** at your older brother's haircut. Why not?

14. Don't shake hands with an **octopod**. Why not?

Name

WHAT WOULD YOU DO WITH IT?

ENTER
LAND OF THRILLS AMUSEMENT PARK
featuring "THE AVALANCHE"

Define the following words in bold type. Then circle the one choice that is appropriate for each word.

1.	**cygnet**	take it on a carousel	put a leash on it	take a picture of it	fry it
2.	**fricassee**	sleep in it	bandage it	eat it for supper	curl it
3.	**acronym**	write it down	weigh it	sit on it	cut it
4.	**bijou**	water it	put it on a sundae	dust it	broil it
5.	**incisor**	put it in the bank	color it	swallow it	brush it
6.	**felon**	slice it	wash it	arrest it	save it
7.	**bok choy**	paint it	cook it	sing to it	sign it
8.	**hellion**	give it a bath	burn it	paint it	discipline it
9.	**bialy**	plant it	take it swimming	sew it up	butter it
10.	**heirloom**	insure it	destroy it	dance with it	bury it
11.	**annuity**	cage it	run from it	invest it	blow it up
12.	**oxymoron**	bandage it	measure it	laugh at it	cure it
13.	**bugaboo**	give it a haircut	fear it	fill it with helium	pet it
14.	**gazette**	put it in a zoo	put jam on it	swat a fly with it	mow it
15.	**decapod**	blow-dry it	put it in a salad	put sunscreen on it	fold it
16.	**foil**	fight with it	tickle it	melt it	memorize it
17.	**serum**	have a party in it	read to it	put it in a jar	broil it
18.	**pique**	get over it	climb it	put it in an envelope	lasso it

Name

A FRAPPÉ ON A FERRIS WHEEL?

Use your dictionary to find out what the words in bold type mean. Then write your answer to each question. On the back of this page, explain why you answered each one as you did.

1. Should a **farrier** be allowed to take a **frappé** on a Ferris wheel? __________
2. Is a monkey likely to **eschew** a banana? __________
3. Why would someone wear a **peruke**? __________
4. Would you style your hair with a **catacomb**? __________
5. Who would you call to **abate** a **conflagration**? __________
6. Describe two times that you have been **bellicose.** __________

   ____
7. Could a **gargoyle** gargle? __________
8. Do you know any teenagers with **comedos**? __________
9. Would you sit on a **sitar**? __________
10. Is **gamboling** illegal in your state? __________
11. Would you babysit with an **oaf**? __________
12. Does a **maxim** belong in a salad? __________
13. Is a **boffin** likely to carry a gun to work? __________
14. Do you know any **somnambulists**? __________
15. Does **abstemious** describe a **glutton**? __________
16. Would you kiss someone with **carbuncles** on his or her face? __________
17. Could a baby with **colic** have a **bucolic** life? __________
18. Who would you expect to find **glissading**? __________
19. Would you like to talk to someone who is **brusque**? __________
20. Have you ever been around a **braggadocio**? __________
21. Can you name someone who is **affable**? __________
22. Name three things you might find on a **carpus.** __________

    ____

    ____

Name __________

CLUE IN TO CONTEXT

CLUELESS
Take a Swing on the "WHIPPER"

Context is the "setting" for a word in a sentence. A word's context often gives you clues to its meaning. Look at the sentence below. What clues might help you figure out that **dauntless** means **fearless**?

Only **dauntless** patrons should try this dangerous ride.

Find context clues to help you guess the meanings of the words in bold type. Then use your dictionary to compare the actual meaning to your guess.

1. Your **ingenious** scheme worked to get us near the front of this line to The Whipper.

   Guess ______________________ Definition ______________________

2. It hurt Miss Candide when we were **candid** about how awful her cotton candy tasted.

   Guess ______________________ Definition ______________________

3. Since my sister has a **dearth** of tickets in her pocket, she has gone to buy more.

   Guess ______________________ Definition ______________________

4. Stop pushing in line—you'll **instigate** a fight!

   Guess ______________________ Definition ______________________

5. **Sullen** Tom is not speaking to anyone since I dropped his triple-decker ice cream cone.

   Guess ______________________ Definition ______________________

6. With great **trepidation**, and against my better judgment, I'm getting on The Terminator.

   Guess ______________________ Definition ______________________

7. We're going to be stuffed, because this park has a **plethora** of food and goodies for sale.

   Guess ______________________ Definition ______________________

8. The **patrons** going in to The Mystery Mansion thought their tickets were much too expensive.

   Guess ______________________ Definition ______________________

Name ____

RIDE THE RAGING RIVER

Use **context clues** to guess what each word in bold type means. Then find the actual definition and compare it to your guess.

1. I'm nervous about the **sinister** grin on that crocodile's face. I don't trust him one bit.

   Guess ______________________ Definition ______________________

2. We were lucky that our guide was **adept** at steering our raft down the river.

   Guess ______________________ Definition ______________________

3. Scott's mouth was **agape** and his face was white when he saw the wave coming toward us.

   Guess ______________________ Definition ______________________

4. The **arrogant** Carlyle Crocodile thinks he's the fiercest crocodile in the river.

   Guess ______________________ Definition ______________________

5. The park officials do not **condone** standing up in the rafts.

   Guess ______________________ Definition ______________________

6. I didn't believe you, but now I **concede** that no one can keep dry on this ride.

   Guess ______________________ Definition ______________________

7. After that embarrassing stunt in the river raft, Andrea's friends **ostracized** her for an hour.

   Guess ______________________ Definition ______________________

8. Amazing! Look at those muscles on our **herculean** raft guide!

   Guess ______________________ Definition ______________________

9. Don't breathe the **noxious** fumes from that boat.

   Guess ______________________ Definition ______________________

10. "Oh, I **abhor** screaming tourists," said Cassy Crocodile. "Let's scare them away!"

    Guess ______________________ Definition ______________________

Name ____

MORE THAN MEETS THE EYE

ARRGG-H!
MOM
WALK-THE-PLANK
$ 2.00
I DARE YOU TO TRY IT!

The **dictionary definition**, or **denotation**, of *pirate* is "one who robs on the high seas."

But there is more than meets the eye. Much more is suggested by the word *pirate* than you find by just looking at the definition. This word stirs up all kinds of images and ideas of . . . adventure, danger, mystery, swords, wooden legs, people walking planks, big black ships, buried treasure, gold, colorful parrots, and patches over eyes . . .

All these images suggested by a word are called its **connotation.**

Find the denotation of each of these words.
Then, write the connotation that is suggested by the word.

1. robber ______________________________

   ____

2. hero ______________________________

   ____

3. laughter ______________________________

   ____

4. argument ______________________________

   ____

5. party ______________________________

   ____

6. giant ______________________________

   ____

7. dark ______________________________

   ____

Name ______________________________

CONNOTATIONS TO CONTEMPLATE

Sam felt uneasy as he waited to get on The Tornado.
What if this said: Sam felt dread as he waited . . .
Sam felt distressed as he waited . . .
Sam felt terrified as he waited . . .
. . . wouldn't you get a stronger feeling that he was really scared?

That's because the connotation of these words suggests more fear than the word *uneasy* suggests. Even when words have similar meanings, the connotations can give entirely different impressions.

For each example, tell how the connotation of the word in the second sentence changes the meaning.

1. Sam felt **sick** when he got off The Tornado.
   Sam felt **nauseated** when he got off The Tornado.

   ____

2. Those musicians are very **slender**.
   Those musicians are very **scrawny**.

   ____

3. Tom showed **pride** after winning the prize.
   Tom showed **conceit** after winning the prize.

   ____

4. Anne gave her little sister a **disapproving** look.
   Anne gave her little sister a **hateful** look.

   ____

5. The teenagers **discussed** their neighbors.
   The teenagers **gossiped** about their neighbors.

   ____

6. This ice cream is **tasty**.
   This ice cream is **luscious**.

   ____

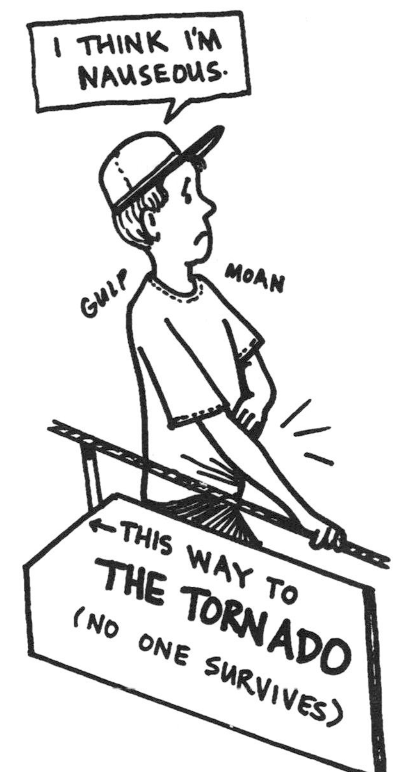
I THINK I'M NAUSEOUS.
GULP
MOAN
←THIS WAY TO
THE TORNADO
(NO ONE SURVIVES)

Name ______________________________

THE IMPOSTORS

Synonyms are words that have the same or nearly the same meanings.

An imposter has shown up in each of the mirrors. All the words are synonyms except one. Get rid of the imposter word by crossing it out with an X.

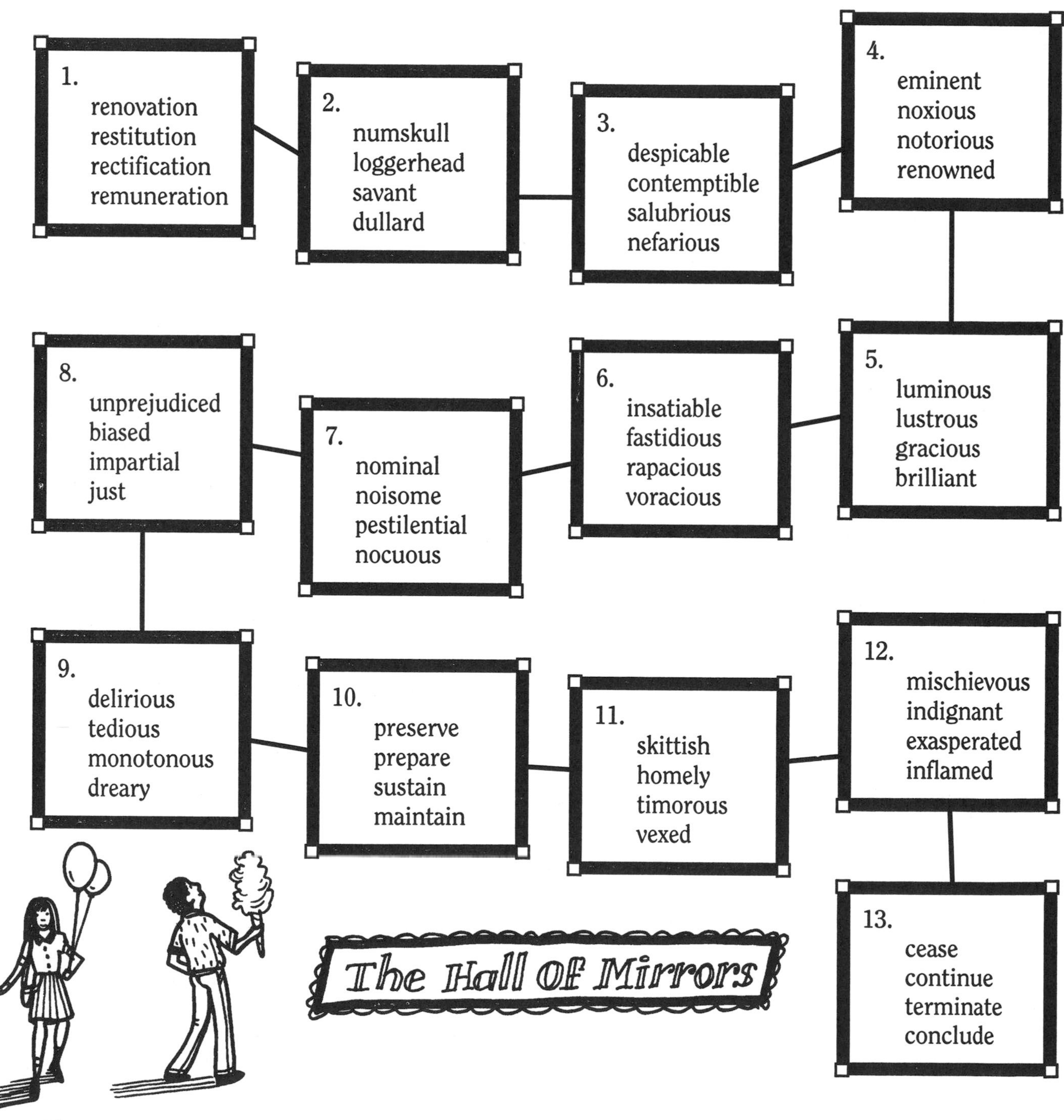
1.
renovation
restitution
rectification
remuneration
2.
numskull
loggerhead
savant
dullard
3.
despicable
contemptible
salubrious
nefarious
4.
eminent
noxious
notorious
renowned
5.
luminous
lustrous
gracious
brilliant
6.
insatiable
fastidious
rapacious
voracious
7.
nominal
noisome
pestilential
nocuous
8.
unprejudiced
biased
impartial
just
9.
delirious
tedious
monotonous
dreary
10.
preserve
prepare
sustain
maintain
11.
skittish
homely
timorous
vexed
12.
mischievous
indignant
exasperated
inflamed
13.
cease
continue
terminate
conclude
The Hall of Mirrors

Name

DOUBLE TROUBLE

Synonyms are words that have the same or nearly the same meanings.

Circle the synonym for each word in bold type.

The Stomach Wrencher

1. You get **ebullient** on The Stomach Wrencher roller coaster—are you ecstatic or nauseous?
2. The lady next to you on that ride is looking **languid**—is she robust or weak?
3. A **grueling** job—is it torturous or leisurely?
4. You enjoy a **canapé**—have you eaten an appetizer or watched a good comedy?
5. A person full of **avarice** has trouble with which—indigestion or greed?
6. When you **gore** a shrimp—do you stab it or sell it?
7. Your mom says that you **masticate** loudly—are you too noisy when you snore or chew?
8. You laugh at a **fatuous** friend—is he clever or foolish?
9. When you **gnash** your teeth—do you brush or grind them?
10. If your studying is **futile**—is it productive or useless?
11. Your hat is **garish**—is it tasteful or flashy?
12. Your neighbor is **churlish**—is she funny or grumpy?
13. A pain in your side is **acute**—is it ticklish or severe?
14. You grow up to be **renowned**—are you famous or handsome?
15. You are **glutted** after lunch—are you tired or stuffed?
16. Someone **fidgets** during the opera—do they wiggle or snore?

Name

SCRAMBLED SYNONYMS

Synonyms are words that have the same meaning.

Each pair of words below was a pair of synonyms, but The Brain-Scrambler scrambled them up. Now the pairs are all wrong. Unscramble them and match up the synonyms correctly. Write the pairs on the lines below.

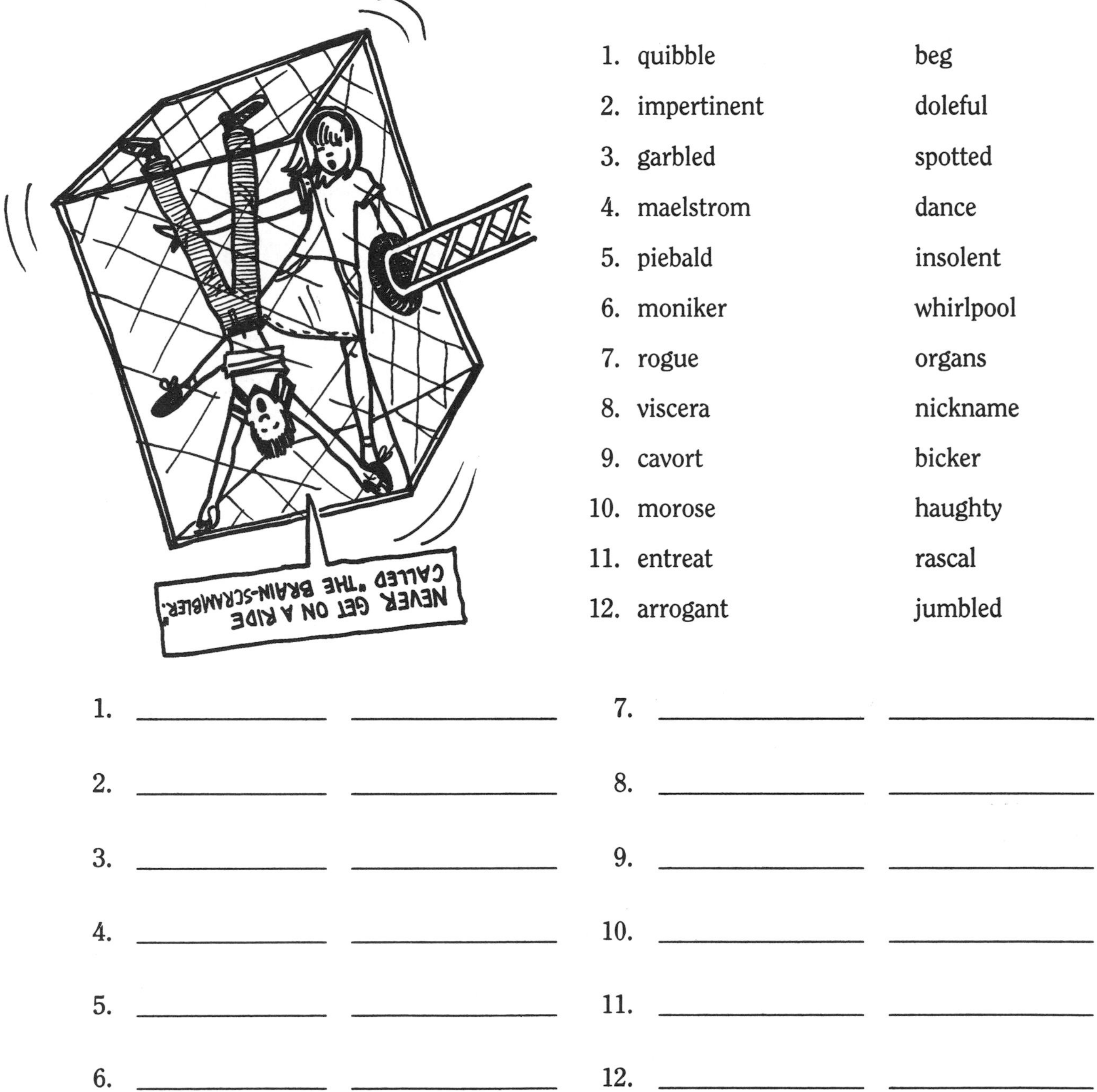
NEVER GET ON A RIDE
CALLED "THE BRAIN-SCRAMBLER."

1. quibble — beg
2. impertinent — doleful
3. garbled — spotted
4. maelstrom — dance
5. piebald — insolent
6. moniker — whirlpool
7. rogue — organs
8. viscera — nickname
9. cavort — bicker
10. morose — haughty
11. entreat — rascal
12. arrogant — jumbled

1. __________ __________
2. __________ __________
3. __________ __________
4. __________ __________
5. __________ __________
6. __________ __________
7. __________ __________
8. __________ __________
9. __________ __________
10. __________ __________
11. __________ __________
12. __________ __________

Name ____________________

TWISTED WORDS

The Twister has caught some words and "twisted" them into **antonyms** (opposites). Find the original word for each antonym (1–12) by searching on The Twister's path. Write the correct antonym in each box. (The Twister's path has more words than you'll use.)

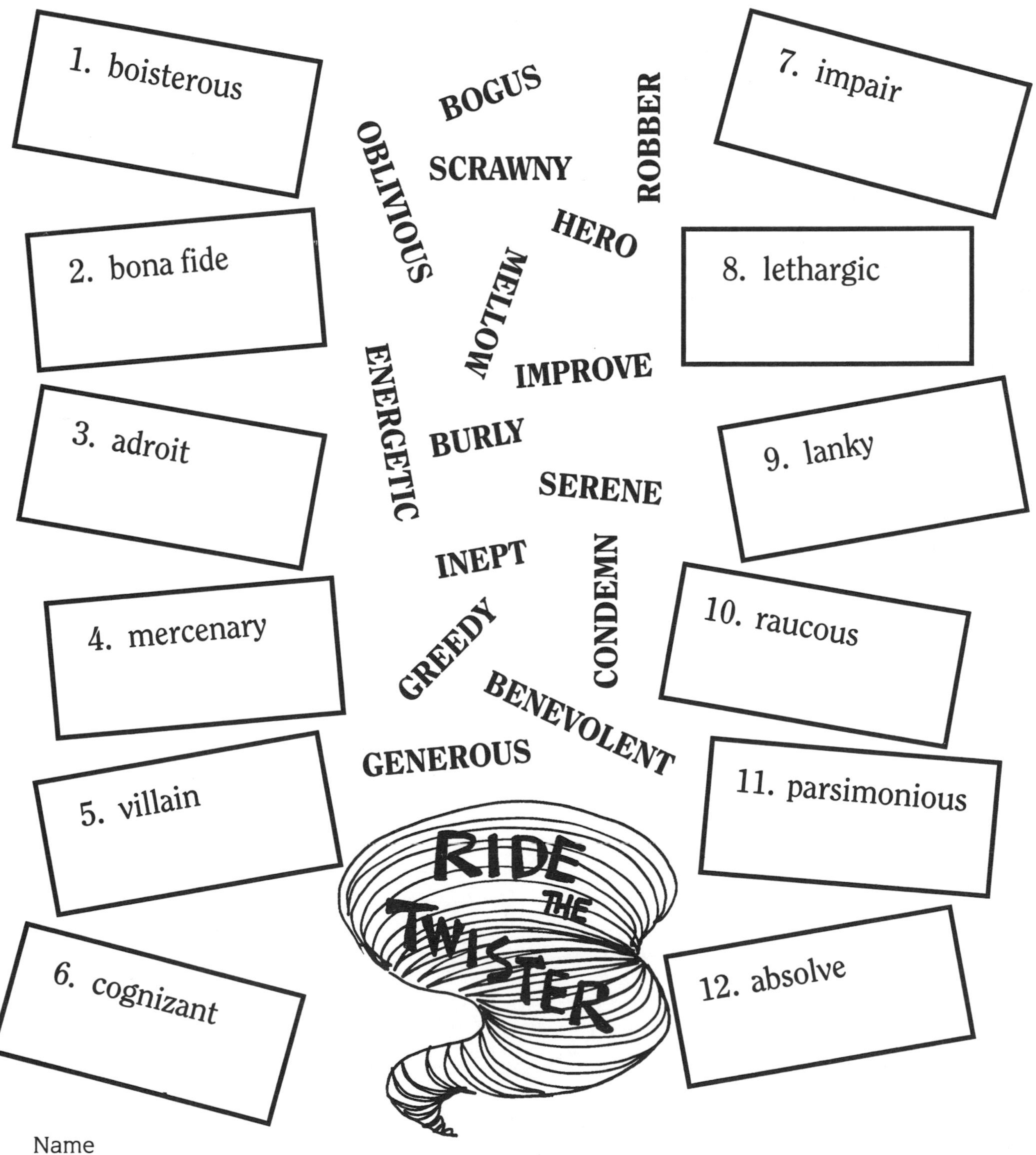
1. boisterous
2. bona fide
3. adroit
4. mercenary
5. villain
6. cognizant
7. impair
8. lethargic
9. lanky
10. raucous
11. parsimonious
12. absolve
BOGUS
ROBBER
OBLIVIOUS
SCRAWNY
HERO
MELLOW
IMPROVE
ENERGETIC
BURLY
SERENE
INEPT
CONDEMN
GREEDY
BENEVOLENT
GENEROUS
RIDE THE TWISTER

Name

OPPOSITES ATTRACT

Antonyms are words that are "attracted" to each other because they are opposites.

Look around the page and find the antonym for each of the words below.

1. conjecture ________________
2. wicked ________________
3. boorish ________________
4. fabrication ________________
5. rejoice ________________
6. disagreeable ________________
7. expense ________________
8. arrogance ________________
9. preserve ________________
10. informal ________________
11. luxury ________________
12. elude ________________
13. radical ________________
14. sacrilegious ________________
15. hovel ________________

confront

creation

castle

JUBILATION

evil

MODESTY

ruin

casual

amiable

lament

UNHOLY

pesty

truth

guess

virtuous

richness

moderate

sacred

EVADE

hardship

proof

prim

revenue

polite

extreme

cost

Name

A KNIGHT IN THE NIGHT

Homophones are words that sound alike but have different spellings and meanings.

IT'S AS BLACK AS NIGHT INSIDE THE BLACK KNIGHT'S CASTLE!
MOAT RIDES $2.00

Use a pair of homophones to complete each sentence. The first one is done for you. On the back of the page, create five (or more) sentences of your own using at least two homophones in each sentence. Use the back of the page.

1. Jenny ________ that she has cotton candy on her ________ .
2. ________ ! Do I really ________ you some money?
3. The lost man was in a ________ after wandering ten ________ in the desert.
4. The ________ in that phone booth has a shirt with a turtle-necked ________ .
5. ________ ! Don't pull all the ________ out of my barn!
6. The campers in their ________ are ________ about reports of bears.
7. Did that pirate ________ gold on the high ________ ?
8. She forgot to ________ her closet door after getting her ________ out.
9. Don't show your ________ while on board a ________ ship.
10. The army ________ choked on a ________ of popcorn.
11. I ________ my dog out to catch a ________ of a rabbit.
12. The sailor sheepishly admitted that he does ________ know how to tie a ________ .
13. Should we ________ her because she drinks twelve different kinds of ________ ?

Name ______________________________

HAVE YOU EVER SEEN?

EEEEEEEEEEEK

HAVE YOU EVER SEEN YOUR AUNT TAKE HER PET ANT FOR A WALK?

HAVE YOU EVER WONDERED IF THE BRAKES WOULD BREAK ON THE "ROCKETING COASTER" RIDE?

HAVE YOU EVER SEEN A BEET MARCH TO THE BEAT?

Homophones are words that sound alike but have different spellings and meanings.

Here are clues for some pairs of homophones. One of each pair is scrambled in the line below. Figure out what the homophones are, and fill in the blanks.
yads . . . esab . . . ripa . . . sayr . . . ekep . . . wrohtn . . . ode . . . frus . . . tarorc . . . ese . . . wob . . . ote

HAVE YOU EVER SEEN . . .

1. a ________ get a ________ ?
   (part of a foot get pulled along?)
2. a ________ get to first ________ ?
   (a stringed instrument run after a hit?)
3. a ________ that could ________ ?
   (an ocean which has vision?)
4. a ________ wear a ________ ?
   (an orange vegetable wear a diamond?)
5. some ________ get a ________ ?
   (sunshine get higher pay?)
6. a ________ take a ________ ?
   (a mountaintop take a squinty look?)
7. a ________ get ________ ?
   (a king's chair get tossed?)
8. a ________ eat a ________ ?
   (two friends eat a juicy fruit?)
9. a ________ with a ________ ?
   (a boyfriend with a necktie?)
10. a ________ jump in the ________ ?
    (a slave jump in the ocean?)
11. a ________ go ________ ?
    (seven days lose strength?)
12. a ________ spend ________ ?
    (a female deer spend money?)

Name

Excuse me! What's your excuse for cutting in line ahead of me?

EXCUSE ME!

Homographs are words that are spelled the same but have different meanings. They often differ in their pronunciation. Choose a pair of homographs from the box at the bottom of the page to complete the sentences. For each sentence, there is a set of clues.

THIS WAY TO THE SUPER AVALANCHE!

1. I ______________ (surmise or guess) that you'll find the ______________ (alleged culprit) hiding in one of the cars on The Avalanche roller coaster.

2. Why did you ______________ (insist against) to throw your ______________ (garbage) in the trash?

3. We might ______________ (happen to) up sailing into the ______________ (air current).

4. Please don't ______________ (abandon) me in the ______________ (dry wasteland).

5. Will the lady with a ______________ (fancy ribbon) please take a ______________ (curtsy)?

6. Scott wanted to ______________ (argue against, disagree with) the results of the ______________ (competition).

7. I ______________ (disagree, protest) to your pointing that dangerous ______________ (gadget, article) at me!

8. Are you going to ______________ (give to) me with a ______________ (gift) at the ______________ (current time)?

9. It only took a ______________ (60 seconds) to eat this ______________ (tiny) cream puff.

10. We got into a huge ______________ (fight) over whose turn it was to ______________ (ship) the boat.

refuse	wind	contest	bow	present	row
suspect	desert	reject	object	minute	read

Name ______________________________

WHAT'S UP?

ARE YOU UP FOR AN ADVENTURE?

I WENT UP TWICE, BUT NEVER THREW UP

We woke up at six o'clock this morning, got dressed up, locked up the house, started up the old car, and headed up the road to The Land of Thrills Amusement Park. (Tom got up on the wrong side of the bed and was stirring up trouble. Everyone was upset with him, so we got held up a bit and got a late start.) If we hadn't gotten tied up in traffic, we would have been here before the place opened up. But since we were late, we quickly lined up for tickets and raced up to our favorite ride. I was about to give up on Sara joining us on The Terminator, but she finally built up her courage and joined us. The upshot of that was that she was up to it after all and held up well. She didn't even throw up.

We wound up running around from ride to ride making up for our lost time. It's noon and we've used up four hours already. I'm mixed up about how many rides we've been on. But I bet by the time this place closes up we'll have ridden up to forty rides. If it were up to me, we wouldn't finish up until we've ridden them all ten times.

Well, hurry up! I've worked up an appetite, so let's look up the eating area and order up some food!

Some words, like the little word *up,* have many meanings and uses. Read the story. Then count all the different uses of the word *up* included in the story. How many did you find? There are many other words that have as many meanings and uses as *up*. Choose one of the words below. Begin collecting a list of as many different ways to use that word as you can. Write your ideas below. If you need more space, continue on the back of the page. Then use the back of the page to write a story. Try to include twenty-five or more uses of your word. Get some friends to help you.

go . . . . run . . . . time . . . . out . . . . up . . . . set . . . . down . . . . town . . . . back . . . . way . . . .

______________ ______________ ______________ ______________ ______________

______________ ______________ ______________ ______________ ______________

Name ________________________________

MORE THAN ONE

Many words have more than one meaning. Here are some examples. Can you figure them out?

1. ______________________ 2. ______________________ 3. ______________________

Write the answers above each picture. Now, choose six of the words below. For each one you choose, illustrate two or more meanings of the word in the boxes below.

spring	light	stall	spot	relish	pen	game
arms	bridge	swallow	date	count	track	bow
shower	beat	bar	down	fire	sling	fence
sow	tackle	back	line	run	tick	quarter
pupil	box	bat	lap	back	ride	chip

Name ______________________________

SOMETHING'S CHANGED

MEANINGS OF PREFIXES

anti	(against)	in	(in, into, not)	pre	(before)
bi	(two)	micro	(small)	semi	(half, part)
bene	(good)	mal	(wrong)	re	(again)
bio	(life)	mid	(middle)	sub	(under)
co	(together)	mini	(small)	super	(above)
dis	(wrong, bad)	mis	(wrong)	trans	(across)
il	(not)	non	(without, not)	un	(not)
im	(not)	post	(after)	uni	(one)

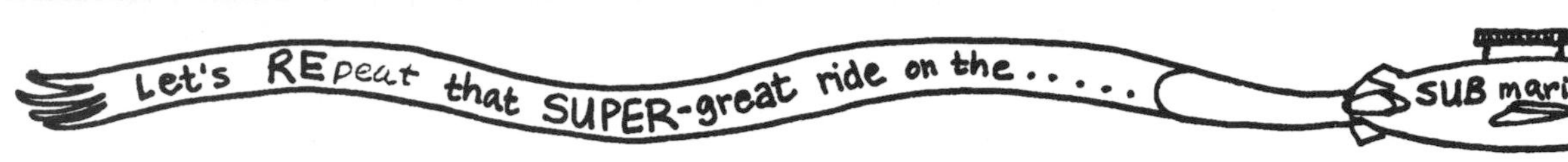
Let's REpeat that SUPER-great ride on the . . . . .
SUB marine

A **prefix** is a word part added to the beginning of a word. Whenever a prefix is added to a root word, the meaning of the root word is changed in some way.

Tell the meaning of each of these words with prefixes.

1. coworker ____________
2. midstream ____________
3. unfit ____________
4. distaste ____________
5. benefit ____________
6. submarine ____________
7. biorhythms ____________
8. transatlantic ____________
9. misbehave ____________
10. uniform ____________
11. malfunction ____________
12. indecent ____________
13. rewrite ____________
14. pretest ____________
15. postgame ____________
16. superpower ____________
17. impolite ____________
18. minibike ____________
19. semicircle ____________
20. antipoverty ____________
21. nonvoter ____________
22. unicycle ____________

Name ____________

WINNING PREFIXES

Find the bottle that will give you the right prefix to make each word. Add the prefix to the root word given or defined in the example. Use each bottle only once.

MID
QUADR NON
MICRO SUB PRE
RE UN UNI IM
FORE ANTI MIS TRI TRANS
MID CO MAL INTER SEMI NON

1. fix again ________________
2. across the ocean ________________
3. three angles ________________
4. wrong take ________________
5. not a worker ________________
6. bad nourishment ________________
7. four-footed ________________
8. write together ________________
9. middle of the way ________________
10. before surgery ________________
11. below standard ________________
12. not tied ________________
13. against drugs ________________
14. front of head ________________
15. without toxins ________________
16. small computer ________________
17. not proper ________________
18. part professional ________________
19. between planets ________________
20. one-wheeled cycle ________________
21. middle size ________________

Name ____

JUICY ENDINGS

SUFFIXES

Suffixes	Meanings	Examples
ion, tion	(state of being, act of)	action, exploration
er, or, ar, ist	(one who does something)	teacher, actor, liar, artist
able, ible	(able to be)	lovable, edible
ness	(state or condition of)	goodness
less	(without)	windowless
ful	(full of, like)	tearful
en	(to be made of, to make)	golden
ly, y	(when, how, like, in the manner of)	kindly, noisy
ize, fy	(to cause to be)	vaporize, dignify

A **suffix** is a word part added at the end of the root word. It changes the root's meaning. These words have been formed by adding suffixes to the roots. Write the meaning of each word.

JUICY WATERMELON
$1.00 per slice

1. supervisor ______________________
2. terrorist ______________________
3. juicy ______________________
4. careful ______________________
5. buyer ______________________
6. sleepless ______________________
7. wooden ______________________
8. tenderly ______________________
9. sadness ______________________
10. beggar ______________________
11. fantasize ______________________
12. purify ______________________
13. addition ______________________
14. breakable ______________________

Name ______________________

SUFFIX SEARCH

DARE TO RIDE!

What is the name of this wild train ride?

You can find out by solving the suffix puzzle. Find the right suffix and add it to the root word to form an answer to each of the clues below. When you have all the answers, transfer the letter that matches each number to the spaces at the bottom of the page. If you have the answers right, these letters will spell the name of the ride!

1. full of thanks ___ ___ ___ ___ ___ ___ ___ [14]
2. one who lies [1] ___ [12] [15]
3. state of being bald ___ [2] ___ ___ ___ ___ ___ ___
4. one who does dental work [18] ___ ___ ___ ___ [3] ___
5. act of acting ___ ___ [4] ___ ___ ___
6. like a creep [5] ___ ___ ___ ___ ___
7. able to be taught ___ ___ ___ ___ [6] ___ ___ ___ ___
8. without age [7] ___ ___ ___ ___ ___ ___
9. act of injecting ___ [8] ___ ___ [9] ___ ___ ___ ___
10. made of silk ___ ___ ___ ___ [10]
11. one who robs ___ ___ ___ ___ ___ [11]
12. to cause to have a motor ___ [16] ___ ___ ___ [13] ___ ___
13. in a brave manner ___ ___ [17] ___ ___ ___ ___

[1] [2] [3] [4] [5] [6] [7] [8] [9] [10] [11] [12] [13] [14] [15] [16] [17] [18]

Name

UNBELIEVABLE !

The word *unbelievable* is formed from the root word *believe* plus a prefix and a suffix. Here are the meanings of some word roots. They can be used to form many words.

Form twenty words from these roots by adding prefixes and suffixes where you need them.

MEANINGS OF ROOTS

act	—	(act or do)
cycle, cir	—	(circle, wheel)
dorm	—	(sleep)
fer	—	(bring or carry)
form	—	(shape)
graph	—	(write)
labor	—	(work)
lib	—	(book)
morph	—	(form)
mov, mob, mot	—	(move)
oper	—	(work)
ped	—	(foot)
phon	—	(sound)
port	—	(carry)
son	—	(sound)
tele	—	(far)
therm	—	(heat)
verb	—	(word)
vis, view, vid	—	(see)
vit, viv	—	(life)

1. ______
2. ______
3. ______
4. ______
5. ______
6. ______
7. ______
8. ______
9. ______
10. ______
11. ______
12. ______
13. ______
14. ______
15. ______
16. ______
17. ______
18. ______
19. ______
20. ______

SPACE SHIP
RIDES
25 cents

Name ______

DUNK THE DUDE

This page is full of word parts. Find the right word parts in the tub and combine them to make a word which matches the definition. You may need to use a prefix and a suffix to make a word, or even two suffixes. Also, you'll need to make slight spelling changes as you make some of the new words.

Try to get at least fifteen right. That's what it takes to push the button that dumps this dude into the tub.

week
LY
DIS
ION
kind
en
port
ize
legal
trans
bi
ness
ABLE
un
MOBIL
il
mis
in
vis
manage
er
mov
heart
RE
success
friend
form
believe
use
ible
im

1. the act of seeing something again
2. two times a week
3. to carry across
4. a condition that is not kind
5. to cause to be mobile
6. to manage poorly
7. not being able to be believed
8. not able to be moved
9. made to feel wrong at heart
10. not in a legal manner
11. full of success
12. able to be used again
13. condition of being like a friend
14. one who forms something again
15. one who does not believe
16. able to be carried across
17. to cause to be legal
18. not able to be seen

Name

MISSING LINKS

The Strong Man's chain has some missing links. So do these chains of words. In each "chain," every word can form a compound word when combined with the word in front and in back of it. A **compound word** is a word formed by combining two other words.

The first two examples are done for you. In the rest, you'll need to figure out what words should be in the missing blanks.

SEE THE
FABULOUS
MISSING
LINK!
SHOWTIMES —
2 - 4 - 6 P.M.
URRRGH

1. eye ____ brush
2. busy ____ guard
3. black ____ man
4. match ____ car
5. boy ____ ship ____ stick
6. drive ____ side ____ case
7. sun ____ town ____ boat
8. pop ____ meal ____ out
9. tea ____ cake ____ man
10. tender ____ note ____ worm ____ chuck
11. chain ____ horse ____ ball ____ mate
12. roller ____ board ____ way ____ show ____ town
13. bubble ____ drop ____ side ____ ball ____ way
14. copy ____ fish ____ up ____ side ____ child

Name ______________________________

COMPOUND LINE-UP

A **compound word** is a word formed from the combination of two other complete words. Butterfly, sunshine, and upstairs are examples.

Everyone in line for The Cosmic Crusher is holding a word that can be combined with the word *head* to make a compound word. (The word may come before or after *head*.) But you can't see the word. You can only see a clue for the word. Use the clues to figure out what each compound word is. The first one is done for you.

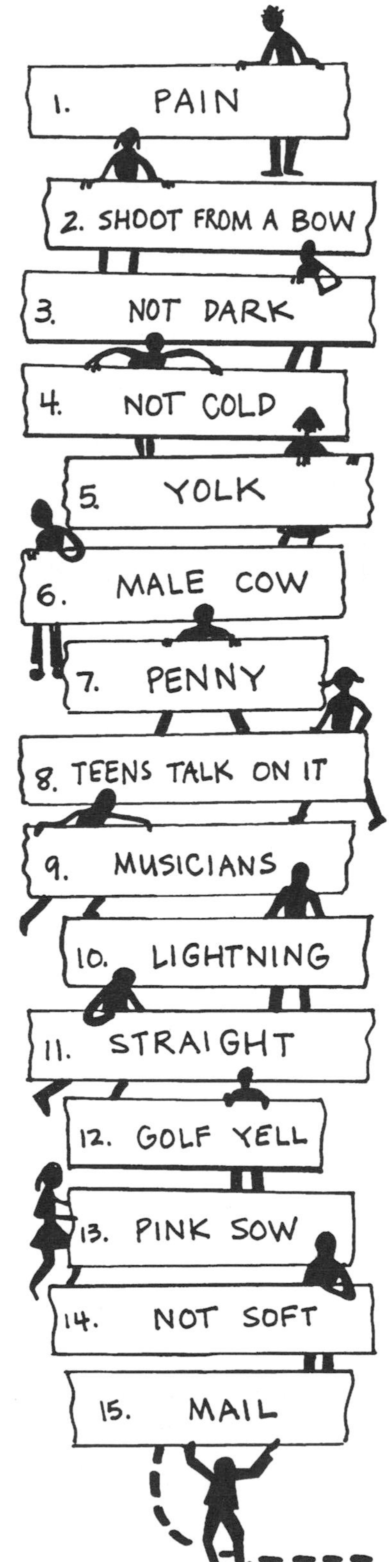

1. PAIN
2. SHOOT FROM A BOW
3. NOT DARK
4. NOT COLD
5. YOLK
6. MALE COW
7. PENNY
8. TEENS TALK ON IT
9. MUSICIANS
10. LIGHTNING
11. STRAIGHT
12. GOLF YELL
13. PINK SOW
14. NOT SOFT
15. MAIL

1. headache 2. ____________

3. ____________ 4. ____________

5. ____________ 6. ____________

7. ____________ 8. ____________

9. ____________ 10. ____________

11. ____________ 12. ____________

13. ____________ 14. ____________

15. ____________

Name ____________

LOOK-ALIKE WORDS

There are many words that look and sound a lot alike. It's hard to keep from being confused about these unless you are clear about their meanings.

Here are some pairs of words that look and sound similar. For each pair, decide which meaning matches which confusing word. You will need help from your dictionary. Write the letter of the correct meaning in front of the word.

1. ________ affect ________ effect
   a. a result b. to influence
2. ________ loath ________ loathe
   c. hate, detest d. reluctant
3. ________ allude ________ elude
   e. mention f. evade
4. ________ credible ________ credulous
   g. believable h. too trustful
5. ________ averse ________ adverse
   i. opposed j. unfavorable
6. ________ scrumptious ________ sumptuous
   k. magnificent l. delicious
7. ________ rigorous ________ vigorous
   m. energetic n. demanding
8. ________ perpetuate ________ perpetrate
   o. preserve p. commit, enact
9. ________ tortuous ________ torturous
   q. painful r. winding
10. ________ illusion ________ allusion
    s. reference to something t. false perception
11. ________ elicit ________ illicit
    u. illegal v. draw forth
12. ________ persecute ________ prosecute
    w. bring legal action against x. torment
13. ________ explicit ________ implicit
    y. implied or suggested z. clearly stated

THE HALL
OF CONFUSING
LOOK- ALIKES

Name ____________________

WORDS THAT CONFUSE

There are many words that people confuse with other words. Here are some of them. Use your dictionary to help you sort them out. Circle the right answer for each question.

1. Molly predicts that Jake will get over his nausea from The Tower of Confusion.
   Is this a **prognosis** or a **diagnosis**?

2. Ten friends vote on which ride to try first. There are two votes for The Scrambler, three for The Twister, five for The Death Drop. Does The Death Drop win by a **majority** or a **plurality**?

3. Sam said, "I tell you! I do not want to go on The Heartstopper."
   Is his message **explicit** or **implicit**?

4. Your fear seems to be spreading to everyone.
   Is it **contagious** or **infectious**?

5. Scott's enthusiasm about this ride is growing by the minute.
   Is his enthusiasm **waxing** or **waning**?

6. I'm just wild about rollercoasters. I've been on them all!
   Does Jayne have a **mania** or a **phobia**?

7. There's a woman showing off her fearlessness by standing up on the seat of the ALPINE PLUNGE.
   Is she **flaunting** her courage or is she **flouting** it?

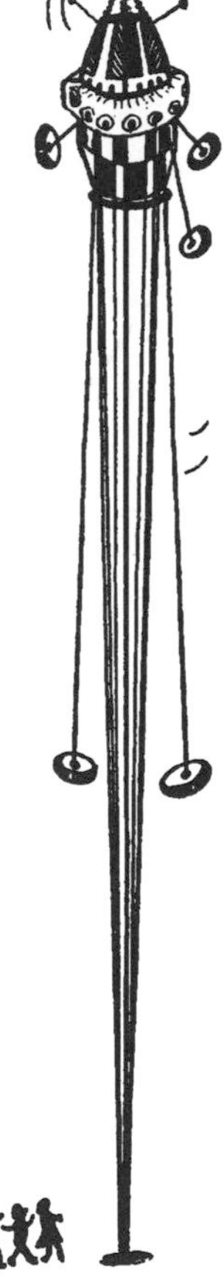

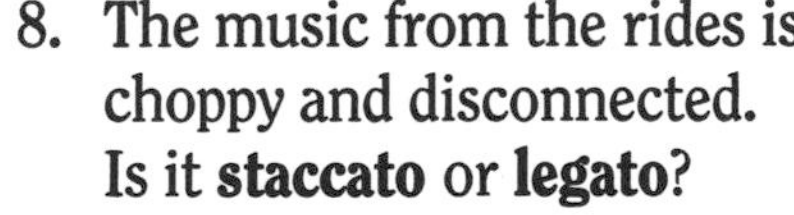

8. The music from the rides is choppy and disconnected.
   Is it **staccato** or **legato**?

9. You've been shouting a lot of false statements that will damage my reputation.
   Is this **slander** or **libel**?

10. Kids have thrown stuff overboard from the rafts in the river.
    Is this floating material **jetsam** or **flotsam**?

11. Tom is full of energy as he climbs up The Tower of Confusion.
    Is he feeling **rigorous** or **vigorous**?

12. The end of the ride is very near.
    Is the end **eminent** or **imminent**?

13. The roller coaster is climbing up to the top of the mountain.
    Is it heading for its **nadir** or **zenith**?

14. From watching you on these rides, I conclude you're not afraid of heights.
    Am I **inferring** or **implying** this?

15. The famous Captain Hook is featured in the Walk-the-Plank ride.
    Is he **notorious** or **nefarious**, or both?

TOWER OF CONFUSION - OPEN!

Name

STICK OUT YOUR NECK

Figurative language is language in which the words do not mean exactly what they say. Instead of giving the literal, or actual, meaning, the words create an interesting or dramatic image that makes a point. There are hundreds of examples of figurative speech in the English language. It's good to know what they mean. It is also fun to think about or illustrate the literal meaning of the words.

Can you figure out what saying each of these pictures represents? Write the answer. Then, on the back of the paper, tell what each expression means.

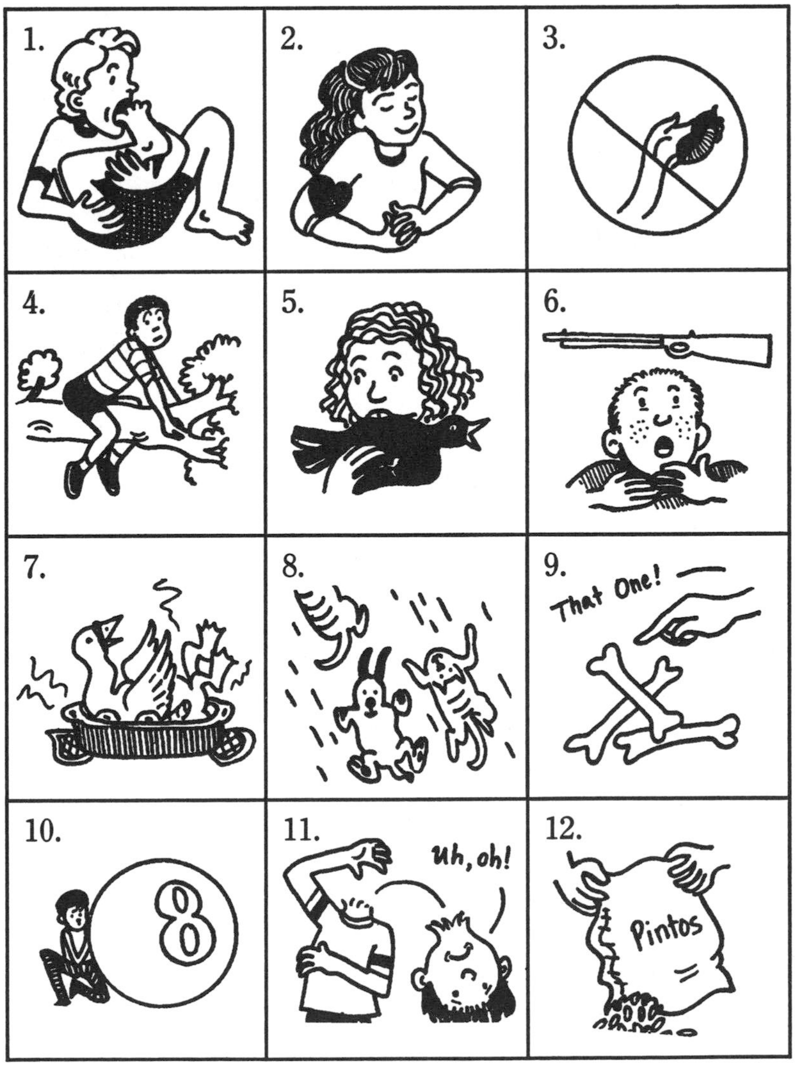

1.	2.	3.
4.	5.	6.
7.	8.	9.
10.	11.	12.

1. ______________________
2. ______________________
3. ______________________
4. ______________________
5. ______________________
6. ______________________
7. ______________________
8. ______________________
9. ______________________
10. ______________________
11. ______________________
12. ______________________

Name ______________________

OVER THE EDGE

MOLLY'S GONE OVER THE EDGE

Poor Molly has gone off her rocker. We've decided that she's lost all of her marbles and has bats in her belfry. This day at the amusement park started off as a red letter day. We got off on the right foot with a great ride on The Wild Mouse. The group was really hitting it off and we were having more fun than a barrel of monkeys on all the rides.

But, by ten o'clock, the tide had turned for Molly. She had blown her top at least 8 times. First, on The Screaming Eagle, she lost her cool when she had to sit in the last car. Then, she got as sick as a dog on The Scrambler and gave us all a tongue-lashing for taking her on the ride. Next, she got madder than a wet hen when her hair and clothes got soaked on The Raging River Rampage. And when Scott put his foot in his mouth and said her hair looked gruesome, she lost her head completely and started screaming bloody murder.

I think the last straw was the snowcone down her back. She ran around like a chicken with her head cut off, raking us over the coals and yelling about how we were driving her up the wall. We really tried hard to get her to cool her jets, but she just kept telling us to get off her back.

Finally, she chilled out a little and wandered around in a fog for a while. We tried to keep the lid on things so she wouldn't flip out completely. Just when it seemed like the heat was off, some out-to-lunch little kid cut right ahead of her in line to The Submarine, her favorite ride. Molly went totally bananas. She got on her high horse and tried to knock the tar out of this kid. But instead, she knocked herself into the mermaid pond. Lucky for her, Scott pulled her out in the nick of time, just as an oncoming submarine was about to cream her.

How many examples of figurative speech can you find in this story? ____________________

Choose one of the paragraphs above and rewrite it in your own words. Try to replace the sayings and expressions in the paragraph with your own fresh, creative images.

Name ____________________

WORDS WITH A PAST

The histories, or **etymologies**, of many words can be found in most dictionaries. A word's etymology is usually found in brackets before or after the definition. The most recent source of a word is given first.

WELCOME TO THE "CASTEL"
A MUSEUM OF ETYMOLOGIES

cas•tle (ka-səl) *n.* 1. A fortified building or group of buildings designed to defend a town, route, or territory, especially in medieval Europe. 2. A mansion. 3. A place that provides security. [Middle English *castel*, from Old English *castel*, from late Latin *castlellum*, village, from Latin *castellum*, castle, diminutive of *castrum*, fortified place.]

You can see that the word *castle,* most recently, comes from the Middle English word *castel* and that its original meanings were *village* and *fortified place.*

Find etymologies for these words. Tell the most recent source and original meaning.

1. carousel ______
2. tsar ______
3. gourmet ______
4. pajama ______
5. piano ______
6. octopus ______
7. acrobat ______
8. athlete ______
9. comet ______
10. juvenile ______

Name ______

ETYMOLOGIES YOU CAN EAT

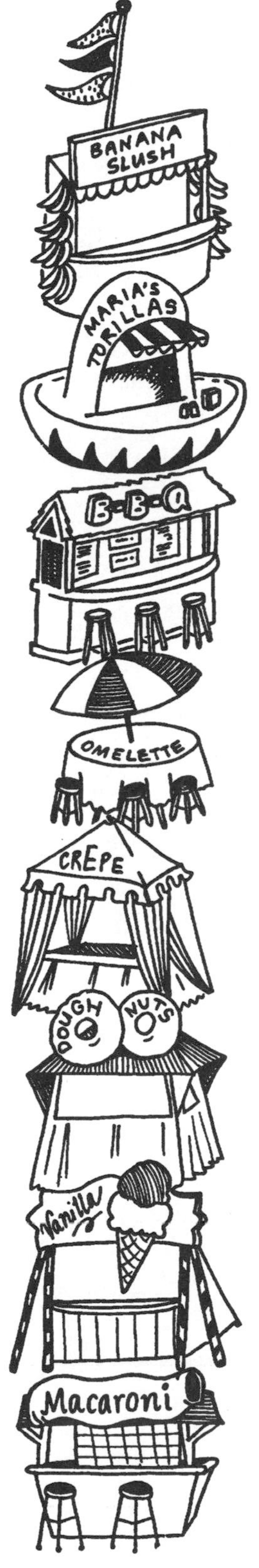
BANANA SLUSH
MARIA'S TORILLAS
B-B-Q
OMELETTE
CREPE
DOUGH NUTS
Vanilla
Macaroni

If you look in a dictionary for the **etymology** (history) of the word *waffle*, you'll find it in brackets before or after the definition. It will usually tell you what language (or languages) this word is borrowed from and something about the original meaning. What can you find about the etymology of the word *waffle*?

language of origin ____________________

original meaning ____________________

____

Look up the history of each of these food words. For each one, tell its language of origin and something about its original meaning.

1. banana ____________________
2. crepe ____________________
3. tortilla ____________________
4. doughnut ____________________
5. barbecue ____________________
6. vanilla ____________________
7. omelette ____________________
8. sauerkraut ____________________
9. molasses ____________________
10. macaroni ____________________

Name ____________________

WHICH ONE FITS?

An **analogy** shows a relationship between two sets of words. The relationship between the first two words is the same as the relationship between the second set of words.

A. Adventure is to daring as villain is to scoundrel.
B. Terror is to fearlessness as power is to weakness.

In example A, both sets of words are **synonyms** (similar meanings).

In example B, both sets of words are **antonyms** (opposite meanings).

CHEAP
DANGER
BOLD
ENDING
GARBAGE
MUTE
INITIAL
GENEROUS
RETAIN
VALUABLES
ALLY
SUPERB
QUIET
SHY
DULL
FUN
COPY
GREEDY
THRILL
ANALOGY
RING
TOSS

Find the word that fits to complete each analogy.
Choose one of the words on the bottles.

1. Quarrel is to argument as rubbish is to ______________ .
2. Sullen is to glum as timid is to ______________ .
3. Peril is to ______________ as hectic is to chaotic.
4. Noisy is to clamorous as ______________ is to splendid.
5. Minimize is to maximize as ______________ is to expensive.
6. ______________ is to mimic as impeccable is to faultless.
7. Friend is to ______________ as enemy is to opponent.
8. ______________ is to release as evidence is to conjecture.
9. Freedom is to slavery as ______________ is to final.
10. Savory is to tasty as boring is to ______________ .

Name

ANALOGIES AREN'T SCARY

In an **analogy**, the words in the first pair must have the same relationship as the words in the second pair. When you try to solve an analogy, begin by deciding what the relationship is between the two words you are given.

scary : terrifying AS _______ : freezing

What is the relationship between scary and terrifying? Terrifying is an extreme form of scary. So, in the next pair, freezing must be an extreme form of something. An answer such as cool would complete the analogy.

GORY: GRUESOME
HAIR-RAISING: BONE-CHILLING
UGLY: GROTESQUE
SCARED: FRANTIC
The Haunted Mansion of Scary Analogies

Explain the relationship between the two words in the complete pair. Then finish the analogy by making the second pair have the same relationship. Circle the correct choice.

1. insolvent : rich AS penniless : _______________
   poor   flush   millionaire   pauper
2. mischief : violence AS _______________ : insult
   attack   harmless   compliment   teasing
3. squirrel : nuts AS _______________ : money
   miser   wallet   selfish   spendthrift
4. pebble : _______________ AS minnow : fish
   gravel   rock   sand   mountain
5. blush : embarrassed AS fume : _______________
   smile   temper   angry   worried
6. _______________ : drip AS mitt : baseball
   bat   water   bucket   tennis
7. perfume : fragrant AS garbage : _______________
   trash   fetid   sweet   smell
8. seasoned : _______________ AS inexperienced : novice
   young   experienced   veteran   amateur

CALL ME 'CHICKEN', BUT I'M NOT GOING IN THERE!

Name ____

ON THE SAME TEAM

TUG O'WAR
TODAY
PRIZES
ROBUST
BRAWNY
Groan
DOCILE
ERG
VIGOROUS
Grunt
HEARTY

The words on this team all have something in common.
All except one, that is! Can you find the one word that doesn't fit?

In each of these lines, four of the five words have something in common.
Decide what the classification is that fits them. Write it at the end of the line.
Then put an X through the word that does not belong.

1. snipe ouzel shrew plover rook ________________
2. vole narwhal addax meristem dingo ________________
3. vicar rector stoic abbot friar ________________
4. sword derringer rapier sacrum foil ________________
5. miter balalaika flageolet tabor sitar ________________
6. paella zwieback capriole tempura borscht ________________
7. basilisk injunction adjudicate barrister jurisprudence ________________
8. gibe witticism bon mot quip bribe ________________
9. patella clavichord phalanges scapula sternum ________________
10. lexicon physiognomy image visage countenance ________________
11. scabies pertussis novella rubella gout ________________

Name ________________________________

WORDS & VOCABULARY
ASSESSMENT AND ANSWER KEYS

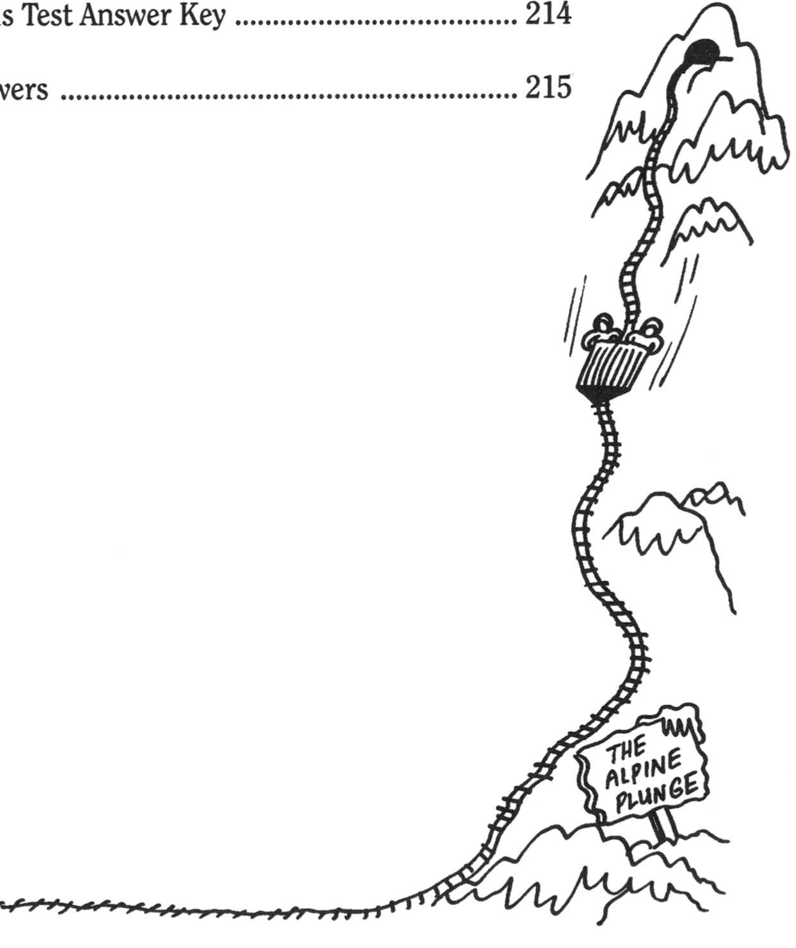

THE ALPINE PLUNGE

WORDS AND VOCABULARY
SKILLS TEST

Questions 1–79 are worth 1 point. Questions 80–86 are worth 3 points. Total possible points: 100.

Write the correct answer.

_______________ 1. A person who eats large quantities of food is a . . .
gourmand   gluten   cygnet   hellion

_______________ 2. What are you likely to find in a gazette?
plants   coffee   coins   stories & articles

_______________ 3. Which word would describe a very talkative person?
bucolic   garrulous   restive   brackish

_______________ 4. With which one of these does a farrier work?
groceries   blood cells   lawyers   horses

_______________ 5. A jetty would be found near . . .
water   a desert   a bedspread   a school

_______________ 6. Which of these would you gnash?
potatoes   your bank account   teeth   cheese

_______________ 7. One of these names a bone. Which one?
clavicle   contrail   cliché   clavichord

_______________ 8. Which word would describe a rowdy, noisy child?
boisterous   abstemious   luminous   savory

_______________ 9. One of these would almost certainly NOT be tasty. Which one?
a query   a tempura   a fricassee   a canapé

_______________ 10. Which one of these means "to slow something down"?
abase   abbot   abate   abhor

Choose a synonym for each word from the word box.

Word box
stab
quibble
greed
grumpy
awful
terminate
rogue
whirlpool
customers
arrogant

_______________ 11. avarice

_______________ 12. maelstrom

_______________ 13. patrons

_______________ 14. haughty

_______________ 15. villain

_______________ 16. abominable

_______________ 17. gore

_______________ 18. bicker

_______________ 19. cease

_______________ 20. churlish

Name ____

Write the correct antonym in each blank.

______________	21. benevolent	fabrication
______________	22. energetic	stingy
______________	23. truth	lethargic
______________	24. polite	burly
______________	25. lanky	boorish

Add a prefix to make a word fitting the definition.

26. ________ cycle — three wheels
27. ________ port — carry across
28. ________ term — middle of the term
29. ________ open — open again
30. ________ appear — not appear
31. ________ read — read wrong
32. ________ practice — bad practice

Add a suffix to make a word fitting the definition.

33. read________ — able to be read
34. pian________ — one who plays piano
35. guilt________ — without guilt
36. lonli________ — state of being lonely
37. visita________ — act of visiting
38. wood________ — made of wood

Write the letter that matches the meaning of the root in each word.

_____ 39. uniform	a. sound		_____ 43. dormitory	e. shape
_____ 40. portable	b. write		_____ 44. sonar	f. carry
_____ 41. pedal	c. see		_____ 45. video	g. foot
_____ 42. autograph	d. sleep			

Find the five compound words in the word box, and write them on the lines.

______________ 46.
______________ 47.
______________ 48.
______________ 49.
______________ 50.

wearable	unicycle
townhouse	operator
thermometer	telephone
mailbox	bodyguard
teakettle	headache

Name ______________________________

Skills Test

Choose the correct pair of homophones to fit each sentence.

a. rain-reign
b. bald-bawled
c. bow-bough
d. hole-whole
e. tease-teas
f. cents-sense
g. would-wood
h. find-fined
i. brake-break
j. nose-knows
k. blew-blue
l. hire-higher

_____ 51. The ____-headed man ____ when he lost his dog.

_____ 52. I could ____ you at a ____ wage than you now get.

_____ 53. Did it ____ much during the king's 40-year____ ?

_____ 54. I ate the ____ doughnut, even the ____ !

_____ 55. The wind ____ my kite across a ____ sky.

_____ 56. I ____ that I've just been ____ fifty dollars for speeding.

_____ 57. Don't ____ Aunt Margaret about the strange ____ she drinks.

Choose the correct pair of homographs to fit each sentence.

a. suspect-suspect
b. object-object
c. refuse-refuse
d. wind-wind
e. contest-contest
f. read-read
g. desert-desert
h. present-present

_____ 58. I'll give you just one ____ for the ____ time.

_____ 59. Why would I ____ a book that I've already ____ ?

_____ 60. If you ____ me in the ____ , I just may die of thirst.

_____ 61. If you sail into that ____ , you'll ____ up capsizing.

Write one word in each blank that can be defined by both of the two meanings given.

______________ 62. bird's beak, a statement of cost

______________ 63. season after summer, to trip

______________ 64. base of a tree, back of a car

______________ 65. time off from work, an injury to a bone

______________ 66. get sent away from a job, a disaster with smoke and flames

For each group, write the one that does NOT belong.

______________	67. tsar	emperor	pauper	monarch
______________	68. roar	bellow	shout	chide
______________	69. lanky	burly	brawny	husky
______________	70. physician	acrobat	magician	contortionist

Name ______________________________

Choose a figure of speech that fits each meaning.

a. in the doghouse
b. get cold feet
c. go out on a limb
d. blow your top
e. in mint condition
f. sick as a dog
g. knock it off
h. put your foot in your mouth

_____ 71. to get angry

_____ 72. stop it

_____ 73. take a risk

_____ 74. in trouble

_____ 75. say something stupid

Choose an answer for each question.

a. pleasant sounds for dancing
b. an untrustworthy scoundrel
c. one who tells untruths
d. scary Halloween creature
e. a domestic animal
f. a lazy, stubborn, slow animal
g. a framework of bones
h. the science of ordering tones

_____ 76. Which shows the connotation for **donkey**?

_____ 77. Which shows the denotation for **skeleton**?

_____ 78. What is the denotation of **music**?

_____ 79. What is the connotation of **skeleton**?

From the context, decide what each word in bold type means. Write the word in the blank. 3 points each.

_______________ 80. Would you like to **repose** on the couch after your long day?
eat rest jump complain

_______________ 81. The mother gorilla was **rebuking** her child for stealing bananas.
scratching hugging teaching scolding

_______________ 82. The **pugilist** knocked out his opponent in one minute in the ring.
boxer doctor thief manager

_______________ 83. That **vociferous** man is going to be thrown out of the library for making so much noise.
greedy hungry loud-voiced fearful

Solve each analogy. Write the correct answer on the line. 3 points each.

_____ 84. proboscis : nose AS phobia : ________ ear fear elephant human

_____ 85. child : children AS mouse : ________ rat adult trap mice

_____ 86. ________ : gum AS tree : ground tooth chew roots grow

SCORE: Total Points ______________ out of a possible 100 points

Name ______________________________

WORDS AND VOCABULARY

SKILLS TEST ANSWER KEY

1. gourmand
2. stories & articles
3. garrulous
4. horses
5. water
6. teeth
7. clavicle
8. boisterous
9. a query
10. abate
11. greed
12. whirlpool
13. customers
14. arrogant
15. rogue
16. awful
17. stab
18. quibble
19. terminate
20. grumpy
21. stingy
22. lethargic
23. fabrication
24. boorish
25. burly
26. tri
27. trans
28. mid
29. re
30. dis
31. mis
32. mal
33. able
34. ist
35. less
36. ness
37. tion
38. en
39. e
40. f
41. g
42. b
43. d
44. a
45. c

46-50. townhouse
mailbox
teakettle
bodyguard
headache

51. b
52. l
53. a
54. d
55. k
56. h
57. e
58. h
59. f
60. g
61. d
62. bill
63. fall
64. trunk
65. break
66. fire
67. pauper
68. chide
69. lanky
70. physician
71. d
72. g
73. c
74. a
75. h
76. f
77. g
78. h
79. d
80. rest
81. scolding
82. boxer
83. loud-voiced
84. fear
85. mice
86. tooth

ANSWERS

page 174

(Some answers will vary.)

1. not a good idea
2. no
3. no
4. probably not
5. no
6. probably
7. no
8. probably not
9. no
10. probably
11. probably not
12. no
13. yes
14. no
15. no
16. you may want to
17. probably not
18. probably not
19. yes
20. probably
21. possibly dangerous
22. yes
23. yes
24. probably
25. possibly
26. no
27. no

page 175

(Explanations will vary.)

1. An abutment would be hard.
2. Brackish water is unclean.
3. Bedlam is not restful.
4. Bumping into a hippo could be dangerous.
5. A quagmire, or swamp, is dangerous for swimming.
6. Deceiving a professional boxer could get you beat up!
7. Loud talking is not allowed in libraries.
8. A whirlpool could sink you.
9. This could get you in trouble with the law.
10. Hiring a thief is illegal.
11. You are too weak to run.
12. The lion may eat you!
13. Your brother might get mad at you for laughing at him.
14. An octopod has 8 "hands" with suckers on them!

page 176

1. take a picture of it
2. eat it for supper
3. write it down
4. dust it
5. brush it
6. arrest it
7. cook it
8. discipline it
9. butter it
10. insure it
11. invest it
12. laugh at it
13. fear it
14. swat a fly with it
15. put it in a salad
16. fight with it
17. put it in a jar
18. get over it

page 177

1. varies
2. no
3. varies
4. no
5. a fire fighter
6. varies
7. yes
8. varies
9. varies
10. no
11. varies
12. no
13. varies
14. varies
15. no
16. varies, probably not
17. yes
18. varies
19. no
20. varies
21. varies
22. varies

page 178

(Guesses will vary.)
Definitions:

1. ingenious - clever
2. candid - honest
3. dearth - shortage
4. instigate - start
5. sullen - gloomy
6. trepidation - fear
7. plethora - abundance
8. patrons - customers

page 179

(Guesses will vary.)
Definitions:

1. sinister - evil
2. adept - skilled
3. agape - wide-open with amazement
4. arrogant - conceited
5. condone - approve of
6. concede - agree
7. ostracized - shut out
8. herculean - brave and strong
9. noxious - poisonous
10. abhor - hate

page 180

(Connotations will vary.)
Denotations:

1. robber - thief
2. hero - idealized person
3. laughter - noise caused by a laugh
4. argument - a dispute
5. party - a celebration
6. giant - something very huge
7. dark - absence of light

page 181

(Answers will vary.)

page 182

1. renovation
2. savant
3. salubrious
4. noxious
5. gracious
6. fastidious
7. nominal
8. just
9. delirious
10. prepare
11. homely
12. mischievous
13. continue

page 183

1. nauseous
2. weak
3. torturous
4. appetizer
5. greed
6. stab
7. chew
8. foolish
9. grind
10. useless
11. flashy
12. grumpy
13. severe
14. famous
15. stuffed
16. wiggle

page 184

1. quibble - bicker
2. impertinent - insolent
3. garbled - jumbled
4. maelstrom - whirlpool
5. piebald - spotted
6. moniker - nickname
7. rogue - rascal
8. viscera - organs
9. cavort - dance
10. morose - doleful
11. entreat - beg
12. arrogant - haughty

page 185

1. boisterous - serene
2. bona fide - bogus
3. adroit - inept
4. mercenary - benevolent
5. villain - hero
6. cognizant - oblivious
7. impair - improve
8. lethargic - energetic
9. lanky - burly
10. raucous - mellow
11. parsimonious - generous
12. absolve - condemn

page 186

1. proof
2. virtuous
3. polite
4. truth
5. lament
6. amiable
7. revenue
8. modesty
9. ruin
10. prim
11. hardship
12. confront
13. moderate
14. sacred
15. castle

page 187

1. knows - nose
2. oh - owe
3. daze - days
4. caller - collar
5. hey - hay
6. tents - tense

7. seize - seas
8. close - clothes
9. navel - naval
10. colonel - kernel
11. sent - scent
12. not - knot
13. tease - teas

page 188

1. toe - tow
2. bass - base
3. sea - see
4. carrot - carat
5. rays - raise
6. peak - peek
7. throne - thrown
8. pair - pear
9. beau - bow
10. serf - surf
11. week - weak
12. doe - dough

page 189

1. suspect
2. refuse
3. wind
4. desert
5. bow
6. contest
7. object
8. present
9. minute
10. row

page 190

There are 31 uses of *up*.
Student stories will vary. Check for uses of the words they choose.

page 191

1. trunk
2. coaster
3. saw

Student drawings will vary.

page 192

1. one who works with others
2. middle of the stream
3. not fit
4. bad taste
5. good fit
6. under the sea
7. life rhythms
8. across the Atlantic
9. behave wrong
10. one form
11. function wrong
12. not decent
13. write again
14. before the test
15. after the game
16. power above others
17. not polite
18. small bike
19. half a circle
20. against poverty
21. not a voter
22. vehicle with one wheel

page 193

1. refix
2. transocean
3. triangles
4. mistakes
5. nonworker
6. malnourishment
7. quadruped
8. cowrite
9. midway
10. presurgery
11. substandard
12. untied
13. anti-drugs
14. forehead
15. nontoxic
16. microcomputer
17. improper
18. semiprofessional
19. interplanet
20. unicycle
21. midsize

page 194

1. one who supervises
2. one who terrorizes
3. like juice or with juice
4. full of care
5. one who buys
6. without sleep
7. made of wood
8. in a tender manner
9. state of being sad
10. one who begs
11. to dream about
12. to make pure
13. act of adding
14. able to break

page 195

1. thankful
2. liar
3. baldness
4. dentist
5. action
6. creepy
7. teachable
8. ageless
9. injection
10. silken
11. robber
12. motorize
13. bravely

Answer to puzzle:
Last Chance Railroad

page 196

Answers will vary.

page 197

1. revision
2. biweekly
3. transport
4. unkindness
5. mobilize
6. mismanage
7. unbelievable
8. immovable
9. dishearten
10. illegally
11. successful
12. reusable
13. friendliness
14. reformer
15. unbeliever
16. transportable
17. legalize
18. invisible

page 198

1. eye - tooth - brush
2. busy - body - guard
3. black - mail - man
4. match - box - car
5. boy - friend - ship - yard - stick
6. drive - in - side - show - case
7. sun - down - town - house - boat
8. pop - corn - meal - time - out
9. tea - cup - cake - walk - man
10. tender - foot - note - book - worm - wood - chuck
11. chain - saw -horse - fly - ball - room - mate
12. roller - skate - board - walk - way - side - show - down - town
13. bubble - gum - drop - out - side - kick - ball - park - way
14. copy - cat - fish - hook - up - hill - side - step - child

page 199

1. headache
2. arrowhead
3. headlight
4. hothead
5. egghead
6. bullhead
7. copperhead
8. headphone
9. headband
10. thunderhead
11. headline
12. forehead
13. pigheaded
14. hardhead
15. letterhead

page 200

1. b, a
2. d, c
3. e, f
4. g, h
5. i, j
6. l, k
7. n, m
8. o, p
9. r, q
10. t, s
11. v, u
12. x, w
13. z, y

page 201

1. prognosis
2. plurality
3. explicit
4. contagious
5. waxing
6. mania
7. flaunting
8. staccato
9. slander
10. flotsam
11. vigorous
12. imminent
13. zenith
14. inferring
15. both

page 202

1. put your foot in your mouth
2. wear your heart on your sleeve
3. don't give me any of your lip
4. go out on a limb
5. eat crow
6. under the gun
7. cook your goose
8. raining cats and dogs
9. a bone to pick
10. get behind the 8 ball
11. lose your head
12. spill the beans

page 203

Answer: There are 34 figures of speech in the story. Student stories will vary.

page 204

(Answers may vary due to differing dictionary information.)

1. French - a kind of tournament
2. Russian - emperor
3. French - wine taster
4. Persian - leg, foot, garment
5. Italian - short for pianoforte, which means soft and loud
6. New Latin - eight-footed
7. French - one who walks on tiptoe
8. Middle English - contestant
9. Middle English - long-haired star
10. Latin - young, a youth

page 205

(Answers may vary due to differing dictionary information.)

1. Portuguese and Spanish - taken from a native plant name in Guinea
2. Old French - crisp or curly
3. American Spanish - a round cake
4. New Latin - a round swelling
5. American Spanish - framework of sticks set on posts
6. Spanish - little sheath
7. French - thin plate
8. German - sour cabbage
9. Portuguese - honey
10. Italian - food made from barley

page 206

1. garbage
2. shy
3. danger
4. superb
5. cheap
6. copy
7. ally
8. retain
9. initial
10. dull

page 207

1. flush
   (insolvent is opposite of rich; penniless is opposite of flush)
2. teasing
   (mischief is a mild form of violence; teasing is a mild form of insult)
3. miser
   (a squirrel hoards nuts; a miser hoards money)
4. rock
   (a minnow is a small fish; a pebble is a small rock)
5. angry
   (someone who is embarrassed may blush; someone who is angry may fume)
6. bucket
   (a mitt catches a baseball; a bucket catches a drip)
7. fetid
   (perfume smells fragrant; garbage smells fetid)
8. veteran
   (a novice is new at something and is therefore inexperienced; someone who is seasoned, or experienced, is a veteran)

page 208

1. shrew - birds
2. meristem - animals
3. stoic - heads of churches
4. sacrum - weapons
5. miter - musical instruments
6. capriole - food
7. basilisk - legal terms
8. bribe - funny sayings or jokes
9. clavichord - body parts or bones
10. lexicon - words meaning appearance
11. novella - diseases

GRAMMAR & USAGE

Skills Exercises

GRAMMAR IN
A BOTTLE

SKILLS CHECKLIST FOR GRAMMAR & USAGE

✔	SKILL	PAGE(S)
	Identify declarative, interrogative, imperative, exclamatory sentences	220
	Find subjects and predicates	221
	Correct sentence fragments and run-on sentences	222
	Identify parts of speech	223, 224, 238, 239
	Identify simple, complex, and compound sentences	224
	Identify and use common and proper nouns	225
	Identify and use singular and plural nouns	226
	Identify, form, and use possessive nouns	227
	Identify and use different kinds of pronouns	228–230
	Identify and use proper pronoun-antecedent agreement	229
	Properly use *who, whom, who's,* and *whose*	230
	Identify and use verb tenses	231
	Identify and use action verbs and verbs of being (linking verbs)	231, 232
	Identify and use regular and irregular verbs	233
	Identify and use transitive and intransitive verbs	234
	Identify and use direct and indirect objects	235
	Properly use special verbs such as *lie* and *lay, sit* and *set, rise* and *raise*	236
	Understand and use subject-verb agreement	237
	Identify and use adjectives	238
	Identify and use adverbs	239
	Identify and use comparative and superlative adjectives and adverbs	240
	Identify and correct dangling modifiers	241
	Use negatives correctly; correct double negatives	242
	Identify and use prepositions and prepositional phrases	243
	Identify and use participles and participial phrases	244
	Identify and use gerund and infinitive phrases	245, 246
	Identify and use independent and dependent clauses	247
	Identify and use noun, adjective, and adverb clauses	248
	Use proper capitalization for proper nouns and adjectives	249
	Properly use a variety of punctuation marks	250-258
	Use proper punctuation and capitalization for a variety of situations	249-258
	Make corrections in improper punctuation	249-258
	Use commas properly in a variety of situations	254
	Use quotation marks properly in dialogue	255
	Use colons and semicolons properly	256
	Use hyphens, dashes, and parentheses properly	257
	Create, explain, and properly punctuate common contractions	258

SURF'S UP!

When surfers yell, "Surf's up!" they're using a particular kind of sentence. Do you know which kind?

There are four kinds of sentences: **declarative (D), interrogative (?), imperative (I)** and **exclamatory (E).**

Use the appropriate mark to identify each sentence below. Then add the correct punctuation at the end of each line.

_____ 1. Surf's up

_____ 2. We're off to the beach

_____ 3. Skiers should watch for shark activity

_____ 4. Has anyone seen the lifeguard

_____ 5. Watch out for the jellyfish

_____ 6. If you want to jet ski, get to the dock by noon

_____ 7. Did you know there was recently a Loch Ness Monster sighted in this area

_____ 8. The trouble with beaches is that they are so sandy

_____ 9. Watch for fiddler crabs

_____ 10. They pinch

_____ 11. I love to walk on the beach at sundown

_____ 12. Anybody up for beach volleyball

_____ 13. What a thrill to get an Olympic gold medal

_____ 14. The sign says, "No dogs on the beach," so we better take Phil home

_____ 15. Thought for a night on the boardwalk: a fool and his money are soon parted

_____ 16. Who's ready for an Awesome Hot Dog

_____ 17. He or she who suns unprotected is seriously lacking in intellectual capacity

_____ 18. We creamed those girls in our surf contest

_____ 19. You can really chill out on a hot beach

_____ 20. How can you be cold and hot at the same time, silly

Name ____________________

ONE OF EACH

Every two-piece bathing suit has a top and a bottom—one of each! Every sentence has two parts, too—a subject and a predicate.

> The **subject** is the part of the sentence which is doing something or about which something is being said.
> The **predicate** is the part of the sentence that tells something about the subject.

I. In each sentence below, draw a single line under the complete subject; draw a double line under the complete predicate.

1. Hundreds of gulls were flying around the dock.
2. On rainy days, does the fog obliterate your view?
3. A whale's big, bulky body can be a fearsome sight.
4. A huge animal does not necessarily have a huge brain.
5. The giant whale leaped into the air and startled everyone.
6. Gory scenes on television have frightened some people away from ocean swimming.
7. Yesterday, three high school kids and two pelicans had a fishing contest.
8. Can you guess the results of the contest?
9. In spite of fair warning, the boys took the jet skis beyond the breakwater.
10. Why do teenage boys often ignore good advice?

II. In the numbered spaces below, write only the simple subject and simple verb for each sentence. Don't get fooled by one or two compound subjects or verbs!

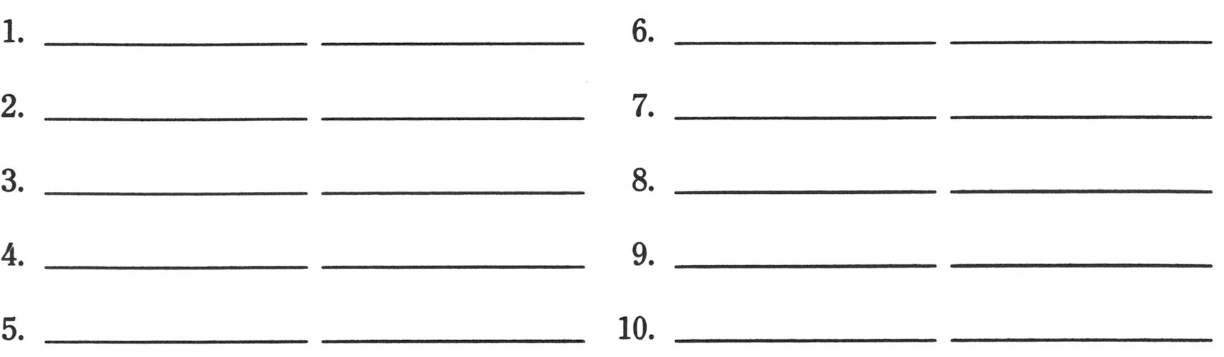

1. ______________ ______________ 6. ______________ ______________

2. ______________ ______________ 7. ______________ ______________

3. ______________ ______________ 8. ______________ ______________

4. ______________ ______________ 9. ______________ ______________

5. ______________ ______________ 10. ______________ ______________

Name

S.O.S. (SAVE OUR SENTENCES!)

At sea, distress is often expressed by signal flags. Fragments and run-on sentences are clearly in distress. For each sentence fragment or run-on, write the distress code S.O.S. For each sentence that is correct, write A.O.K. Save the distressed items by making the necessary corrections.

☐☐☐ 1. I dated a girl, she dumped me.

☐☐☐ 2. I like hamburgers with mustard, catsup, pickle, and rock music.

☐☐☐ 3. When I get pumped and ready for a great game.

☐☐☐ 4. Beach music on the boardwalk by the sea.

☐☐☐ 5. Are you heading for the Ferris wheel count me in?

☐☐☐ 6. Dancing in the moonlight with a handsome hunk of the male species.

☐☐☐ 7. All day, I lie in the sun and dream in golden bronze.

☐☐☐ 8. Where did those bikers come from, San Francisco?

☐☐☐ 9. Putting sand crabs in people's shoes.

☐☐☐ 10. There's nothing I love more than wild surf, it is incredibly invigorating!

A B C D E F G
H I J K L M N
O P Q R S T U
V W X Y Z

The flags on the left show the International Alphabet in Flag Code. Use the flags to write a short message below. Draw a flag for each letter of each word.

Name

WHAT'S FOR LUNCH?

On a cold, foggy day at the seashore, there is nothing more comforting than a bowl of hot soup. Discover what soup is the special on today's menu by solving the puzzle and transferring the numbered letters to the corresponding spaces at the bottom of the page.

First, you must place each word in this list in its appropriate space:

yesterday	loiter	there	tough	nobody
fishing	skinny	regurgitate	illustrate	everything
wise	lighthouse	disappear	Maine	slowly

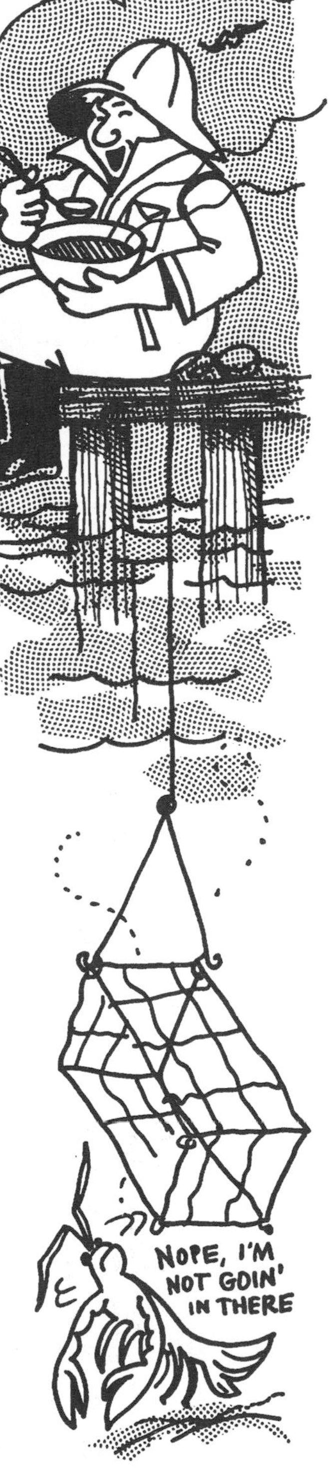
NOPE, I'M NOT GOIN' IN THERE

1. NOUN ___ ___ ___ ___ ___ ___ ___ ___ ___(4) ___
2. VERB ___ ___(2) ___ ___ ___ ___
3. ADJECTIVE ___(8) ___ ___ ___ ___ ___
4. ADVERB ___ ___ ___ ___ ___ ___
5. PRONOUN ___ ___ ___ ___ ___ ___ ___ ___ ___ ___
6. ADJECTIVE ___(11) ___ ___ ___
7. ADVERB ___ ___ ___ ___ ___
8. VERB ___ ___ ___ ___ ___ ___ ___ ___ ___ ___ ___(6)
9. NOUN ___ ___ ___ ___ ___ ___ ___
10. PRONOUN ___ ___ ___(3) ___ ___ ___
11. VERB ___ ___ ___ ___ ___ ___ ___ ___ ___(7)
12. ADJECTIVE ___(9) ___ ___ ___ ___
13. ADVERB ___ ___ ___ ___(5) ___ ___ ___ ___ ___
14. NOUN ___ ___ ___ ___ ___(10)
15. VERB ___ ___(1) ___ ___ ___ ___ ___ ___ ___ ___

Soup of the day: ___(1) ___(2) ___(3) ___(4) ___(5) ___(6) ___(7)   ___(8) ___(9) ___(10) ___(11)

Name ______________________

A-MAZE-ING POSSIBILITIES

The bottom of the sea is like a maze. Many interesting things are hidden among the rocks, plants, and coral.

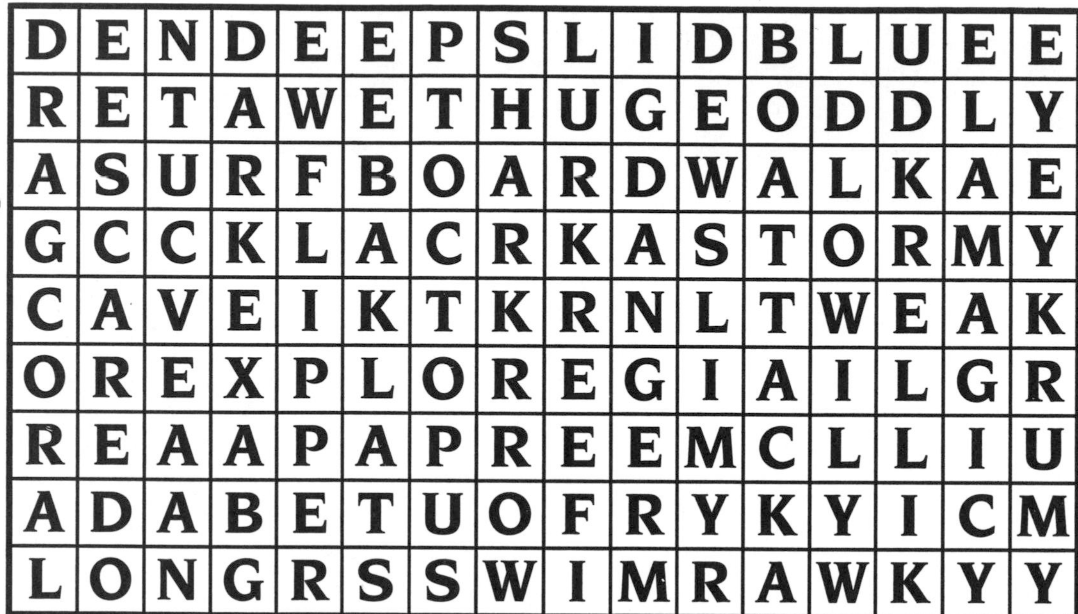

D	E	N	D	E	E	P	S	L	I	D	B	L	U	E	E
R	E	T	A	W	E	T	H	U	G	E	O	D	D	L	Y
A	S	U	R	F	B	O	A	R	D	W	A	L	K	A	E
G	C	C	K	L	A	C	R	K	A	S	T	O	R	M	Y
C	A	V	E	I	K	T	K	R	N	L	T	W	E	A	K
O	R	E	X	P	L	O	R	E	G	I	A	I	L	G	R
R	E	A	A	P	A	P	R	E	E	M	C	L	L	I	U
A	D	A	B	E	T	U	O	F	R	Y	K	Y	I	C	M
L	O	N	G	R	S	S	W	I	M	R	A	W	K	Y	Y

I. This maze is hiding nouns, verbs, adjectives, and adverbs. As you find them, list them in the proper category below. (Several words may fit in more than one category!)

NOUNS *(about 30)*	VERBS *(about 16)*	ADJECTIVES *(about 23)*	ADVERB *(only 1!)*

II. On the back side of this paper, use combinations of words from the lists above to create **two simple sentences**, **three complex sentences**, and **three compound sentences**. Check your grammar text to review the properties of each kind of sentence.

Name

TWO BY THE SEA

Crusty Old Pirate Patch-Eye has hidden his "treasures" in his chest. For each category, write two common nouns that tell what could be in there. All items must have some association with the beach or sea. The name of each item must begin with the letter at the top of each column.

Category		***C***	***S***
something to eat	1.	______________	______________
item of clothing	2.	______________	______________
animal	3.	______________	______________

KEEP
AWAY
FROM
ME
TREASURE

Write any two sea-related common nouns for each of these:

Category		***T***	***M***
method of travel	4.	______________	______________
game or sport	5.	______________	______________
something belonging to a teenager	6.	______________	______________

Write any two sea-related proper nouns for each of these:

Category		***R***	***A***
titles of songs, books, poems, or movies	7.	______________	______________
name of a famous person (real or fictional)	8.	______________	______________
something belonging to a teenager	9.	______________	______________

Name ______________________________

SEE YOU AT THE CLUB

The signs at the beach clubhouse are covered with plural nouns. Find them all! Then write each plural on a line below, followed by the matching rule (1, 2, 3, or 4) that governs that plural.

Rules for Forming Plural Nouns

1. Form most plurals by adding *s* to the singular noun.
2. If the singular noun ends in *s, ss, sh, ch,* or *x,* add *es* to form a plural noun.
3. If the noun ends in *y* preceded by a consonant, change the *y* to *i* and add *es.*
4. Some nouns, such as *man* or *mouse,* are formed irregularly.

	Plural	*Rule*		*Plural*	*Rule*
1.	____________	___	12.	____________	___
2.	____________	___	13.	____________	___
3.	____________	___	14.	____________	___
4.	____________	___	15.	____________	___
5.	____________	___	16.	____________	___
6.	____________	___	17.	____________	___
7.	____________	___	18.	____________	___
8.	____________	___	19.	____________	___
9.	____________	___	20.	____________	___
10.	____________	___	21.	____________	___
11.	____________	___	22.	____________	___

DUNE BUGGIES for rent
CLUB HOUSE
BEACH SUPPLIES
RENTALS
OPEN WEEKDAYS 8 AM- 8PM WEEKENDS 7AM – 10PM
REST ROOMS Men Women
SHAKES & DRINKS
SANDWICHES
CANDIES
ADMISSION
Adults $5
Children (under 12) $3
Babies No Charge
NO cans, bottles, or drinking glasses
PLEASE WASH TAR off your FEET
KEEP BEACHES FREE OF TRASH
NO coolers
NO lunch boxes

Name ____________________

SEASHORE SNAPSHOTS

The sights and sounds of the seashore make you want to grab your camera.

> To show that something belongs to a singlular person, place, or thing, add *'s* to the noun. To show ownership by more than one person, place, or thing add *s'* unless the plural ends in *s*. Then add only an apostrophe.

Close your eyes and pay attention to the mental snapshots created by each of these phrases. Then rephrase each one to make it show ownership.

1. Fin belonging to a shark ____________________
2. Whistles belonging to the lifeguards ____________________
3. Radio belonging to Gus ____________________
4. Surfboard belonging to somebody ____________________
5. Laughter of the children ____________________
6. Sounds made by the surf ____________________
7. Cries of the gulls ____________________
8. Suntans belonging to teenagers ____________________
9. Warnings sounded by bell buoys ____________________
10. Strength of ocean swimmers____________________
11. Soles of sandals ____________________
12. The colorful sails of boats ____________________
13. The stories of footprints ____________________
14. Beach belonging to no one ____________________

Use the lines below to write a very short sea story in which you use at least ten possessive nouns, none of which are mentioned above. Underline each possessive in your story.

A VERY SHORT SEA STORY

____

____

____

____

____

Name ____

PICK A PRONOUN

You can't escape pronouns. They're everywhere. In the dunes, on the sand, under the water. They're usually little words, but there's a lot to remember about these little things. Show what you know about pronouns.

I. Match each item in Column A with its appropriate companion in Column B.

	A		B
1. _____	pronoun	A.	NOT referring to a particular person or thing
2. _____	relative pronoun	B.	word for which the pronoun stands
3. _____	demonstrative pronoun	C.	the self-selves forms of personal pronouns
4. _____	antecedent	D.	used in questions
5. _____	compound pronoun	E.	used to introduce adjective clauses
6. _____	indefinite pronoun	F.	takes a plural verb
7. _____	interrogative pronoun	G.	used to point out a specific person or thing
8. _____	each	H.	used in place of one or more nouns
9. _____	personal pronoun	I.	takes a singular verb
10. _____	reflexive pronoun	J.	I, we, you, your, she, it, their

II. In each sentence, circle the antecedent for the pronoun(s) written in bold type.

1. Margaret lost her bathing suit; do you suppose an octopus ate **it**?
2. Jim watched the frisbee as **it** disappeared behind the dunes.
3. The ball touched the player's hands before he noticed the wasp perched on **it.**
4. Megan, stop chasing the boys; **you** boys stop chasing **her.**
5. The girl **who** had been hit by the dune buggy regained consciousness.

III. Copy each pronoun in bold type in the corresponding space below and tell what kind of pronoun it is.

1. **Who** is yelling from the cliffs?
2. It was Jeff's irresponsible action **that** caused the accident.
3. Now he hates **himself.**
4. **Those** are wonderful hot dogs.
5. **Whoever** put this crab in my bag is dead meat!

1. ______________ ______________________________
2. ______________ ______________________________
3. ______________ ______________________________
4. ______________ ______________________________
5. ______________ ______________________________

Name ____

THE AGREEABLE PRONOUN

Crabs aren't always agreeable. (People often see them fighting.)

A pronoun must agree with its antecedent (the word it refers to) in number and gender.

I. Write the antecedent for each pronoun printed in bold.

1. Some of the students brought **their** lunches to the beach. ____________
2. Ken took Meg home on **his** new motorcycle. ____________
3. John and Eric blamed **themselves** for the accident. ____________
4. The members of the class turned in **their** term papers. ____________
5. We found a chambered nautilus and kept **it.** ____________
6. Would you lend me **one** of your sweaters? ____________
7. We keep the priceless vase in **its** special cabinet. ____________
8. The divers found pieces of coral and brought **them** back to the boat. ____________
9. We surprised **ourselves** by winning the sailing race. ____________
10. We could have kept the trophy, but we shared **it.** ____________

Two or more singular antecedents joined by *or* or *nor* should be referred to by a singular pronoun. Two or more antecedents joined by *and* should be referred to by a plural pronoun.

II. Underline the correct pronoun and circle the antecedent(s).

1. None of the trees were destroyed in the storm, but (they, it) lost many branches.
2. The cats have (their, its) own personalities.
3. Someone put (their, her) sunglasses in the wrong bag.
4. The winds of the storm may blow (themselves, itself) out.
5. Both of Sue's sisters lost (her, their) purses.
6. Did either Libby or Danielle call about (their, her) appointment?
7. Neither Erin nor Scott ate (their, his) lunch.
8. Jim and Troy have made up (his, their) own minds.
9. Since when has a J-24 won (its, their) first race?
10. Every ship in the race chooses (its, their) own course.

WELL, HE'S AN AGREEABLE GUY

Name ____________________

WHO'S WHO?

Who's on the line? **Who's** calling for **whom? Who** wants to talk to **whose** friend?

> **Who** is used as the subject of a verb; **whom** is used as a direct object or the object of a preposition.
> **Who's** is the contraction for *who is*; **whose** is a possessive pronoun.

Circle the correct choice for each item.

IS THIS THE PARTY
TO WHOM I AM SPEAKING?

1. (Who, Whom) ordered this pizza?
2. (Who's, Whose) wet towel is this?
3. For (who, whom) did you sacrifice your dill pickle?
4. (Who's, Whose) that joker with the sunburn?
5. The girl with (who, whom) I danced is very light on her feet.
6. (Who, Whom) may I say is calling?
7. (Who, Whom) do you think left this mess on the table?
8. The cousin about (who, whom) I spoke is going to college in the fall.
9. Did you ever hear of Hemingway, (who, whom) wrote *The Old Man and the Sea?*
10. (Who's, Whose) the author of *Jaws?*
11. (Whose, Who's) book is *Treasure Island?*
12. Do you know (who, whom) wrote *The Rime of the Ancient Mariner?*
13. The writer to (who, whom) you are referring is Coleridge.
14. I admire sailors of old (who, whom) I never met.
15. I remember best the teacher (who, whom) is responsible for my love of poetry.
16. I'm scared of anyone (whose, who's) not scared of *Jaws.*
17. The fish of (whom, who) you speak isn't even real!
18. Look (who's, whose) talking! You got out of the water when a minnow nibbled your feet.
19. Hey! (Who, Whom) do you think you are?
20. I'm someone (whom, who) everyone believes!

Name

TENSE TIMES

These pictures show some tense situations at sea. Tell each story by conjugating the verb in all its active tenses. The verb can be found near each picture.

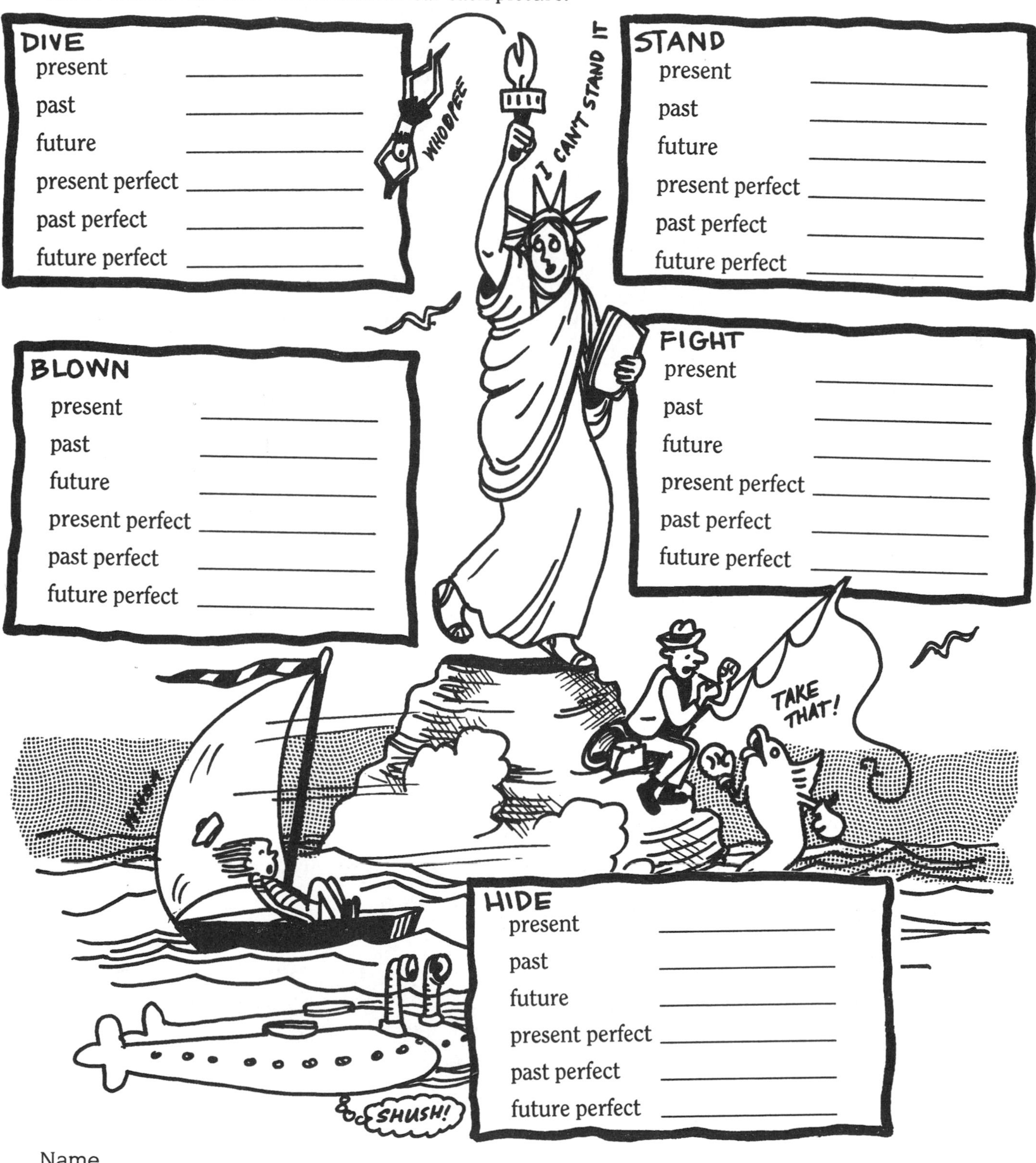
DIVE
present
past
future
present perfect
past perfect
future perfect
WHOOPEE
I CAN'T STAND IT
STAND
present
past
future
present perfect
past perfect
future perfect
BLOWN
present
past
future
present perfect
past perfect
future perfect
FIGHT
present
past
future
present perfect
past perfect
future perfect
TAKE THAT!
HIDE
present
past
future
present perfect
past perfect
future perfect
SHUSH!

Name

WILD ABOUT VERBS

Victor is obsessed with verbs. No one knows how he got started, but he just can't stop going wild over verbs. You don't have to be a verb nerd to figure out which verbs are linking verbs and which are active verbs. Just remember this:

A **linking verb** is a verb that does not show action, but serves as a link between two words. Linking verbs are sometimes called **verbs of being.**

Underline the verb in each sentence below.
If the verb is an **action verb**, write **A** on the line provided. If it is a **linking verb**, write **L.**

_____ 1. Victor is a verb nerd.

_____ 2. A verb nerd responds ecstatically to his favorite words—verbs.

_____ 3. Victor grows restless if he is deprived of a grammar book or dictionary.

_____ 4. He appears jittery when away from the sounds of verbs.

_____ 5. Victor often becomes hoarse from reciting lists of linking verbs.

_____ 6. He seems enervated from constantly demonstrating action verbs.

_____ 7. He rejoices gleefully when he hears a crowd yell, "Go!" to a team.

_____ 8. He's wild when a pitcher pitches and a catcher catches.

_____ 9. He watches flowers grow.

_____ 10. He listens to roosters crow.

_____ 11. Victor has plans for starting a verb choir.

_____ 12. The choir will sing only verbs.

_____ 13. He teaches verbs to his pet cockatiel.

_____ 14. He can sleep only with his verbaphone playing soft predicate phrases.

_____ 15. He often looks tired in the morning.

I'M JUST WILD ABOUT VERBS.
I DOZED
I ATE.
I LISTENED.
I WALKED.
I FLOATED
I RESTED

Name ____________________

FIN FAN FUN

Fisherman Franz **will throw** this little fish back in the water. He **threw** the last three back. In fact, he **has thrown** all the fish back that he's caught today.

Throw is an irregular verb. The past and past participle forms do not follow the usual rules. For each of the irregular verbs below, write the missing form(s). You may need your grammar text to help with the answers.

	verb	*past*	*past participle*
1.	catch	____________	have caught
2.	swim	swam	____________
3.	____________	rose	have risen
4.	bite	bit	____________
5.	dive	____________	have dived (dove)
6.	fly	____________	have flown
7.	freeze	____________	____________
8.	sit	sat	____________
9.	hang (execute)	hanged	____________
10.	hang (suspend)	____________	have hung
11.	drink	drank	____________
12.	shake	____________	have shaken
13.	____________	shrank	____________
14.	____________	spoke	have spoken
15.	swear	____________	have sworn
16.	____________	grew	____________
17.	sink	sank	____________
18.	drown	____________	have drowned
19.	sing	sang	____________

Franz's Fish

Whew!

Can you solve this riddle, using parts of the verbs **lay**, **lie**, and **lie**?

IF YOU ________ DOWN AND SAY YOU HAVE ________ DOWN, YOU WILL HAVE ________ .

Name ______________________________

SEASIDE SCENES

A **transitive** verb shows action and is always followed by an object which receives the action.

An **intransitive** verb does not have an object which receives action.

Example: The whale **swallowed** the diver. *(transitive)*
The diver **escaped** through the blow hole. *(intransitive)*

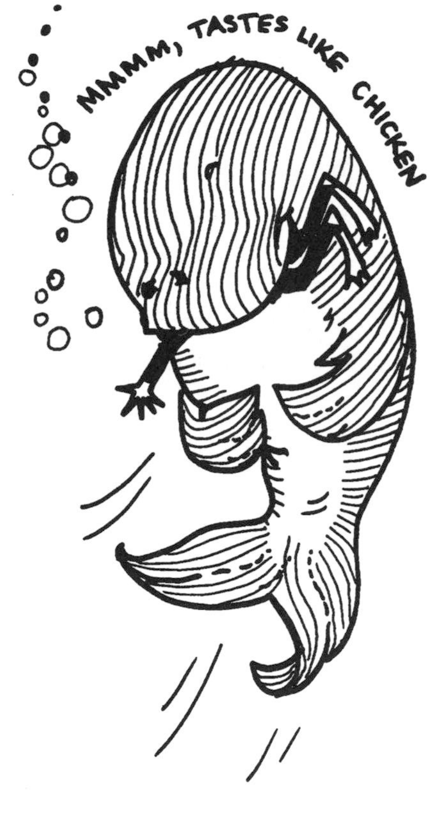
MMMM, TASTES LIKE CHICKEN

Picture each of the following scenes from the sea in your mind. Mark sentences with a T if they contain a transitive verb and with an I if they contain an intransitive verb. Circle the objects of the transitive verbs.

_____ 1. Kites fly high over the crystal waters.

_____ 2. Rays float like large pancakes in the shallow waters.

_____ 3. Divers spear fish for a lunch on the beach.

_____ 4. A ship sails west into the sunset.

_____ 5. Waves wash the rocky shoreline.

_____ 6. A mother manatee nurtures her young.

_____ 7. Jet skis play with the waves.

_____ 8. A pilot fish swims alongside a sand shark.

_____ 9. Children gather shells on the sand.

_____ 10. An octopus teases a starfish.

_____ 11. A nervous lifeguard watches five young children in the waves.

_____ 12. Three frightened swimmers avoid large jellyfish.

_____ 13. Sunburned tourists find shade under umbrellas.

_____ 14. Gulls disappear into the clouds.

_____ 15. She sells seashells at the seashore.

Name ______________________________

OBJECT OVERLOAD

Hector is off to the beach, slightly overloaded, wouldn't you say? He's got a few too many beach objects. While he's looking for places to set up all his objects, you can be looking for direct and indirect objects.

> A **direct object** is a noun or pronoun to which the action of a verb is done, answering the question *what?* or *whom?*
> Example: The kids bounced beach balls. (*Balls* is the direct object.)
>
> An **indirect object** is a noun or pronoun that comes between the verb and the direct object. It tells *to whom* or *to what* the action is done.
> Example: Greg threw his friend a beach ball. (*Friend* is the indirect object.)

For each sentence below, underline the object(s). Then, above each one you underline, write **D** for **direct** object or **I** for **indirect** object.

1. Hector needed a wheelbarrow for his trip to the beach.
2. Under the boardwalk, I found shelter from the sun (and from Hector).
3. Unfortunately, Hector found me under the boardwalk.
4. He gave me the job of watching his stuff while he went swimming.
5. Along the way down the beach, he picked up many shells.
6. As he plunged into the water, the waves gave him a beating.
7. Hector had put his faith in his new floating device. (It didn't help him much.)
8. As the lifeguards watched Hector struggle in the surf, he gave them a serious scare.
9. It was two hours before he returned, hollering, "I came to get my stuff."
10. In the meantime, I had loaned a kind old lady his umbrella.
11. It provided her sunburned husband some relief from the sun.
12. I confess, I shared most of the other objects, too.
13. Hector bombarded me with threats and insults for a long, loud time.
14. "Hey, I don't even know this guy," I told amused onlookers.
15. I think I'll find another beach for my next sea visit.
16. Shall I introduce you to Hector?

IT TAKES NO GENIUS TO KNOW THAT I'M FREQUENTLY SEEN AROUND THE BEACH SCENE.
I ♥ the Sea

Name

TROUBLESOME VERBS

Do you lie or lay on the beach? Unless you are a hen,
it would probably be more conventional to lie!

NOT A BAD
LIFE FOR A
CHICKEN

Lie (to rest or recline) .... **Lay** (to put or place)

Sit (to rest in a seated position) .... **Set** (to place or put something)

Rise (to go upward) ..... **Raise** (to make something else go upward)

I. Circle the correct choice for each sentence.

1. We (lay, laid) on the beach.
2. We (lay, laid) our towels on the beach.
3. We (raised, rose) our awning for shade.
4. While we were (rising, raising) the tent, Josh (sat, set) his radio on the towel.
5. "Don't (lay, lie) those bottles there," hollered the beach patrol.
6. Sue (lay, lied) down on the lounge chair while the rest of us (set, sat) by the pool.
7. Niki got splashed by a dive bomb and (rose, raised) so quickly that she upset a book she had (laid, lain) on the chair, and it fell into the water.
8. "Why didn't I (set, sit) that on the table?" she moaned.
9. Ted was (laying, lying) on a chaise nearby.
10. When he saw the submerged book, he quickly (raised, rose) to the occasion.
11. The smile he got from Niki as he (lay, laid) the book in her hands was his reward.
12. Later, we enjoyed (setting, sitting) on the beach, watching the winds (raise, rise) and fall against the far-off spinnaker sails.

II. Fill in the blank with the form of the verb specified in parentheses.

Rise/Raise

1. The flag will be ____________ at sunrise. *(past participle)*
2. The sun ___________ slowly over the horizon. *(past tense)*

Lie/Lay

3. The bricks were __________ in a zigzag pattern. *(past participle)*
4. Mike had to ___________ on his stomach because his back was burned. *(present tense)*

Sit/Set

5. We were ___________ on the deck when lightning struck. *(present participle)*
6. The students ___________ on the beach for the concert. *(past tense)*

Name

AGREE OR DISAGREE

Deep-sea divers usually get along with most of the sea creatures they meet. If they don't, it could be disastrous. Subjects and verbs in clauses need to get along, too. If they disagree, sentences will sound strange or be confusing.

The **subject** and **verb** of any clause must **agree in number.** If a subject is singular, the verb must be singular. Example: The lobster's claw *(singular)* is *(singular)* dangerous. If a subject is plural, the verb must be plural. Example: Divers *(plural)* dress *(plural)* carefully.

I. Do these subjects and verbs get along? YES or NO? Correct each sentence where the subject and verb do not agree.

_____ 1. Neither Pete nor Doug are going water skiing. ____________________

_____ 2. Sand fleas are disgusting pests. ____________________

_____ 3. A gull's favorite meal is not macaroni and cheese. ____________________

_____ 4. Tracy's pants is blowing overboard. ____________________

_____ 5. The boys boast broad muscles and big tattoos. ____________________

_____ 6. Baked peanut butter and moldy cheese makes a cooler stink! ____________________

_____ 7. Each of the contestants are required to model bathing suits. ____________________

_____ 8. Half of the drinks was missing. ____________________

_____ 9. Everybody is invited to the clambake. ____________________

_____ 10. Lots of singers and dancers is on the program. ____________________

_____ 11. One of the musicians are doing a comedy act. ____________________

_____ 12. Where are the bongo players? ____________________

_____ 13. The group, The Sandpipers, wasn't any good. ____________________

_____ 14. What if one of the hula dancers trip and falls. ____________________

II. Match each subject with an agreeable verb.
(You will need to use only about half the verbs!)

SUBJECTS	**VERBS**	
geese	hides	surfaces
a submarine	scurry	fly
the sea captain	pinches	honks
angel fish	swim	commands
sand crabs	dive	salute

Name ____________________

REEF RIOT

The reef is loaded with sea life. This story about the reef is loaded with adjectives. Adjectives should answer the questions **"How many?" "What kind?"** or **"Which one?"** Identify and circle the adjectives in the story below.

A leisurely, 100-yard swim brought us to the off-shore reef. We were looking for loose shells, unusual coral formations, flowering anemones, and brightly colored fish; we were looking out for sea spines, fire coral, moray eels, and unfriendly sharks. Jason had brought some bread crusts to entice the tiny reef fish, and Jen hoped that her can of cheese curls would attract some of the larger, hungry inhabitants. Dan and Joe had tucked some leftover chum in their pockets, just in case they saw a nosy squid or a scouting ray. Excited by the unexplored wonders of the reef and energized by the cool, clear Caribbean waters, we skimmed along the shallower, in-shore edges of the reef. Jess and I poked contentedly at the buzzing population of colorful creatures hidden in the cracks and crevices of the craggy coral. Jen, Jason, Dan, and Joe had rounded the ocean side of the reef and were out of sight. However, a cloud of chum and crumbs, propelled by voluminous bubbles, churned near the turn in the reef. It appeared to be the detritus of a fracas that was taking place on the other side. Jess and I raced recklessly toward the troubled waters. As we rounded the reef, we discovered a mass of frenzied fish swarming around our friends. On the deep, blue, ocean edge of this frightening scenario circled a dark, foreboding shape . . .

In each blank, add one or more adjectives that describe some of the sights you might have seen on the reef. Try to choose words that draw strong visual images and have not been used in the story.

1. ______________ tails
2. ______________ rocks
3. ______________ shapes
4. ______________ body
5. ______________ waves
6. ______________ eyes
7. ______________ creature
8. ______________ claws
9. ______________ caves
10. ______________ surface
11. ______________ fish
12. ______________ grasses
13. ______________ scales
14. ______________ teeth
15. ______________ coral
16. ______________ skies
17. ______________ sounds
18. ______________ divers

Name

"ADD" VERBS

Where is a shark? **When** did it show up? **How** will we escape? **How often** do they come here? **To what extent** should they be allowed?

> Remember that an adverb modifies a verb, an adjective, or another adverb.
> It answers the questions: **Where? When? How? How often? To what extent?**

I. Add to each sentence an adverb that strongly supports the word it modifies.

1. "Please help me!" cried the child ________________ .
2. "Watch that broken glass," ________________ warned the girl.
3. ________________ , she struck at the intruder.
4. ________________ , he gained on his opponent.
5. The examination showed he was improving extremely ________________ .
6. ________________ , Joy ran to tell the good news.
7. A ________________ powerful prince presided over the proceedings.
8. ________________ , the flight is on time.
9. The concert is ________________ sold out.
10. Hoards of bees swarmed ________________ around their heads.
11. ________________ , I ate a monstrous meal.
12. ________________ , a person can find solitude.

II. Write a news story that has at least one adverb in each sentence. Underline the adverbs in your story. Circle the words they modify.

SHARK SIGHTING CLOSES BEACHES

WHERE? ________________________________

WHEN? ________________________________

HOW? ________________________________

HOW OFTEN? ________________________________

TO WHAT EXTENT? ________________________________

Name ________________________________

FAST, FASTER, FASTEST

You can't compare the speeds of the boats without using comparatives and superlatives.

A **comparative adjective** or **adverb** is used to describe a comparison between two things, person, places, or actions.

A **superlative adjective** or **adverb** compares three or more things, persons, places, or actions.

I. Decide whether each word listed below is an adjective or adverb. Then enter it on the appropriate chart and add its comparative and superlative forms.

good	*late*	*happy*	*easy*	*happily*	*easily*
badly	*many*	*bad*	*stubborn*	*loud*	*well (how something is done)*

ADJECTIVES:	Positive	Comparative	Superlative
1.	______	______	______
2.	______	______	______
3.	______	______	______
4.	______	______	______
5.	______	______	______
6.	______	______	______
7.	______	______	______
8.	______	______	______

ADVERBS:	Positive	Comparative	Superlative
1.	______	______	______
2.	______	______	______
3.	______	______	______
4.	______	______	______

THE SEA SHARP
THE WHIZ
MOTHER'S WORRY

II. Fill in each blank with a word that makes the proper comparisons about the picture above, using a form of the word in parentheses.

1. *The Whiz* is slightly ____________ than *The Sea Sharp.* (fast)
2. *Mother's Worry* is the ______________ boat of the three. (fast)
3. *The Whiz* is _____________ to *The Sea Sharp* than to *Mother's Worry.* (near)
4. *The Sea Sharp* is the _______________ boat in the race. (big)
5. *Mother's Worry* is the racer _________________ to the finish line. (close)

Name ______________________________

NO DANGLING, PLEASE

TICKLE-TICKLE
HEE, HEE

It's not a good idea to dangle your feet off the pier unless you're sure about what's lurking below the surface of the water. It's also not a good idea to dangle modifiers in sentences.

> When sentences or phrases are combined, the relationship between them must be clear. If a modifying clause or phrase does not clearly and sensibly modify a word in the sentence, or if it is not placed close to the word it modifies, it is called a **dangling modifier.**
>
> Crabs were served to the guests *covered with butter.*

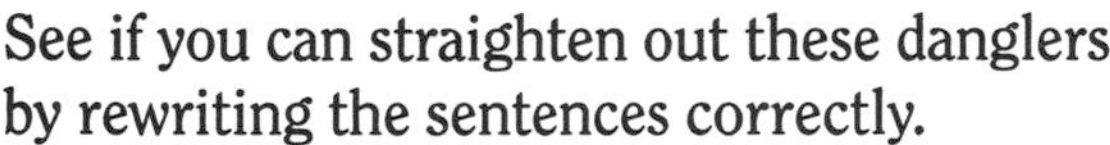

See if you can straighten out these danglers by rewriting the sentences correctly.

1. While riding a bicycle, a stray dog bit me.

2. Jutting out of the sea, the swimmers were shocked to see a fin.

3. While eating its food, I suddenly noticed how fat our dog was becoming.

4. Riding horseback along the beach, the ocean looked very peaceful.

5. Why did you buy saltwater taffy from a store that was unwrapped?

6. Joe lost the music he had written by mistake.

7. My mother told me to put on sunscreen at least ten times this week.

8. I repaired the raft that was punctured by the shark with great care.

Name

A DOUBLE NEGATIVE IS A NO-NO!!

Scuba diving alone is a no-no. So is using double negatives. Never get caught doing either of these!

A **double negative** is a construction in which two negatives are used when one is sufficient!

Underline the double negatives you find in the following sentences. Then rewrite each of those sentences, correcting the error(s). Several sentences are correct. In the spaces at the bottom of the page, record the first letter of each correct sentence, and your wise choices will reveal a double positive!

1. You have only five minutes of air in your tank.
   ____
2. Tina couldn't hardly move her arm after the jellyfish sting.
   ____
3. Didn't you ever do nothing about that leak in the boat?
   ____
4. Evan can hardly see through his clouded mask.
   ____
5. We haven't but two days of vacation left.
   ____
6. I can't find no shipwrecks around here.
   ____
7. Scuba diving alone makes no sense.
   ____
8. Bob never dives in no dangerous places.
   ____
9. Yesterday, we had scarcely any free time to swim.
   ____
10. There isn't no ice left in the cooler.
    ____
11. Everyone searched for treasure, but there was none.
    ____
12. Seven divers have searched, but haven't found anything.
    ____
13. I haven't ever seen no barracuda.
    ____
14. If you aren't seeing one now, you're not seeing nothing!
    ____

I HAVEN'T NEVER SEEN SO MANY PRETTY FISHIES!

___ ___ ___ , ___ ___ ___ ___ !

Name ______________________________

POSITIONS, PLEASE!

The little starfish is next to the fat starfish. The skinny starfish is not near the little one. But none of them are inside a predator.

Next, near, and **inside** are prepositions. A **preposition** is a word that shows the relationship of a noun or pronoun to some other word in the sentence.

I. Locate only the prepositions in the following list. Write each preposition in a place on the drawing which illustrates its proper relationship to the drawing. (You may use arrows when necessary.)

around	*above*	*the*	*beside*	*toward*
below	*neither*	*over*	*between*	*after*
on	*nor*	*either*	*across*	*yet*
against	*and*	*through*	*underneath*	*within*
behind	*instead*	*both*	*near*	*you*

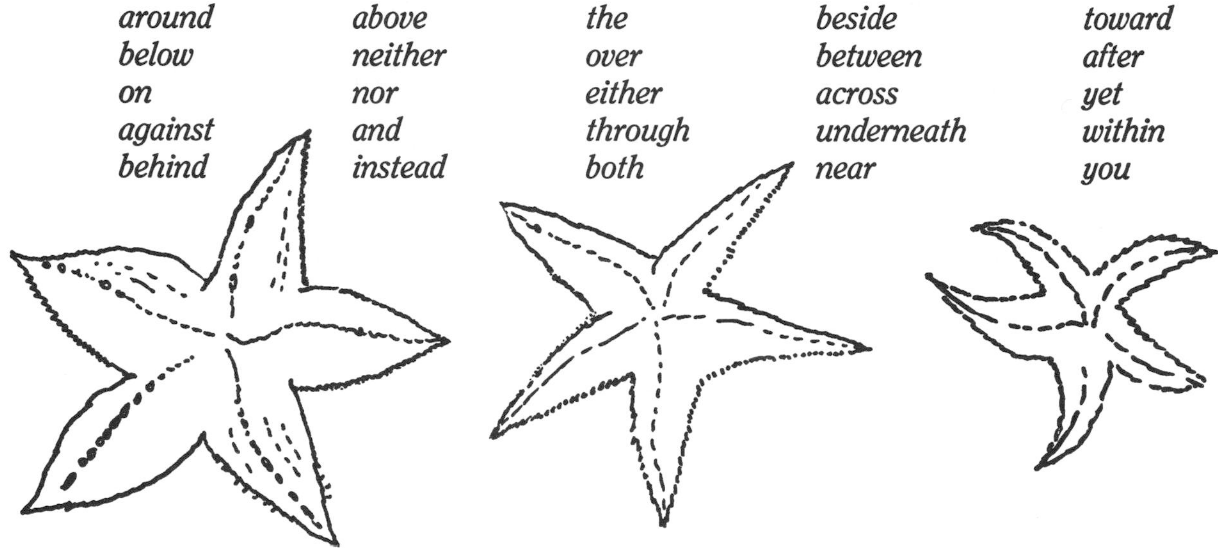

A **prepositional phrase** is a phrase that begins with a preposition and ends with a noun.

II. Write a prepositional phrase to go with each noun. Use each preposition only once!

1. ______________________________ rickety stairs
2. ______________________________ burning sand
3. ______________________________ a melting igloo
4. ______________________________ a wacky tea party
5. ______________________________ a dancing bear
6. ______________________________ chicken soup
7. ______________________________ crashing waves
8. ______________________________ sticky syrup
9. ______________________________ an ugly octopus
10. ______________________________ two slippery eels

Name ______________________________

A WHALE OF A TALE

This tale about a whale is loaded with participles and participial phrases. (Most tales are!) Can you find them all?

A **participle** is a verb form that is used as an adjective.

A **present participle** usually consists of the verb plus **ing.**

A **past participle** usually consists of the verb plus **d** or **ed** and occasionally **t, en,** or **n**.

I. Underline the participles in the sentences below.

1. Caught by a storm, a large whale was washed ashore by the waves.
2. Jumping up and down with delight, the children gathered around the beached animal.
3. The mammal, given the right care, could be saved.
4. The marine biologists worked carefully, keeping the animal wet as they examined it.
5. Encouraged by the crowd, the whale was able to return to his ocean home.
6. Moving out to sea, he tipped his tail to his landlubber friends.
7. Pleased with their accomplishment, the crowd cheered.

A **participial phrase** is the participle and its related words, acting together as an adjective.

II. Fill each space below with a participial phrase.

1. The whale ____________________________ was a female.
2. The waves ____________________________ were complicating the rescue efforts.
3. ____________________________, the whale finally got turned around.
4. The rescuers, ____________________________, were able to coax the whale forward.
5. ____________________________, the children waved joyfully as the whale swam out to sea.
6. The people, ____________________________, cheered the rescuers.
7. ____________________________, everyone made his way home happily.

Name

JUGGLING GERUNDS

Swimming, diving, snorkeling, burning, screaming, chasing—these are some of the many gerunds you might find at the beach.

> A **gerund** is a verb form, ending in **ing**, that is used as a **noun.**
> Like nouns, gerunds can be used as **subjects, predicate nominatives, direct** or **indirect objects,** or **objects of prepositions.**

I. Circle the gerund in each sentence; then, on the line provided, tell how it is used.

1. Juggling on water skis is a nearly impossible feat. ____________
2. I like jet skiing better. ____________
3. At the point of breaking, waves are most powerful. ____________
4. Body surfing can be dangerous. ____________
5. The most popular beach sport is watching people. ____________
6. The girls gave sunning most of their time and energy. ____________
7. The boys loved playing volleyball. ____________
8. Are there any rules for boating here? ____________
9. I have lain here all day and given my reading not one thought. ____________
10. A rocking boat makes taking pictures difficult. ____________

> A **gerund phrase** is a gerund with all of its related words, acting together as a noun.

II. Write a gerund phrase to complete each sentence below.

1. ____________ is a difficult task.
2. Most kids love ____________.
3. ____________ seemed to excite the fish.
4. The problem ____________ was one we had to solve quickly.

Name ____________

TO SWIM IS TO SURVIVE

The title of this page has two infinitives. This sentence has two more: "If this swimmer is going to live through the day, she needs to make it to the island." Can you find them?

An **infinitive** is a verb form, usually preceded by the word **to.** It may be used as a **noun, adjective,** or **adverb.**

I. Circle the infinitives in the sentences below.

1. I love to eat clams.
2. To locate one tiny boat on the ocean is difficult.
3. We hope to sail to Bimini this winter.
4. The captain seemed to be ill.
5. The motor sounds as if it is about to quit.
6. To swim is to survive.

An **infinitive phrase** is an infinitive together with all of its related words.

II. For each picture below, write a sentence that includes an infinitive phrase.

1. 

2. 

3. 

4. 

Name

LONERS AND LEANERS

"<u>If you are alone</u>, <u>you can lean on me</u>!!"
(dependent) *(independent)*

An **independent clause** expresses a complete thought and can stand by itself. (It's a LONER!)

A **dependent (subordinate) clause** does **not** express a complete thought and **cannot** stand alone. (It's a LEANER!)

Choose from the following list of "loners" and "leaners" five pairs of clauses that can be used to create five sentences. Write your sentences on the lines below. Each sentence should contain one independent and one subordinate clause.

after he had swallowed a gold ring
while he was changing
when my family vacationed in Bermuda
while she was cleaning his fish
his pants blew away
his date fainted

he fell off the dock
after he kissed her
they witnessed a drowning
the fish was so big
that I will never forget it
a giant sea turtle washed ashore

1. ______________________________

2. ______________________________

3. ______________________________

4. ______________________________

5. ______________________________

Name ______________________________

CLAUSE CAUGHT IN CLAWS???

Don't get caught in confusion about clauses. Practice finding clauses that **depend** on others.

A **dependent clause** is a group of words that has a subject and predicate but does not express a complete thought. It **depends** on an **independent clause** to complete its meaning.

FORTUNE: THE CRAB WHO HOLDS PAPER FORTUNE SHALL BE CAUGHT BEFORE SUNDOWN!

Underline the dependent clause in each sentence. Then, in the numbered space, tell whether it is used as a noun, adjective, or adverb.

_______________ 1. The lobster who had the biggest claws won the fight.

_______________ 2. The fish that Meg caught was 21 inches long.

_______________ 3. Before the sun was up, we had our equipment ready.

_______________ 4. Yvette, who has been fishing since she was a child, won the contest.

_______________ 5. That big barracuda knows what our fishing secrets are.

_______________ 6. Because he felt seasick, Kirk hung over the stern.

_______________ 7. Here is the pole for which you have been looking.

_______________ 8. Whoever wins the battle gets a date with a mermaid.

_______________ 9. After we had fished all day, we got dressed up for dinner and dancing.

_______________ 10. We often dream that we live in an underwater castle.

_______________ 11. When that happens, we usually have just fallen asleep in the bathtub!

_______________ 12. Who knows what the future will bring?

_______________ 13. We may be living in an underwater kingdom where everything is peaceful.

_______________ 14. If you should find a genie in a bottle at sea, what three wishes would you ask for?

Name ____

COOL OR OBTUSE???

Cal, the lifeguard, gave himself the name Cool Cal. He thinks he is cool for many reasons. One of them is that he's a whiz at capitalization—or so he thinks! If Cal has correctly capitalized an item below, give it a C (for COOL); if it is incorrect, give it an O (for OBTUSE). If you don't know the meaning of the word *obtuse*, look it up. Then transform the Os to COOL by making proper corrections.

C

_______________ 1. a small Catholic church on Shelby Avenue

_______________ 2. fingerprints taken by officer Wiley

_______________ 3. You'll love victorian literature!

_______________ 4. See you on Labor Day!

_______________ 5. the Washington monument

_______________ 6. We visited the great Smoky mountains.

_______________ 7. My high school teacher went to Duke University.

_______________ 8. traveling East on U.S. I-40

_______________ 9. my father's sister, Cleopatra

_______________ 10. buddhists worship in temples

_______________ 11. I hope she won't tell mom!

_______________ 12. He went to the Southwest to school.

_______________ 13. American red cross

_______________ 14. I flunked Spanish, but I passed chemistry.

_______________ 15. the Canadians won the gold medal!

_______________ 16. I've read the holy bible, cover to cover.

_______________ 17. I love new England in the fall.

_______________ 18. Welcome to the senior Class Picnic.

_______________ 19. He drives a red pickup truck.

_______________ 20. He drives a Mighty Man Brand truck.

Name ____

CLEARLY CLOUDY

I. Correct the errors in punctuation and capitalization on this envelope and business letter.

i m tickt
124 opaque cr
waterless ia 69843

ms. crystal clear
happy day dive supply corporation
133 see weed blvd
miami, florida 47856

124 opaque circle
waterless ia 69843
may 15

ms crystal clear marketing manager
happy day dive supply corporation
133 see weed boulevard
miami, fl 47856

dear ms clear

I am returning under separate cover a happy day diving mask which I purchased from your company thirty days ago. It was advertised as cloud proof and leak proof it clouds it leaks I would like to have my money returned and I would respectfully suggest that you withdraw your advertising from all markets until you can deliver the product you describe. You might also consider changing your name and the name of your company

sincerely yours

i. m. tickt

II. Use this space to create a correct response from the company to I. M. Tickt. Double check your capitalization and punctuation.

HAPPY DAY DIVE SUPPLY

Name

TITLE-WISE

When you're reading a good book or magazine at the beach, you don't have to worry about its title—at least not after you've picked the one you're going to read. But when you write titles, it gets a little tricky, and you need to know the rules.

MOBY DICK

Titles of books, plays, movies, periodicals, works of art, long musical compositions, and book-length poems are underlined or written in italics.

Titles of magazine articles, short stories, poems, songs, chapters, and other parts of books or periodicals are enclosed in quotation marks.

Capitalize the first letter in the first and last words as well as in nouns, verbs, adverbs, adjectives, and pronouns in titles. Do not capitalize prepositions, articles, or conjunctions.

Write at least two appropriate titles (real ones) for each category below. Use reference materials if you need help in identifying real titles.

CITY NEWSPAPERS ______________________________

FAMOUS WORKS OF ART ______________________________

BOOKS ______________________________

SONGS ______________________________

PERIODICALS ______________________________

SHORT STORIES ______________________________

SHORT POEMS ______________________________

MOVIES ______________________________

CHAPTER TITLES ______________________________

MAGAZINE ARTICLES______________________________

Name ______________________________

PUNCTUATION REPAIR

Some of the signs in this town are in need of repair. Fix each sign by adding needed punctuation or by crossing out marks used in error.

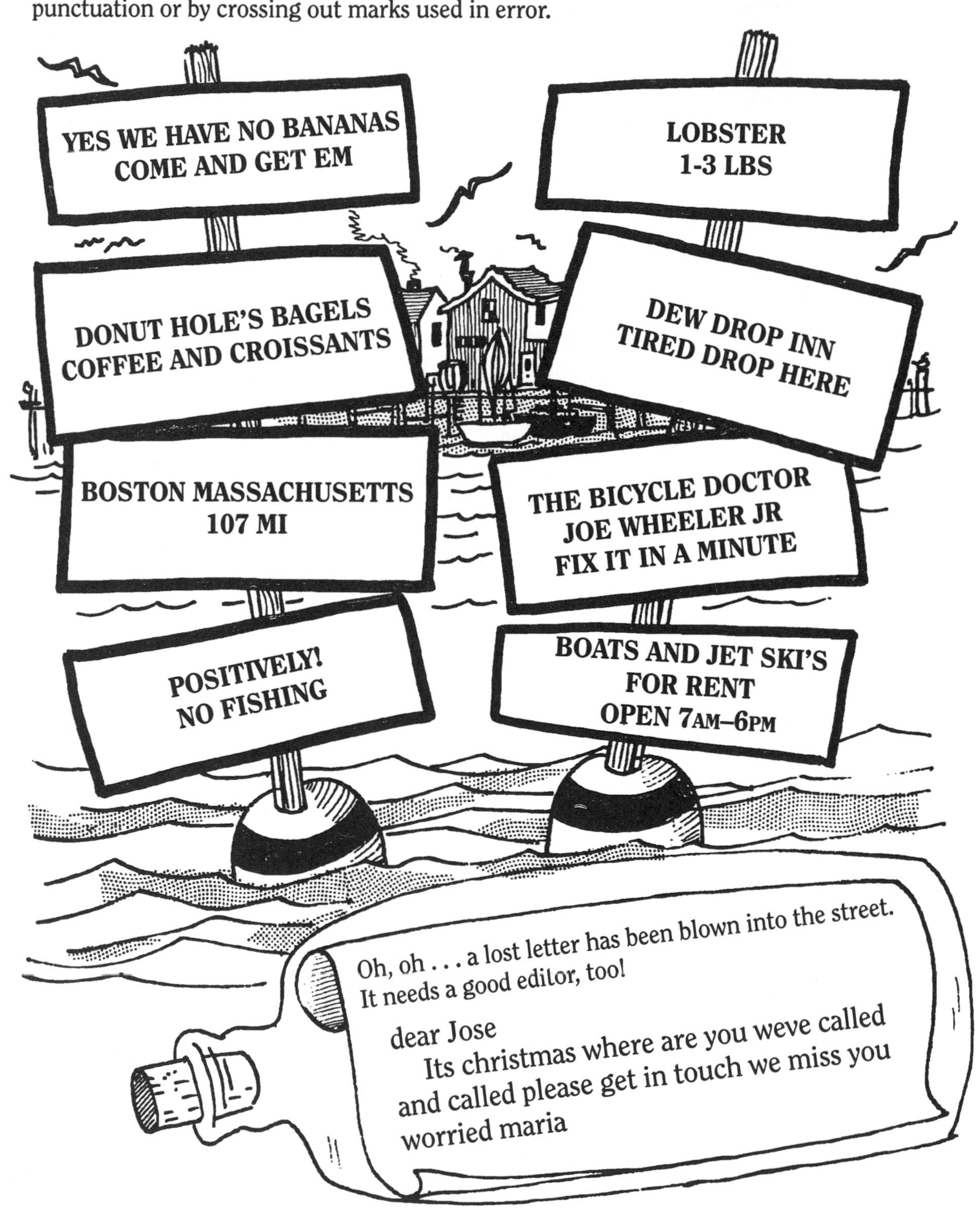
YES WE HAVE NO BANANAS
COME AND GET EM
LOBSTER
1-3 LBS
DONUT HOLE'S BAGELS
COFFEE AND CROISSANTS
DEW DROP INN
TIRED DROP HERE
BOSTON MASSACHUSETTS
107 MI
THE BICYCLE DOCTOR
JOE WHEELER JR
FIX IT IN A MINUTE
POSITIVELY!
NO FISHING
BOATS AND JET SKI'S
FOR RENT
OPEN 7AM–6PM
Oh, oh . . . a lost letter has been blown into the street.
It needs a good editor, too!
dear Jose
Its christmas where are you weve called
and called please get in touch we miss you
worried maria

Name

A PERFECT DAY FOR DIVING

This is the story of seven snorkelers going off to take advantage of a perfect day. But the story is a mess. It's in need of a proofreader—that's you! Use proofreaders' marks to make the necessary insertions and corrections in capitalization and punctuation on the copy below. Then use the rest of the page to rewrite the story. If you need more space, use the back of the page.

the day was clear and calm extraordinary for off shore diving we packed wet suits towels masks snorkels flippers soft drinks and chips and threw in some squeeze cheese for the fish

last man into the trucks a flat flounder yelled jed

Oh no whered I put my new watch I asked it was waterproof and had a luminous dial I got it 'specially for diving

honk

coming yes there it is OK

I jammed my super sharks baseball cap onto my head

a moment later seven of us were crammed into the 4 X 4 headed to the emerald waters of eden rock off to coral reefs caves and fluorescent fish maybe wed see a ray or a barracuda or a sand shark maybe wed tease a fat old moray eel out of his cave

adventure here we come

A PERFECT DAY FOR DIVING

Name

LOST IN THE WAVES

This tale has gotten caught up in a big wave. Unfortunately, all the commas have been lost. Find all the places where commas have been washed away. Use a colored pen or pencil to insert them where they belong.

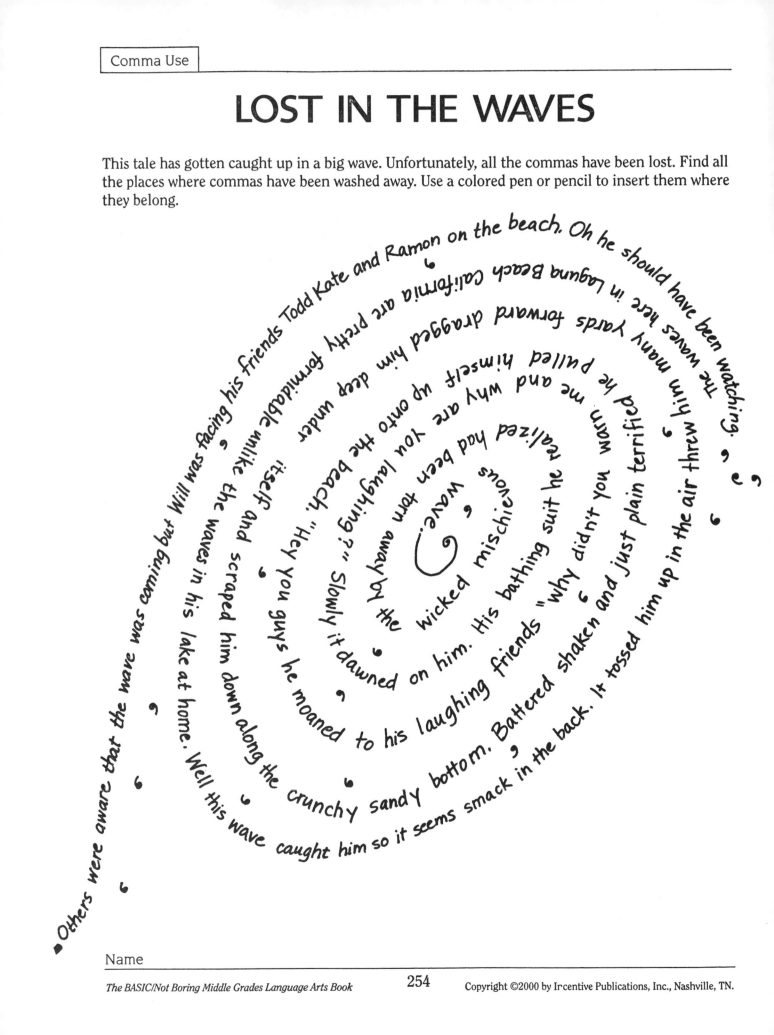

Others were aware that the wave was coming but Will was facing his friends Todd Kate and Ramon on the beach. Oh he should have been watching.
The waves here in Laguna Beach California are pretty formidable unlike the waves in his lake at home. Well this wave caught him so it seems smack in the back. It tossed him up in the air threw him many yards forward dragged him deep under itself and scraped him down along the crunchy sandy bottom. Battered shaken and just plain terrified he pulled himself up onto the beach. "Hey you guys" he moaned to his laughing friends "why didn't you warn me and why are you laughing?" Slowly it dawned on him. His bathing suit he realized had been torn away by the wicked mischievous wave.

Name

QUOTABLES

Old Carlotta Crocodile says that if you should meet a crocodile, you should not take a stick and poke him. (This is an indirect quote.) See the direct quote below.

WHAT DID OLD CARLOTTA SAY?
"IF YOU SHOULD MEET A CROCODILE, DON'T TAKE A STICK AND POKE HER."

I. The sentences below contain indirect quotations. Rewrite each sentence, changing the quote to a direct quotation, correctly punctuated.

1. Mark Twain once said that a lie can travel halfway around the world while the truth is putting on its shoes.

2. You will probably agree with Roger Lewin's observation that, too often, we give children answers to remember rather than problems to solve.

3. Do you know what H. G. Wells meant when he proposed that civilization is a race between education and catastrophe?

4. Thomas Jefferson stated that he was a great believer in luck, and found that the harder he worked, the more he had of it.

5. Will Rogers says everybody is ignorant, only on different subjects!

II. Punctuate these sentences:

1. Look cried Louis its a rainbow
2. I can hardly wait chattered Benita Tomorrow is my birthday
3. Do you know how old I'll be she asked Thirteen—a real teenager

Name

COLON & COMPANY

Detective Inspector Sharpeye, disguised as a beach bum, is lurking around tracking down missing colons and semicolons. He's hoping for your help.

The slash mark in each item below means a colon or semicolon may be missing from that space. Your mission, should you decide to accept it, is to discover which sentence in each pair needs a colon or a semicolon. Indicate your choice (A or B) on the lines to the right, and mark the correct punctuation in the sentence that is missing a colon or semicolon.

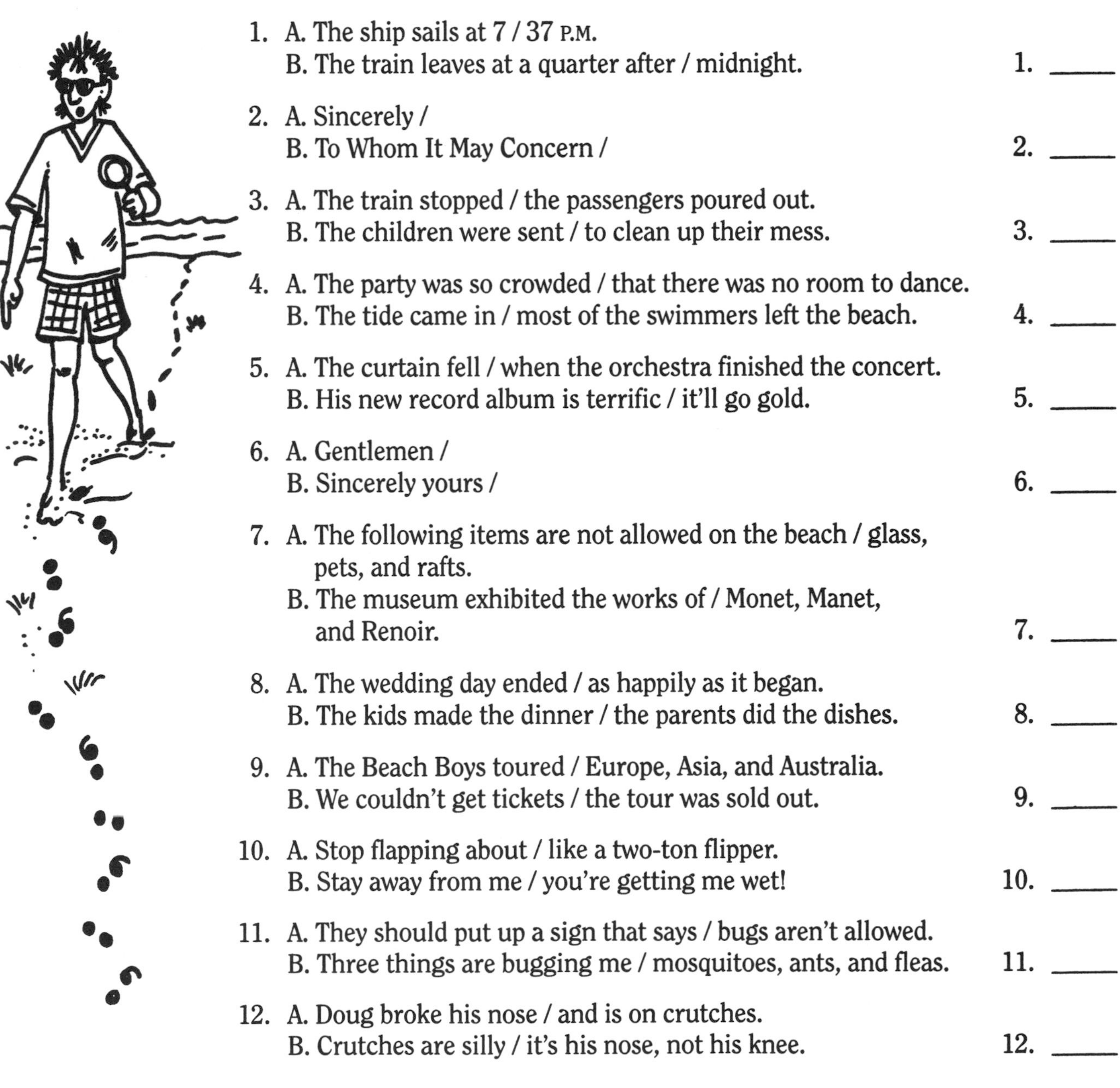

1. A. The ship sails at 7 / 37 P.M.
   B. The train leaves at a quarter after / midnight. 1. _____
2. A. Sincerely /
   B. To Whom It May Concern / 2. _____
3. A. The train stopped / the passengers poured out.
   B. The children were sent / to clean up their mess. 3. _____
4. A. The party was so crowded / that there was no room to dance.
   B. The tide came in / most of the swimmers left the beach. 4. _____
5. A. The curtain fell / when the orchestra finished the concert.
   B. His new record album is terrific / it'll go gold. 5. _____
6. A. Gentlemen /
   B. Sincerely yours / 6. _____
7. A. The following items are not allowed on the beach / glass, pets, and rafts.
   B. The museum exhibited the works of / Monet, Manet, and Renoir. 7. _____
8. A. The wedding day ended / as happily as it began.
   B. The kids made the dinner / the parents did the dishes. 8. _____
9. A. The Beach Boys toured / Europe, Asia, and Australia.
   B. We couldn't get tickets / the tour was sold out. 9. _____
10. A. Stop flapping about / like a two-ton flipper.
    B. Stay away from me / you're getting me wet! 10. _____
11. A. They should put up a sign that says / bugs aren't allowed.
    B. Three things are bugging me / mosquitoes, ants, and fleas. 11. _____
12. A. Doug broke his nose / and is on crutches.
    B. Crutches are silly / it's his nose, not his knee. 12. _____

Name ____________________

BRILLIANT DEVICES

The **dash**, the **hyphen**, and **parentheses** are all brilliant devices to help you write interesting sentences. Check your grammar handbook or textbook to review the purposes and rules for using these devices. Then insert them properly in the examples below.

THE DRAMATIC DASH

1. The boss raged into the office, screamed obscenities at his staff and his pants fell to his knees.
2. The vicar's knickers are thicker and slicker a clever rhyme.
3. Aunt Prunella had a face that matched her personality pinched, pink, and powdery.
4. One hundred-year-old George Galguggener swims eight miles a day an amazing feat!

I KIN DO IT!
I KIN DO IT!

THE HEROIC HYPHEN

5. He raged into the office and screamed at his staff in obscenity laden language.
6. A mad dog debriefed the vicar, making him the ex knick-ered vicar.
7. Aunt Prunella is the seventy six year old mother in law of the president elect, Peter Papagallo.
8. Mr. Galguggener, a one hundred year old ex marine frogman, says he can swim forty six miles a week.

THE PERIPATETIC PARENTHESES

9. When the boss screamed, his pants fell down. I think he popped his belt.
10. The vicar appeared at the beach in a pair of neon knickers. What a nerd!
11. Aunt Prunella was the descendant and, of course, namesake of the great Prosperpina Prunella Piccadilly Pepperdine.
12. The oldest swimmer in town he claims to be one hundred swims eight miles every day.

Name

SAILORS' NOTS

Sailors use very clever, secure knots to tie two things together. **Contractions** are like knots. They tie words together in a shortened or combined form. An **apostrophe** shows where letters have been left out when the knot is tied!

I. In each of the knots below, "tie" the pair of words together to create a contraction.

1. is not
2. are not
3. was not
4. were not
5. do not
6. does not
7. did not
8. could not
9. would not
10. will not
11. can not
12. should not
13. have not
14. has not
15. had not

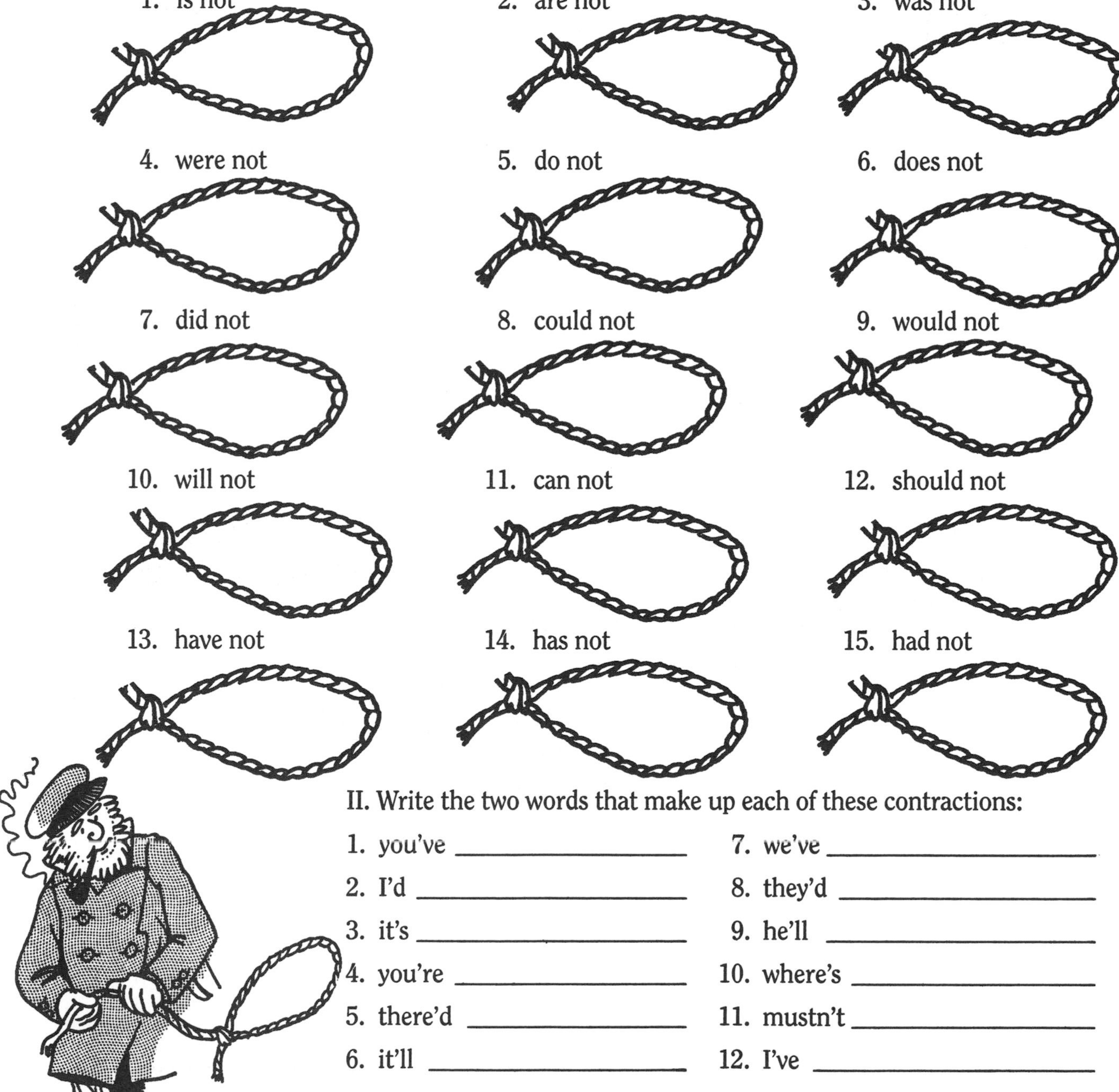

II. Write the two words that make up each of these contractions:

1. you've ____________________
2. I'd ____________________
3. it's ____________________
4. you're ____________________
5. there'd ____________________
6. it'll ____________________
7. we've ____________________
8. they'd ____________________
9. he'll ____________________
10. where's ____________________
11. mustn't ____________________
12. I've ____________________

Name

GRAMMAR & USAGE
ASSESSMENT AND ANSWER KEYS

GRAMMAR & USAGE
SKILLS TEST

Each correct answer is worth 1 point. Total possible score: 100 points.

Use these sentences to answer 1–5.

A. Knowing it might be dangerous, we took a chance and swam at the pier.
B. We took a chance, and, oh, were we sorry!
C. We took our chances.

1. Which is a simple sentence? ______________________
2. Which is a compound sentence? ______________________
3. Which is a complex sentence? ______________________
4. What's the simple subject of **A?** ______________________
5. What's the simple predicate of **C?** ______________________

Use these sentences to answer 6–11.

D. Don't swim too near the reef!
E. Have you ever actually seen a shark?
F. Watch for the divers.
G. Sharks terrify me to death.
H. Don't be such a chicken.
I. Help, that huge shark is after me!

6. Which sentence(s) is / are declarative? ______________________
7. Which sentence(s) is / are interrogative? ______________________
8. Which sentence(s) is / are imperative? ______________________
9. Which sentence(s) is / are exclamatory? ______________________
10. What is the understood subject of **H?** ______________________
11. What is the complete predicate of **G?** ______________________

For sentences 12–15 below, write **C** for **complete, F** for **fragment,** or **R** for **run-on.**

_____ 12. Maria stayed inside all day she had a terrible sunburn.
_____ 13. Because of her severe sunburn.
_____ 14. Feeling miserable, Marie stayed inside all day.
_____ 15. Never having been burned so badly before.

______________ 16. Write the singular form of **mice.**
______________ 17. Write the plural form of **mother-in-law.**
______________ 18. Write the plural form of **beach.**
______________ 19. Write the plural form of **hero.**
______________ 20. Write the possessive meaning **goggles belonging to the swimmer.**
______________ 21. Write the possessive meaning **raft belonging to Jess.**
______________ 22. Write the possessive meaning **the appetites of the lifeguards.**

Name ____

Use these sentences to answer 23-25.

A. Janelle could feel the tension in the rope from the boat pulling her up on the water skis.
B. The Walters family loved spending their vacations at Lake Tahoe.
C. "Who will ski it with me today?" she wondered.

23. Write all the common nouns in **A-C.** ______________________________

24. Write all the proper nouns in **A-C.** ______________________________

25. Write all the pronouns in **A-C.** ______________________________

For 26–37, tell what part of speech each word is as used in sentence **A** or **B**.

A. The yellow lights from the buoys flashed regularly throughout the night.
B. Seventeen lighthouse keepers snored loudly every night.

26. yellow ______________
27. lights ______________
28. buoys ______________
29. flashed ______________
30. regularly ______________
31. throughout ______________
32. lighthouse ______________
33. keepers ______________
34. snored ______________
35. loudly ______________
36. every ______________
37. night ______________

Give the past tense and past participle of each of these irregular verbs:

	past	past participle
38. become	______________	______________
39. say	______________	______________
40. do	______________	______________

The lobster pinches! Write the verb in these tenses:

pinches	present tense	43. ______________	present perfect tense
41. ______________	past tense	44. ______________	past perfect tense
42. ______________	future tense	45. ______________	future perfect tense

Circle the correct word for each sentence.

46. Did Dana or Rachael forget (her, their) raft?
47. The beach shop has raised (their, its) prices.
48. Fish and toddlers (eat, eats) worms.
49. His large claws (give, gives) the crab a bad reputation.
50. In the ocean today (are, is) many whales.
51. The teenagers (lay, laid) down their towel.
52. A mother seal came to (lie, lay) on the rock.
53. Don't (sit, set) your glasses on the sand.
54. Six lifeguards suddenly (raised, rose) up and ran to the water.
55. (Who, Whom) will get me some sunscreen?
56. (Who's, Whose) first to get in the water?
57. She's an awesome diver (who, whom) everyone admires.
58. The octopus is the (scary, scarier, scariest) of all the sea animals.
59. I'm a bad diver, but my brother is (worst, worse).
60. Chad's dune buggy can make it over the dunes (easily, more easily, most easily) than I could climb.

Name ____

Tell whether the verb in sentences 61–64 is transitive (T) or intransitive (I).

_______________ 61. Speedboats raced throughout the bay.

_______________ 62. The lifeguard watched the swimmers.

_______________ 63. Surfers lined up along the beach.

_______________ 64. A strong undertow caused danger.

65. Which sentences below have a dangling modifier? ____________________________________

A. Anne filmed fish holding her underwater camera.
B. Hoping for a great wave, her surfboard was ready to go.
C. While waiting for the storm to pass, Jeff hid his boat in a cove.
D. While floating on my raft, a jellyfish stung me.

66. Which sentences below show correct use of negatives? ________________________________

E. There aren't no sea urchins over there.
F. I've found no sand dollars this week.
G. There is scarcely anybody on the beach.
H. I can't see through my goggles neither.
I. I ain't got no lunch money.

Use the sentences below to answer 67–70.

J. Many fish eat algae for food.
K. Swimming is great exercise.
L. To catch a lobster, you need a good trap.
M. Testing to see if the water was cold, John stuck his toes in slowly.

_____ 67. Which sentence has a prepositional phrase? Name the preposition. ________________

_____ 68. Which sentence has a participle? Name the participle. ________________________

_____ 69. Which sentence has a gerund? Name the gerund. ____________________________

_____ 70. Which sentences have infinitives? Name the infinitives. ______________________

For each sentence, tell whether the clause is **(I) independent,** or **(S) subordinate** (dependent).

_____ 71. the tide is out

_____ 72. when we buried Todd in the sand

_____ 73. since she left the boardwalk

_____ 74. you should get out of the water

Tell whether each clause in bold print is a noun, adjective, or adverb clause.

_______________ 75. Anyone could join the scuba class **which was scheduled for Tuesday.**

_______________ 76. Anna is the teenager **who is the owner of the umbrella.**

_______________ 77. **Before I swim here,** I want to make sure there are no sharks.

_______________ 78. The shop **that rents jet skis** is open all day.

_______________ 79. **Whenever I dive near a sunken ship,** I feel a sense of mystery.

_______________ 80. **Whoever comes to the picnic** will be well fed.

_______________ 81. She screamed **as if she were being swallowed by a whale.**

Name ____

For 82–89, tell whether the word in bold print is a **direct object (D)** or an **indirect object (I)**.

_____ 82. The barracuda ate the **diver.**

_____ 83. The lifeguard signaled **Joe** a warning.

_____ 84. I sent my **boyfriend** a letter in a bottle.

_____ 85. Jonathan ate clam **chowder.**

_____ 86. Brie handed **me** a hermit crab.

_____ 87. The whale gave us a great **show.**

_____ 88. That last wave gave Brad a **ride** all the way to the beach.

_____ 89. An old pirate showed **us** some buried treasure.

For 90–100, correct each sentence to give it the correct capitalization and punctuation.

90. when is high tide james asked the lifeguard at main street beach

____

91. high tide he answered is around 3 15 p m today

____

92. moby dick is my favorite novel of all announced nick

____

93. roberto the oceanographer is from san juan puerto rico

____

94. usually sea anemones starfish and fiddler crabs all hang around tide pools

____

95. governor wilson read the sunday beach times on malibu beach

____

96. there were seven beach chairs left we had eight people

____

97. a canadian diver said he would dive off the golden gate bridge on new years day

____

98. she told me of ginas accomplishments 6 world championships 8 u s championships and 7 olympic gold medals

____

99. the winds are rising and the seas waves are angry it must mean a storm is coming

____

100. wait i left my copy of the old man and the sea on the beach

____

SCORE: Total Points ________________ out of a possible 100 points

Name ____

GRAMMAR & USAGE
SKILLS TEST ANSWER KEY

1. C
2. B
3. A
4. we
5. took, swam
6. G
7. E
8. F, H
9. D, I
10. you
11. terrify me to death
12. R
13. F
14. C
15. F
16. mouse
17. mothers-in-law
18. beaches
19. heroes
20. the swimmer's goggles
21. Jess' raft (or Jess's raft)
22. the lifeguards' appetites
23. tension, rope, boat, skis or water skis, family, vacations
24. Janelle, Walters (used as an adjective), Lake, Tahoe
25. her, their, who, it, me, she
26. adjective
27. noun
28. noun
29. verb
30. adverb
31. preposition
32. adjective
33. noun
34. verb
35. adverb
36. adjective
37. noun
38. became, has become
39. said, has said
40. did, has done
41. pinched
42. will pinch
43. has pinched
44. had pinched
45. will have pinched
46. her
47. its
48. eat
49. give
50. are
51. laid
52. lie
53. set
54. rose
55. Who
56. Who's
57. whom
58. scariest
59. worse
60. more easily
61. I
62. T
63. I
64. T
65. A, B, D
66. F, G
67. J, for
68. M, testing
69. K, swimming
70. L, to catch; M, to see
71. I
72. S
73. S
74. I
75. adjective
76. adjective
77. adverb
78. adjective
79. adverb
80. noun
81. adverb
82. D
83. I
84. I
85. D
86. I
87. D
88. D
89. I
90. "When is high tide?" James asked the lifeguard at Main Street Beach.
91. "High tide," he answered, "is around 3:15 P.M. today."
92. "<u>Moby Dick</u> is my favorite novel of all," announced Nick.
93. Is Roberto, the oceanographer, from San Juan, Puerto Rico?
94. Usually sea anemones, starfish, and fiddler crabs all hang around tide pools.
95. Governor Wilson read the Sunday Beach Times on Malibu Beach.
96. There were seven beach chairs left; we had eight people.
97. A Canadian diver said he would dive off the Golden Gate Bridge on New Year's Day.
98. She told me of Gina's accomplishments: 6 world championships, 8 U.S. championships, and 7 Olympic gold medals.
99. The winds are rising and the sea's waves are angry; it must mean a storm is coming.
100. Wait! I left my copy of <u>The Old Man and the Sea</u> on the beach!

ANSWERS

page 220

1. E	6. I	11. D	16. ?
2. E	7. ?	12. ?	17. D
3. D	8. D	13. E	18. E
4. ?	9. I	14. D	19. D
5. E	10. E	15. D	20. ?

page 221

1. Hundreds of gulls were flying around the dock.
2. On rainy days, does the fog obliterate your view?
3. A whale's big, bulky body can be a fearsome sight.
4. A huge animal does not necessarily have a huge brain.
5. The giant whale leaped into the air and startled everyone.
6. Gory scenes on television have frightened some people away from ocean swimming.
7. Yesterday, three high school kids and two pelicans had a fishing contest.
8. Can you guess the results of the contest?
9. In spite of fair warning, the boys took the jet skis beyond the breakwater.
10. Why do teenage boys often ignore good advice?

I.
1. Hundreds/were flying
2. fog/does obliterate
3. body/can be
4. animal/does have
5. whale/leaped, startled
6. scenes/have frightened
7. kids, pelicans/had
8. you/can guess
9. boys/took
10. boys/ignore

page 222

1. SOS	6. SOS
2. AOK	7. AOK
3. SOS	8. SOS
4. SOS	9. SOS
5. SOS	10. SOS

page 223

1. LIGHTHOUSE
2. LOITER
3. SKINNY
4. SLOWLY
5. EVERYTHING
6. WISE
7. THERE
8. REGURGITATE
9. FISHING
10. NOBODY
11. DISAPPEAR
12. TOUGH
13. YESTERDAY
14. MAINE
15. ILLUSTRATE

Soup of the Day: LOBSTER STEW

page 224

I. **Nouns:** board, surfboard, boardwalk, surf, octopus, flipper, boat, shark, sea, cave, ray, crab, storm, reef, coral, killer, danger, eye, magic, arm, den, rag, bed, dew, tack, war, water, fan, eel, walk

Verbs: kill, row, bet, drag, cut, attack, talk, scare, explore, surf, flip, lurk, slid, swim, stalk, walk

Adjectives: weak, huge, stormy, blue, dark, coral, long, killer, deep, slimy, fat, male, raw, wily, low, old, bad, wet, warm, murky, magic, icy, my

Adverb: oddly

II. Answers will vary.

page 225

Answers will vary.

page 226

1. weekdays (1)	13. men.........(4)
2. weekends (1)	14. women(4)
3. beaches ...(2)	15. shakes .....(1)
4. cans.........(1)	16. drinks......(1)
5. bottles .....(1)	17. sandwiches (2)
6. glasses.....(2)	
7. coolers ....(1)	18. candies....(3)
8. boxes.......(2)	19. supplies...(3)
9. adults ......(1)	20. kites ....(1)
10. children ..(4)	21. rentals.....(1)
11. babies......(3)	22. dune buggies....(3)
12. rooms......(1)	

page 227

1. shark's fin
2. lifeguards' whistles
3. Gus's radio *or* Gus' radio
4. somebody's surfboard
5. children's laughter
6. surf's sound
7. gulls' cries
8. teenagers' suntans
9. bell buoys' warnings
10. ocean swimmers' strength
11. sandals' soles
12. boats' colorful sails
13. footprints' stories
14. no one's beach

A VERY SHORT SEA STORY
Answers will vary.

page 228

I.

1. H	6. A
2. E	7. D
3. G	8. I
4. B	9. J
5. F	10. C

II.

1. suit	4. boys, Megan
2. frisbee	
3. ball	5. girl

III.
1. who, interrogative
2. that, relative
3. himself, reflexive
4. those, demonstrative
5. whoever, indefinite

page 229

I.

1. some	6. sweaters
2. Ken	7. vase
3. John & Eric	8. pieces
4. members	9. we
5. nautilus	10. trophy

II.
1. None–they
2. cats–their
3. someone–her
4. winds–themselves
5. Both–their
6. either–her
7. Neither–his
8. Jim and Troy–their
9. J-24–its
10. ship–its

page 230

1. Who	8. whom	15. who
2. Whose	9. who	16. who's
3. whom	10. Who's	17. whom
4. Who's	11. Whose	18. who's
5. whom	12. who	19. Who
6. Who	13. whom	20. whom
7. Who	14. whom	

page 231

DIVE: she dives, she dived (dove), she will dive, she has dived (dove), she had dived (dove), she will have dived (dove).

STAND: I stand, I stood, I shall stand, I have stood, I had stood, I shall have stood

BLOWN: it is blown, it was blown, it will be blown, it has been blown, it had been blown, it will have been blown

FIGHT: they fight, they fought, they will fight, they have fought, they had fought, they will have fought

HIDE: we hide, we hid, we will hide, we have hidden, we had hidden, we shall have hidden

page 232

1. L	6. L	11. L
2. A	7. A	12. A
3. L	8. L	13. A
4. L	9. A	14. A
5. L	10. A	15. L

page 233

1. catch — caught — have caught
2. swim — swam — have swum
3. rise — rose — have risen
4. bite — bit — have bitten
5. dive — dived (dove) — have dived (dove)
6. fly — flew — have flown
7. freeze — froze — have frozen
8. sit — sat — have sat
9. hang (execute) — hanged — have hanged
10. hang (suspend) — hung — have hung
11. drink — drank — have drunk
12. shake — shook — have shaken
13. shrink — shrank — have shrunk
14. speak — spoke — have spoken
15. swear — swore — have sworn
16. grow — grew — have grown
17. sink — sank — have sunk
18. drown — drowned — have drowned
19. sing — sang — have sung

RIDDLE:
If you lie down and say you have laid down, you will have lied.

page 234

1. I	6. T	11. T
2. I	7. I	12. T
3. T	8. I	13. T
4. I	9. T	14. I
5. T	10. T	15. T

page 235

1. wheelbarrow (D)
2. shelter (D)
3. me (D)
4. me (I) job (D)
5. shells (D)
6. him (I), beating (D)
7. faith (D), him (D)
8. Hector (D), them (I), scare (D)
9. stuff (D)
10. lady (I), umbrella (D)
11. husband (I), relief (D)
12. most (D)
13. me (I), threats, insults (D)
14. guy (D), on-lookers (D)
15. beach (D)
16. you (D)

page 236

I.

1. lay	7. rose, laid
2. laid	8. set
3. raised	9. lying
4. raising, set	10. rose
5. lay	11. laid
6. lay, sat	12. sitting, rise

II.

1. raised	4. lie
2. rose	5. sitting
3. laid	6. sat

page 237

I.
1. NO, is going
2. YES
3. YES
4. NO, are blowing
5. YES
6. NO, make
7. NO, is required
8. NO, are
9. YES
10. NO, are
11. NO, is doing
12. YES
13. YES
14. NO, trips

II.
1. geese fly
2. a submarine surfaces
3. the sea captain commands
4. angel fish swim
5. sand crabs scurry

page 238

I. **Adjectives** to be identified:
a, leisurely, 100-yard, the, off-shore, loose, unusual, coral, flowering, colored, sea, fire, moray, unfriendly, some, bread, the, tiny, reef, cheese, the, larger, hungry, leftover, their, nosy, scouting, the, unexplored, the, the, cool, clear, Caribbean, the, shallower, in-shore, the, the, buzzing, colorful, the, craggy, the, ocean, the, a. voluminous, the, the, the, a, the, other, the, troubled, the, a, frenzied, our, the, deep, blue, ocean, this, frightening, a, dark, foreboding

II. Answers will vary.

page 239

I. Answers will vary.
II. Original response required.

page 240

I.

Adjectives:
1. stubborn, more stubborn, most stubborn
2. good, better, best
3. easy, easier, easiest
4. bad, worse, worst
5. many, more, most
6. late, later, latest
7. happy, happier, happiest
8. loud, louder, loudest

Adverbs:
1. well, better, best
2. happily, more happily, most happily
3. badly, more badly, most badly
4. easily, more easily, most easily

II.
1. faster
2. fastest
3. nearer
4. biggest
5. closest

page 241

1. While I was riding on my bicycle, a stray dog bit me. (A stray dog bit me while I was riding on my bicycle.)
2. The swimmers were shocked to see a fin jutting out of the sea.
3. While our dog was eating its food, I suddenly noticed how fat he was becoming.
4. The ocean looked very peaceful as I was riding horse-back along the beach.
5. Why did you buy, from a store, salt water taffy that was unwrapped?
6. Joe lost, by mistake, the music he had written.
7. My mother told me at least ten times this week to put on sunscreen.
8. I repaired with great care the raft that was punctured by the shark.

page 242

	Incorrect	*Correct*
1.	———	*correct*
2.	couldn't hardly	could hardly
3.	do nothing	do anything
4.	———	*correct*
5.	haven't but	have but
6.	can't . . . no	can't . . . any, can . . . no
7.	———	*correct*
8.	never . . . no	never . . . any
9.	———	*correct*
10.	isn't no	is no, isn't any
11.	———	*correct*
12.	———	*correct*
13.	haven't . . . no	haven't . . . any
14.	not . . . nothing	not . . . anything

double positive: YES, YES

page 243

I. **PREPOSITIONS** which should be identified are:

around	between	underneath
above	after	within
beside	on	behind
toward	across	near
below	against	
over	through	

(Placement on drawing will vary.)

II. Answers will vary.

page 244

I.
1. Caught
2. Jumping, beached
3. given
4. keeping
5. Encouraged
6. Moving
7. Pleased

II. Answers will vary (suggested answers):
1. lying on the sand
2. dashing against the rescuers
3. Given lots of help
4. working together
5. Rejoicing in their success
6. watching the operation
7. Satisfied with a job well done

page 245

I.
1. Juggling, subject
2. skiing, direct object
3. breaking, object of preposition
4. surfing, subject
5. watching, predicate nominative
6. sunning, indirect object
7. playing, direct object
8. boating, object of preposition
9. reading, indirect object
10. taking, direct object

II. Answers will vary.

page 246

I.
1. to eat
2. to locate
3. to sail
4. to be
5. to quit
6. to swim, to survive

II. Original response required.

page 247

Combinations will vary (suggested combinations):
1. A giant sea turtle washed ashore after he had swallowed a gold ring.
2. While he was changing, his pants blew away.
3. When my family vacationed in Bermuda, they witnessed a drowning.
4. While she was cleaning his fish, he fell off the dock.
5. His date fainted after he kissed her.

page 248

1. Adj.	8. Noun
2. Adj.	9. Adv.
3. Adv.	10. Noun
4. Adj.	11. Adv.
5. Noun	12. Noun
6. Adv.	13. Adv.
7. Adj.	14. Adv.

page 249

1. C	6. O	11. O	16. O
2. O	7. C	12. C	17. O
3. O	8. O	13. O	18. O
4. C	9. C	14. C	19. C
5. O	10. O	15. C	20. C

page 250

I. *Envelope:*

I. M. Tickt
124 Opaque Cr.
Waterless, IA 69843

Ms. Crystal Clear
Happy Day Dive Supply
Corporation
133 See Weed Blvd.
Miami, Florida 47856

Letter:

124 Opaque Circle
Waterless, IA 69843
May 15

Ms. Crystal Clear, Marketing
Manager
Happy Day Dive Supply
Corporation
133 See Weed Boulevard
Miami, FL 47856

Dear Ms. Clear,

I am returning under separate cover a Happy Day diving mask which I purchased from your company thirty days ago. It was advertised as cloud-proof and leak-proof. It clouds. It leaks. I would like to have my money returned, and I would respectfully suggest that you withdraw your advertising from all markets until you can deliver the product you describe. You might also consider changing your name and the name of your company.

Sincerely yours,
I. M. Tickt

II. Original response required

page 251

Answers will vary.

page 252

YES, WE HAVE NO BANANAS!
COME AND GET 'EM!

DONUT HOLES, BAGELS,
COFFEE, AND CROISSANTS

BOSTON, MASSACHUSETTS
107 MI.

POSITIVELY
NO FISHING!

LOBSTER
1-3 LBS.

DEW DROP INN
TIRED? DROP HERE!

The BICYCLE DOCTOR
JOE WHEELER, JR.
"Fix It in a Minute!"

BOATS and JET SKIS
FOR RENT
OPEN 7 a.m. - 6 p.m.

Dear Jose,

It's Christmas. Where are you? We've called and called.

Please get in touch. We miss you!

Worried,
Maria

page 253

A PERFECT DAY
FOR DIVING

The day was clear and calm—extraordinary for off-shore diving. We packed wet suits, towels, masks, snorkels, flippers, soft drinks, and chips and threw in some squeeze cheese for the fish.

"Last man into the truck's a flat flounder!" yelled Jed.

"Oh, no! Where'd I put my new watch?", I asked. It was waterproof and had a luminous dial. I got it 'specially for diving.

Honk!

"Coming! Yes, there it is! OK!"

I jammed my Super Sharks baseball cap onto my head.

A moment later, seven of us were crammed into the 4 x 4, headed to the emerald waters of Eden Rock—off to coral reefs, caves, and fluorescent fish. Maybe we'd see a ray or a barracuda or a sand shark. Maybe we'd tease a fat old moray eel out of his cave.

"Adventure, here we come!"

page 254

Others were aware the wave was coming, but Will was facing his friends Todd, Kate, and Ramon on the beach. Oh, he should have been watching. The waves here in Laguna Beach, California, are pretty formidable, unlike the waves in his lake at home. Well, this wave caught him, so it seems, smack in the back. It tossed him up in the air, threw him many yards forward, dragged him deep under itself, and scraped him down along the crunchy, sandy bottom. Battered, shaken, and just plain terrified, he pulled himself up onto the beach. "Hey, you guys," he moaned to his laughing friends, "why didn't you warn me, and why are you laughing?" Slowly, it dawned on him. His bathing suit, he realized, had been torn away by the wicked, mischievous wave.

page 255

1. Mark Twain once said, "A lie can travel halfway around the world while the truth is putting on its shoes."
2. You will probably agree with this Roger Lewin observation: "Too often, we give children answers to remember rather than problems to solve." OR You will probably agree with Roger Lewin that "too often, we give . . ."
3. Do you know what H. G. Wells meant when he proposed, "Civilization is a race between education and catastrophe"?
4. Thomas Jefferson stated, "I am a great believer in luck, and find that the harder I work, the more I have of it."
5. Will Rogers says, "Everybody is ignorant, only on different subjects!"

II. 1. "Look," cried Louis, "it's a rainbow!"
2. "I can hardly wait," chattered Benita. "Tomorrow is my birthday!"
3. "Do you know how old I'll be?" she asked. "Thirteen—a real teenager!"

page 256

1. A :	7. A :
2. B :	8. B ;
3. A ;	9. B ;
4. B ;	10. B ;
5. B ;	11. B :
6. A :	12. B ;

page 257

1. The boss raged into the office, screamed obscenities at his staff—and his pants fell to his knees.
2. The vicar's knickers are thicker and slicker—a clever rhyme.
3. Aunt Prunella had a face that matched her personality—pinched, pink, and powdery.
4. One hundred-year-old George Galguggener swims eight miles a day—an amazing feat!
5. He raged into the office and screamed at his staff with obscenity-laden language.
6. A mad dog debriefed the vicar, making him the ex-knickered vicar.
7. Aunt Prunella is the seventy-six-year-old mother-in-law of the president-elect, Peter Papagallo.
8. Mr. Galguggener, a one-hundred-year-old ex-marine frogman, says he can swim forty-six miles a week.
9. When he screamed, his pants fell down. (I think he popped his belt.)
10. The vicar appeared at the service in a pair of patched knickers. (What a nerd!)
11. Aunt Prunella was the descendant (and, of course, namesake) of the great Proserpina Prunella Piccadilly Pepperdine.
12. The oldest swimmer in town (he claims to be one hundred) swims eight miles every day.

page 258

I.

1. isn't	9. wouldn't
2. aren't	10. won't
3. wasn't	11. can't
4. weren't	12. shouldn't
5. don't	13. haven't
6. doesn't	14. hasn't
7. didn't	15. hadn't
8. couldn't	

II.

1. you have	7. we have
2. I would	8. they would
3. it is	9. he will
4. you are	10. where is
5. there would	11. must not
6. it will	12. I have

STUDY & RESEARCH

Skills Exercises

SKILLS CHECKLIST FOR STUDY & RESEARCH

✔	SKILL	PAGE(S)
	Listen to get information	270
	Understand and follow directions	270, 276, 277
	Find and put words in alphabetical order	271
	Use a dictionary or glossary to find word meanings	271, 279
	Use an encyclopedia to find information	271, 282–284, 290
	Use a table of contents to find information	272, 273
	Use an index to find information	274, 275
	Use and draw maps to find and show locations and information	276, 277
	Find information on copyright pages	278
	Use a thesaurus to find words for a specific purpose	280
	Use an atlas to find information	281, 282
	Use an encyclopedia index	285
	Use a reader's guide to locate information	286
	Use an almanac to find information	287, 288
	Use a biographical dictionary to find information	289
	Use a literary reference book to find information	290
	Find information in *The Guinness Book of World Records*	291
	Locate sections and information in a newspaper	292
	Use and create a bibliography to gather source information	293
	Select the best resource for a task	294–296
	Find and interpret information from charts and tables	297
	Find and interpret information from a graph	298
	Find and interpret information from a diagram	299
	Find and interpret information from a timeline	300
	Gain information by careful observation and logical thinking	301, 303–305
	Form questions to gain information	302
	Find and organize information to give a report	304
	Use scanning and skimming to gain information quickly	306, 307
	Organize information by outlining	306, 308
	Summarize information to use or study	306, 309
	Be familiar with and use the Dewey Decimal System	310
	Use a card catalog or on-line catalog to find books	311

STOLEN JEWELS!

A priceless emerald necklace is missing from the safe of a European monarchy. One of these wily characters below has taken it. Find out who. Here's how:

Cut this page on the dotted line. Give the bottom portion of the page to a friend and ask your friend to read the directions aloud to you, slowly and carefully, one at a time. Do only what the directions tell you to do. Do nothing that you are not told to do. Do not erase. Do not ask questions. Each direction may be read only one time. If you listen well, your answer should solve the mystery!

THE COOK
D
H
THE SWAMI
F
P
THE SNEAKY GUY
T
N
THE OPERA SINGER
C
A
I
B
THE CONVICT
THE HOUND
E

1	2	3	4	5	6	7	8	9	10	11	12	13	14	15	16	17	18	19	20	21	22	23	24	25	26

- -

DIRECTIONS: Read each direction clearly and carefully ONE time. Do not answer questions.

1. Put the letter next to the swami's feather in box 8.
2. Put the letter near the nose of the dog in boxes 3, 7, 13, and 26.
3. Put the letter on the ear of the convict in box 10.
4. Put the letter on the hat of the chef in box 14.
5. Put the letter on the hat of Sneak in boxes 1 and 17.
6. Put the letter next to the opera singer's earring in boxes 11 and 22.
7. Put the letter near the dog's ear in box 12.
8. Put the letter on the chef's chin in boxes 2 and 6.
9. Put the letter on the bald head in boxes 16, 19, and 25.
10. Put the letter on Sneak's lapel in box 20.
11. Put the letter at the end of the singer's nose in box 5.
12. Put the letter at the point of the swami's nose in box 24.

Name

"Z" CONNECTION

Z has always been a somewhat mysterious letter. Be a smart sleuth and connect clues to solve "z" mysteries below.

I. Use your dictionary and encyclopedia to complete "Z" connection between the "Z" words in Column A with their matching identification in Column B.

A	B
1. _____ Zedekiah	A. a Greek god
2. _____ Zambezi	B. a North American Indian
3. _____ Zimbabwe	C. a musical instrument
4. _____ zither	D. a metallic element
5. _____ zinc	E. a sea inlet
6. _____ Zuider Zee	F. a river
7. _____ Zagreb	G. a king
8. _____ ziggurat	H. an imaginary zone in the heavens
9. _____ zoonosis	I. a mineral rock
10. _____ zoology	J. a disease humans get from animals
11. _____ Zeus	K. a form of Buddhism
12. _____ Zola	L. a study of animals
13. _____ Zurich	M. capital of Croatia
14. _____ Zircon	N. a pyramid
15. _____ Zeppelin	O. a plant
16. _____ Zen	P. an African country
17. _____ Zanzibar	Q. a French novelist
18. _____ Zapotec	R. a German scientist
19. _____ zinnia	S. an island of Tanzania
20. _____ zodiac	T. a city in Switzerland

II. Use the space below to write the "Z" words in alphabetical order.

1. ______________	11. ______________
2. ______________	12. ______________
3. ______________	13. ______________
4. ______________	14. ______________
5. ______________	15. ______________
6. ______________	16. ______________
7. ______________	17. ______________
8. ______________	18. ______________
9. ______________	19. ______________
10. ______________	20. ______________

Name ______________________________

MYSTERIES OF THE MIND

HOW TO RELEASE YOUR MIND

One of the most important mysteries you will ever need to solve is the mystery of how your mind works and what you can do to sharpen and assist its processes.

The table of contents on page 273 is taken from a book called *Learning to Learn* by Gloria Frender. The questions below will help you see how you could use this book to increase the efficiency of your brain power and your study skills. See if you can identify pages that will give you the best chance of success. Answer by recording the page numbers.

1. If you wanted to identify the strengths and weaknesses of your study habits, what page(s) would you choose to read? ______
2. What page(s) might help you become a better reader? ______
3. If you have problems remembering what you study, on which page(s) might you find advice? ______
4. If you were trying to improve your spelling study skills, which page(s) might supply some hints? ______
5. You never know whether or not to guess on test questions. Which page(s) might answer this question? ______
6. Where would you find advice on how to make a good study guide? ______
7. Where would you look to gain understanding about how your mind learns? ______
8. Whoops! You had a dental appointment and missed almost ½ day. You've got a test coming up and an assignment due. You don't have the information you need. What page(s) might help? ______
9. It's hard to pay attention when the teacher lectures a long time. You're supposed to take notes, but how do you know what's important? And how can you listen so long? Help is on page(s) ______
10. If you want to be really great at getting information from charts and graphs, you might find some good pointers on page(s) ______
11. Test tomorrow? You didn't know? Ball game tonight? You're in deep trouble. Any pages here you might check out—quickly? ______
12. Several pages offer advice on dealing with main ideas. They are pages ______

Name ______

TABLE OF CONTENTS

Partial Table of Contents from Learning To Learn *by Gloria Frender, © 1990, by Incentive Publications, Inc. Used by permission.*

DETECTIVE'S DOWNTIME DILEMMA

Small-town detectives often have a block of slow days. A pleasant way to pass the time is to give attention to personal hobbies and interests. Detective Hyde has discovered a great book of activities that suit his interests—nature and the environment. Check the index on page 275 to determine on which pages Officer Hyde might find information about the following topics. List the pages he should check for each topic.

DIRT SCULPTURES?

1. How to grow fruit in a bottle ___________
2. Making a necklace ___________
3. How to do grave rubbings ___________
4. Building bird houses ___________
5. Making a backyard water slide ___________
6. Holiday activities ___________
7. Making dirt sculptures ___________
8. Growing plants ___________
9. Making weather instruments ___________
10. How to dry a wedding bouquet for a keepsake ___________
11. Making rain tea ___________
12. Constructing a hideaway ___________
13. Planning a party for the first day of spring ___________
14. Making designs from shells ___________
15. How to fry an egg on a sidewalk ___________
16. Choosing tools for nature activities ___________
17. Ideas for things to make for a party table (other than food) ___________
18. How to make jelly ___________
19. Games to play after dark ___________
20. How to make a talisman (You may need a dictionary to help you find this one!) ___________

Name ___________

Partial Index from Puddles & Wings & Grapevine Swings *by Imogene Forte & Marjorie Frank,*
©1982, Incentive Publications, Inc. Used by permission.

Name

HIDDEN TREASURE HINTS

An anonymous tip has led you to an uncharted island in the Caribbean Sea, where you have located a cave filled with human skeletons and rotting wooden chests. Among the debris, you find an old book which you discover to be a diary. You are able to decipher portions of its last entry . . .

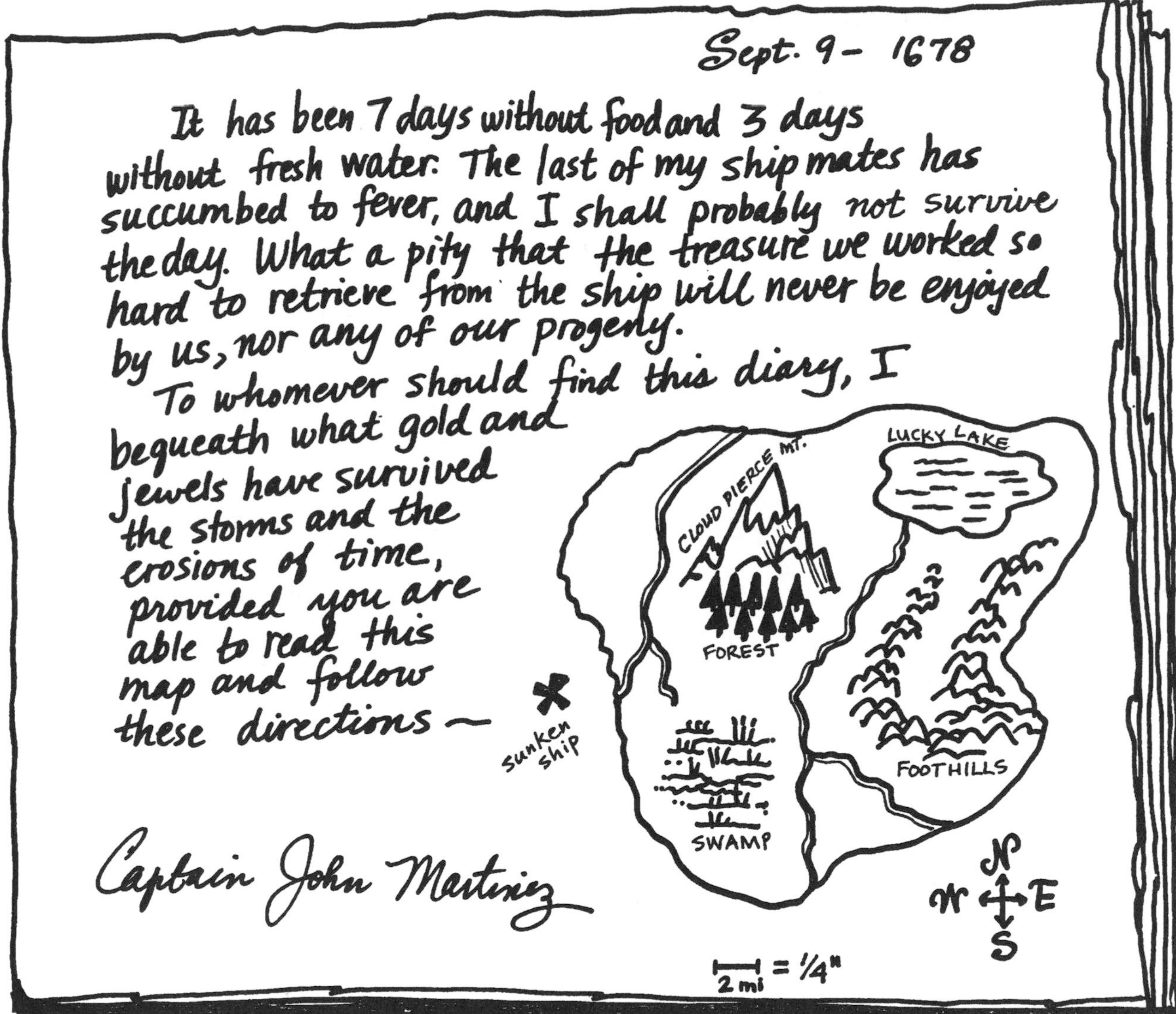
Sept. 9 – 1678
It has been 7 days without food and 3 days without fresh water. The last of my ship mates has succumbed to fever, and I shall probably not survive the day. What a pity that the treasure we worked so hard to retrieve from the ship will never be enjoyed by us, nor any of our progeny.
To whomever should find this diary, I bequeath what gold and jewels have survived the storms and the erosions of time, provided you are able to read this map and follow these directions –
Captain John Martinez
LUCKY LAKE
CLOUD PIERCE MT.
FOREST
sunken ship
SWAMP
FOOTHILLS
N
W
E
S
2 mi = 1/4"

DIRECTIONS: Begin at the wreck of the Sarasota. Travel directly toward land to the mouth of the west fork of the river. Follow this river fork upstream 4 miles to the split of the rivers. Head directly east through the forest which is at the base of a mountain. Go 10 miles and you will hit another river. Follow this river north for 4 miles. Then turn east and walk 4 miles. You will be at the mouth of a valley between two ranges of hills. Travel south for 8 miles between the ranges of hills until you hit the foothills at the south end of the valley. As soon as you hit the foothills, on the southeast edge of the valley, you will find treasure.

Trace your journey on the map Captain John has sketched.

Name

CASE #6

Interpreting Directions/Drawing a Map

DANGEROUS IMPULSE

Would you ordinarily laugh at someone who claims to know where hidden treasure is buried? Maybe you would, but today, a mysterious phone call jump-started your curiosity. The strange voice at the other end of the line gave you these directions for finding a hidden treasure, and your impulse was to follow the directions to the treasure—or, perhaps, to danger!

Read the entire set of directions carefully before you touch a pencil. Look at the compass on the map; then draw a map that will help you picture exactly where the treasure may be. Draw your map in the space below.

YOUR DRIVEWAY
BEECH ROAD

N

W E

S

1 mile

DIRECTIONS: Leave your driveway at sundown. Turn left on Beech Road. After you cross the creek, take the second road on your right. Travel exactly one mile directly south. Then turn left at the old graveyard. Go over the railroad tracks and take the right fork at the grove of trees. Turn left at the first road and follow the black rail fence southeast to the lake. Park by the old cabin and wait for further direction.

Name

COPYRIGHT = NO COPYCATS

Often, clues to mysteries are found in the most unlikely places. A good detective must know how to look for information in unusual places. On this page, you will find information from the copyright pages from six different books. You may be surprised by the things you can learn from these pages. Careful reading of the pages will help you answer the questions below. Before you begin, look up the word **copyright** in a dictionary or encyclopedia.

1. What is a copyright? ______________________________
2. How long is a copyright effective? ______________________________
3. Which books below have a copyright owned by a company? ______________________________
4. Which copyright is most recent? ______________________________
5. Who is the owner of the copyright for *What Every Teenager Should Know?* ______________
6. Which books were printed out of the United States? ______________________________
7. Which book has illustrations copyrighted by someone other than the author? ______________
8. Who is the publisher of *How to Exercise without Lifting a Finger?* ______________
9. Which is the earliest copyright? ______________________________
10. Which book gives some permission to reprint pages? ______________________________

Math in the Real World of Architecture
Author: Shirley Cook
©1996 by Incentive Publications, Inc.
Publisher: Incentive Publications, Inc., Nashville, TN
Printed in the United States
Pages labeled with the statement © 1996 Incentive Publications, Inc., Nashville, TN are intended for reproduction. Permission is hereby granted to the purchaser of one copy of Math in the Real World of Architecture to reproduce these pages in sufficient quantities for meeting the purchaser's own classroom needs.

Brothers and Other Annoyances
Author: Henry Q. Henry, III
©1990 by Bretsone Publishing Co.
Publisher: Bretstone Publishing Co., NY, NY
Printed in Singapore

Training Your Pet Python
Author: J. S. Reptile
©1982 by J. S. Reptile; illus. by A. Copper Head
Publisher: Zoo Press, Chicago, IL
Printed in Australia

How to Exercise Without Lifting A Finger
Author: Russell L. Bow
©1989 by Russell L. Bow
Publisher: Bodyworks Press, Inc., Philadelphia, PA
Printed in the United States

What Every Teenager Should Know
Author: Dr. I. Noahtall
©1983 by Dr. I. Noahtall
Publisher; J. C. Landover, Inc., Wichita, Kansas
Printed in the United States

Tales That Twist Your Tongue
Author: Samantha Cynthia Simms-Smith
©1992 by Samantha Cynthia Simms-Smith
Publisher: C. C. Cooper, Inc., San Francisco, CA
Printed in Hong Kong

Name ______________________________

BLACK AND BLUE

Black and blue is what a sleuth becomes if he or she is not very careful. There are all kinds of black and blue things in our world—some good, some bad. See if you can match each of these blacks and blues with the correct definition. A dictionary and an encyclopedia may help!

_____ 1. blue chip
_____ 2. blue blood
_____ 3. Black Forest
_____ 4. Black Beauty
_____ 5. Blackmun, Harry A.
_____ 6. black hole
_____ 7. blue bonnet
_____ 8. black stump
_____ 9. blue gum
_____ 10. black box
_____ 11. Black Prince
_____ 12. black buck
_____ 13. blueprint
_____ 14. black widow
_____ 15. Black Sea
_____ 16. Blackfoot
_____ 17. blue laws
_____ 18. blacklist
_____ 19. Blue Ridge
_____ 20. blackmail
_____ 21. Black Monday
_____ 22. blues
_____ 23. bluegrass
_____ 24. black magic
_____ 25. Bluebeard

A. a folk tale character who murdered six wives
B. a harmful female spider
C. a criminal offense of extortion
D. stock market crash of October, 1987
E. mountainous wooded region of West Germany
F. member of a Plains American Indian tribe
G. melancholy African American music
H. an antelope of India
I. inland body of water in Southeast Europe
J. name for a unit containing flight recorders
K. Kentucky pasture for horses
L. Colonial New England rules enforcing morals
M. to ban or boycott
N. a Texas flowering plant
O. Australian trees
P. a place in space from which nothing escapes
Q. a stock that sells at a high price
R. story of a horse's life
S. a person of noble or aristocratic descent
T. a range of mountains extending from West Virginia to Georgia
U. U.S. Supreme Court justice, appointed 1970
V. photographic process used in engineering
W. voodoo, witchcraft
X. Prince of Wales—eldest son of King Edward III
Y. an imaginary boundary between civilization and the Australian outback

Name ________________________________

TRIPLE-A DETECTIVES

BORK	SHARK	JESS
Affable	Aggressive	Adventurous
Authoritative	Audacious	Ardent
Absentminded	Agile	Alert
____________	____________	____________
____________	____________	____________
____________	____________	____________
____________	____________	____________
____________	____________	____________

Bork, Shark, and Jess are the three members of the Triple-A Detective Agency. Each has a distinct set of characteristics that make him or her a superb sleuth. Bork is affable, authoritative, and absentminded; Shark is aggressive, audacious, and agile; and Jess is ever adventurous, ardent, and alert. Together, they are unstoppable. Look carefully at the portrait of each detective and add at least **five** additional character traits you guess from each picture.

Use your thesaurus to locate another word that is a synonym for each "A" word listed AND for each of your own word choices. Try to choose words that make these three appear to be a clever, fascinating trio.

Name ______________________________

"B"EELINE TO OBLIVION

Bahamas	Bahrain	Bangladesh	Benin
Barbados	Budapest	Belize	Bhutan
Boston	Botswana	Brazil	Boise
Bulgaria	Burundi	Birmingham	Belgium

When a criminal is trying to hide from authorities, she tries to locate a place in the world where she is unlikely to be easily found. After you have used an atlas or other resources to answer the following questions, decide which of the above "B" places on the globe you think would be the best hiding place and tell why.

1. Circle in the list above each word that does not name a nation.
2. Find an island, not listed above, which is located in the Baltic Sea.
3. Which is located closest to the equator?
   British Isles   Baku
   Brazzaville   Broome
4. Which city has the highest elevation?
   Boston   Beirut
   Belgrade   Bogotá
5. Which city has the lowest population?
   Baffin Island   Bali
   Borneo   Budapest
6. Which is NOT a capital city?
   Bucharest   Bern   Brisbane   Baghdad
7. Which country's border touches the Black Sea?
   Bulgaria   Belize   Brazil   Burundi
8. Which is located farthest inland from an ocean or sea?
   Broken Hill   Bandjarmasin   Bergen   Bhutan
9. Which two cities are closest together?
   Bratislava & Budapest   Brazilia & Beliz   Barcelona & Birmingham
10. Which city is located closest to the Sea of Galilee?
    Brussels   Beirut   Berlin   Bordeaux
11. For a real criminal, I think _______________ would be the best hiding place because
    ____
    ____
    ____.

Name ______________________________

MISS WATSON IS MISSING!

A young woman is missing, and the only clue to her existence is a suitcase found in San Francisco, bearing the name of Miss Jane Watson. You have been authorized by the FBI to open this bag and try to see if it contains any clues to Miss Watson's whereabouts.
It is believed that Miss Watson may have left Boston, Massachusetts two to three weeks ago on a cross-country trip by car, train, and plane to San Francisco. She is known to have been a habitual buyer of souvenirs and it is unlikely that she would pass through any state or major city without securing at least one piece of memorabilia from each place she visited.

USS ALABAMA
The History of the Alamo
NIAGRA FALLS
Oklahoma is O.K
SALT LAKE SALT

As you sort through the items in her luggage, try to determine the origin of each possession and place its number on the map to mark the place each was likely obtained. Perhaps as you mark the map, you will be able to trace Miss Watson's journey from Boston to San Francisco or whatever her last stop may have been. (A U. S. atlas and an encyclopedia will be useful tools for your investigation.)

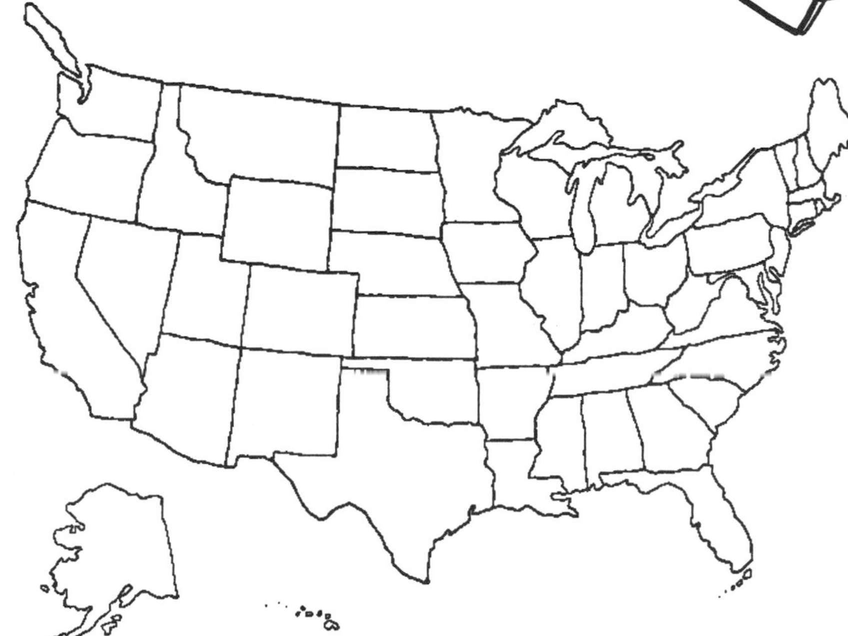

Name

MYSTERIES—UNSOLVED AND OTHERWISE

What's mysterious about a fish, an island, a triangle, a blue book? Find out! Each of these persons, places, or things has some connection to the world of mystery. Use your encyclopedias to help you explain the "mystery" factor of each item listed.

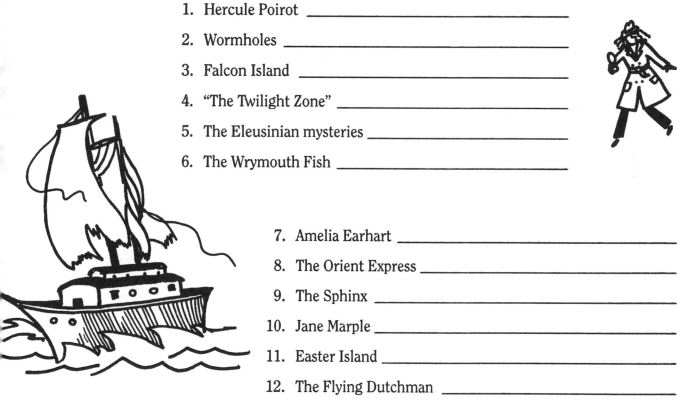

1. Hercule Poirot ______________________
2. Wormholes ______________________
3. Falcon Island ______________________
4. "The Twilight Zone" ______________________
5. The Eleusinian mysteries ______________________
6. The Wrymouth Fish ______________________
7. Amelia Earhart ______________________
8. The Orient Express ______________________
9. The Sphinx ______________________
10. Jane Marple ______________________
11. Easter Island ______________________
12. The Flying Dutchman ______________________
13. Mike Hammer ______________________
14. Henrik Ibsen ______________________
15. The Condon Report ______________________
16. The Bermuda Triangle ______________________
17. The Dead Sea Scrolls ______________________
18. The Mary Celeste ______________________
19. Project Blue Book ______________________
20. Francois Couperin ______________________

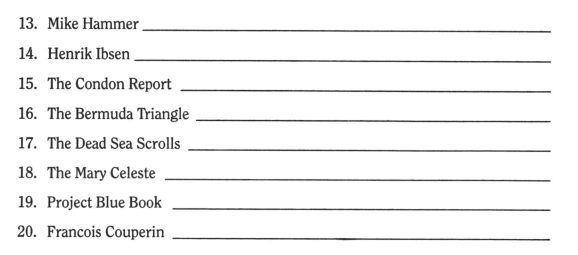

Name ______________________

TORTURES, TOMBS, AND OTHER TRIVIA

The encyclopedia is full of wonderful curiosities. It's your job, detective, to track down these fourteen today.

1. Who threatened to torture Galileo?
   a) a police officer b) his wife c) a monk d) a thief
2. What would you find in Scotland Yard?
   a) a garbage dump b) tombs of famous people c) criminal investigators d) prizewinning roses
3. Where might you meet a white dwarf and a red giant?
   a) at a circus b) in the galaxy c) at a major league baseball game d) in a fairy tale
4. If you had met Jim Jarratt, which of these would he probably be wearing?
   a) a suit of mail c) a deep-sea diver's suit
   b) a space suit d) a priest's robe
5. You've just had lunch with Tutankhamun. You've dined with . . .
   a) a tarantula b) a Chinese emperor c) a mountain d) a mummy
6. Who was with Uri Gagarin on April 13, 1961?
   a) the Russian army b) a monkey c) a ballerina d) no one
7. You watched Dr. John S. Pemberton at his work. What was he doing?
   a) drinking Coca Cola® c) performing brain surgery
   b) examining fish d) floating in space
8. When you're inspecting croup, what are you looking at?
   a) a government overthrow d) the rear end of a horse
   b) a group of engineers e) c and d
   c) an inflamed larynx
9. How long did William Henry Harrison serve as president of the United States?
   a) 1 month b) 1 year c) 7 years d) not at all
10. If you're in the Marianas Trench, where are you?
    a) in a New York City sewer ditch c) in the lowest spot of the ocean
    b) in a pit on a World War II battlefield d) in a whale's mouth
11. Where are the Isles of Langerhans?
    a) in the North Sea b) in your pancreas c) on the moon's surface d) in the Sea of Japan
12. What do you weigh on a Richter Scale?
    a) vegetables b) elephants c) earthquakes d) diamonds
13. What would you do with a scul?
    a) give it to the police c) row it on a lake
    b) chop it onto a salad d) put it on a leash
14. You're in Tunguska, Siberia, in 1908, and you've been hit by something. What is it?
    a) a meteorite c) a UFO
    b) the worst avalanche of the century d) the Black Death

Name ______________________________

INFORMATION FRENZY

Your assignment, Super Sleuth, should you elect (or be forced) to accept it, is to 1) locate the index volume of a set of encyclopedias and 2) use it to decide in which volume you will find the most complete information about the following. (Some topics may be addressed in more than one volume.)

TOPIC	VOLUME LETTER(S) OR NUMBER(S)	PAGE #'S
1. Hurricane warnings		
2. Capital city of Austria		
3. Picture of Alexander Hamilton		
4. Shakespeare's play, *Hamlet*		
5. A cottonmouth snake		
6. Seminole Indian wars		
7. The Goliath frog		
8. The Mormon Tabernacle in Utah		
9. How to set a dinner table		
10. The poisonous plant water hemlock		
11. Equipment for sky surfing		
12. Dr. Seuss		
13. How to give artificial respiration		
14. Ball lightning		
15. Habitats of vultures		
16. The Golden Gate Bridge		
17. What you do with a skeeter boat		
18. Who invented Sunday school?		
19. What's meant by "skin of teeth"?		
20. Bang's disease		
21. Merlin the Magician		

Name ____________________

FUTURE FORECAST

Will detectives and law enforcement agencies still be around in the distant future? Use a *Reader's Guide to Periodicals* to find articles in which writers have made predictions about living in the twenty-first century. For the topics listed below, find at least one quote in a periodical that states an opinion or makes a prediction about that area of life in future years. Then give your own opinion or prediction in answer to the question in each category.

• FAMILY LIFE Quote: ______________________________

____

______________ Source: ______________

Will you have larger or smaller families than your parents? ______________

• JOBS Quote: ______________________________

____

______________ Source: ______________

What new jobs might be created? ______________

____

• EDUCATION Quote: ______________________________

____

______________ Source: ______________

Describe a feature of a future school your children may attend. ______________

____

____

• HEALTH CARE Quote: ______________________________

____

____

Source: ______________

How will you likely be taken care of when you are over age 75?

____

____

____

Name

IT'S A WONDER!

SECURITY FORCE NEEDED: Your agency has been hired to provide security for a worldwide "Celebration of the Seven Natural Wonders of the World." Since you will need to make your own travel arrangements to visit each site, you must determine the geographic location of each and the approximate distance you will have to travel from your home to view each of the seven places.

List the seven wonders of the natural world and their locations in the order (nearest to farthest) that they are located in distance from your city or town. Place a star on the world map below to show each stop on your journey.

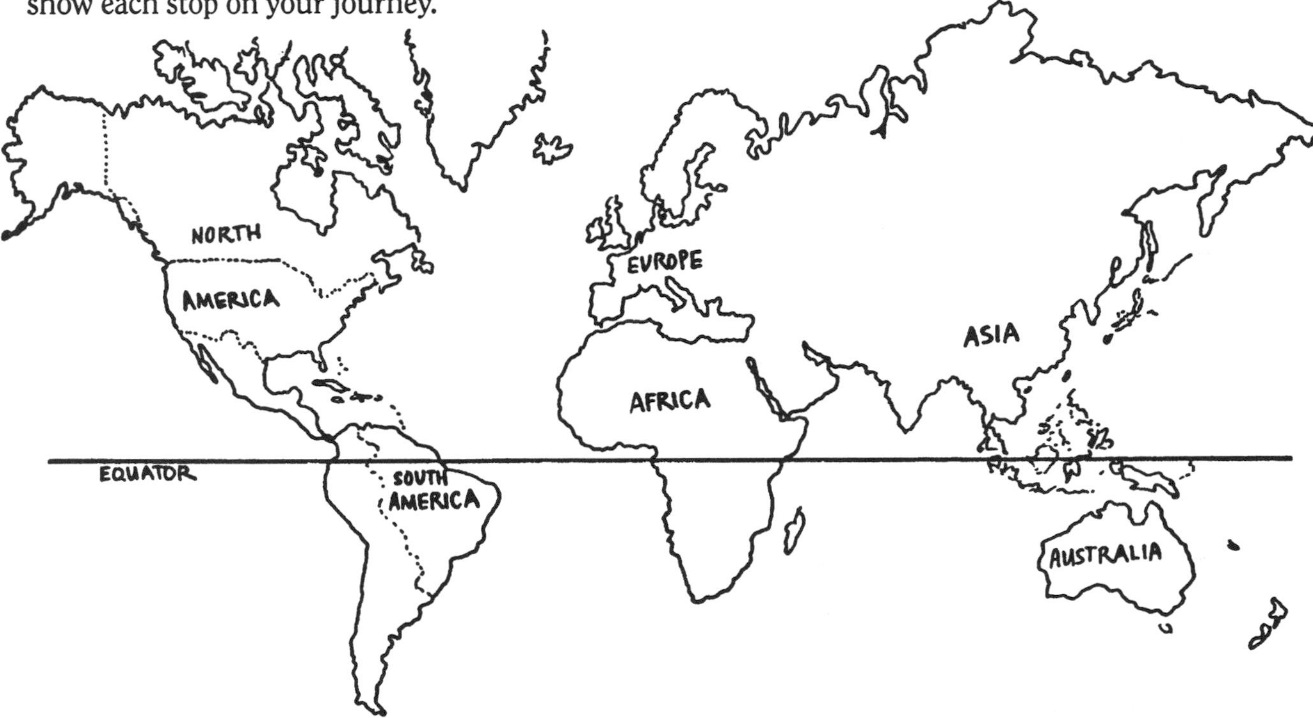
NORTH
AMERICA
EUROPE
ASIA
AFRICA
EQUATOR
SOUTH
AMERICA
AUSTRALIA

THE SEVEN WONDERS OF THE NATURAL WORLD

	NAME	LOCATION
1.	__________	__________
2.	__________	__________
3.	__________	__________
4.	__________	__________
5.	__________	__________
6.	__________	__________
7.	__________	__________

Note: Resources may disagree on which natural wonders are most significant. Choose any seven of those mentioned in your source.

Name ____________________

SPORTS SLEUTHING

Your challenge is to see how quickly and accurately you can find information clues in a world almanac. Locate the answers requested here. Check the box at the bottom of the page that you think best categorizes your skills.

1. What man won the 1992 Olympic Figure Skating Gold Medal?
2. What horse was the Triple Crown winner of thoroughbred racing in 1977?
3. Who was the heavyweight boxing champion of the world from 1952-1956?
4. What is the only country to have won the World Cup Soccer championship four times?
5. What team won the World Series in baseball in the year you were born?
6. What woman won the tennis singles at Wimbledon, England for six consecutive years?
7. For what major sport were each of these names well known?

   Sonja Henie ____________________

   Boris Becker ____________________

   Micky Mantle ____________________

   Olga Korbut ____________________

   Joe Namath ____________________

   Jackie Joyner-Kersee ____________________
8. Who was awarded the Heisman Trophy as outstanding college football player in 1968?
9. What country dominated the Summer Olympic Championship in pole vaulting from 1896-1968?
10. What area of sports does each of these American sports organizations represent?

    NASCAR ____________________

    NRS ____________________

    PGA ____________________

    NFL ____________________

    NBA ____________________

    NHL ____________________

Winner
Champion
SUPER SLEUTH
FINISH LINE

According to my score, I am a

☐ WINNER ☐ CHAMPION ☐ SUPER SLEUTH

Name ____________________

CASE # 18

Using a Biographical Dictionary

UNCOMMON BUT COMMON

What do a nineteenth-century Quaker woman, a Mexican-American migrant worker, a Hawaiian senator, an African American congresswoman, and the cofounder of *Ms.* magazine have in common? Use your detecting skills to figure it out!

Use a biographical dictionary or encyclopedia to learn as much as possible about the lives and achievements of these five people. Record your findings briefly in the spaces below. Then decide what you believe is their common achievement.

	SUSAN BROWNELL ANTHONY	CESAR CHAVEZ	HIRAM FONG	SHIRLEY CHISHOLM	GLORIA ANTHONY STEINEM
Dates:					
Home:					
Job(s):					

Major Life Achievements

SUSAN BROWNELL ANTHONY ______________________________

____

CESAR CHAVEZ ______________________________

____

HIRAM FONG ______________________________

____

SHIRLEY CHISHOLM ______________________________

____

GLORIA ANTHONY STEINEM ______________________________

____

COMMON CONTRIBUTION TO SOCIETY

____

____

____

Name ______________________________

WHO'S WHOSE SLEUTH?

The word *sleuth* came from a shortened form of *sleuth hound*, a Scottish bloodhound, noted for its perseverance in tracking game, suspects, or fugitives.

Below is a list of super sleuths of fiction who were, of course, named by their creators. Your mission is to draw a line to match the name of each sleuth with his or her creator. You will find encyclopedias or literary and biographical dictionaries to be helpful resources.

A Mickey Spillane
B Agatha Christie
C Rex Stout
D P.D. James
E G. K. Chesterton
Charlie Chan
The Saint - Simon Templar
PERRY MASON
Miss Jane Marple
Father Brown
MIKE HAMMER
Hercule Poirot
Nero Wolfe
CORDELIA GRAY
Travis McGee
F Earl Derr Biggers
G Leslie Charteris
H Agatha Christie
I John D. McDonald
J Erle Stanley Gardner

Name

ONE FOR THE RECORD

For five decades, one of the world's best research groups has been the staff of Guinness Publishing Ltd. of Enfield, Great Britain. Each year, they publish a book of information that tells about the biggest and best in all kinds of categories.

I. Spend some time rummaging through the facts and figures in a recent *The Guinness Book of World Records*. In each space below, write an important record that interests you. Each entry must fit the word at the beginning of the line, and your final collection must include facts from at least eight different subject categories (e.g., all examples cannot be sports).

1. Oldest: ______
2. Biggest: ______
3. Smallest: ______
4. Fastest: ______
5. Longest: ______
6. Highest: ______
7. Lowest: ______
8. Greatest: ______
9. Youngest: ______
10. Deepest: ______
11. Worst: ______
12. Heaviest: ______
13. Lightest: ______
14. Most Valuable: ______
15. Strongest: ______

World's Biggest CUPCAKE

II. Check the name index in your record book to see if you can locate a person who shares either your first or last name.

Record the name here: ______

Tell what achievement is attributed to this person: ______

______

______

______

Name ______

THE BIG NEWS

DAILY NEWS
EXTRA!
BABY GIRL
BORN TODAY

You and your parents may think that the big news on the day of your birth was your arrival on the planet, but the newspaper headlines probably missed that very important story and chose something else instead. Sleuth on yourself. Visit your town library or your local newspaper office and see if you can find some of the following information.

On the day you were born:

1. What was the front-page headline? ______________________________

2. What was the weather like? ______________________________
3. How much did the paper cost? ______________________________
4. What sporting event was making news? ______________________________
5. What politicians or world leaders were in the news? ______________________________
6. What were the popular cartoons? ______________________________
7. What movies were playing? ______________________________
8. Copy the headline of an article that tells some bad (unhappy) news. ______________________________
9. What was the "in" style in teen fashions? (See department store ads.) ______________________________
10. What is the range of prices on a new pickup truck? ______________________________
11. Name someone who died that week. ______________________________
12. In this space, copy the most interesting "want ad" from the paper. ______________________________

Name ______________________________

A BRILLIANT BIBLIOGRAPHY

One of a researcher's favorite words is *bibliography*—because in a bibliography, one can find gobs and gobs of information that is not in the usual reference books. Look up *bibliography* in your encyclopedia. Then use a grammar and composition textbook to review how bibliographies are written. You may find one that you can use as a model.

Choose one of the following topics and create a bibliography of at least ten resources that provide information on that topic. *Hint: Be sure to check the* Reader's Guide to Periodicals *for periodical items as well as a card catalog and any bibliographic information following encyclopedia entries.*

Prisoners of London Tower	**Volcanoes**	**Famous Forgeries**
Unsolved Mysteries	**Outlaws of the Old West**	**Leprechauns**
Magic & Magicians	**Castles**	**Indian Legends**

Brilliant Bibliography Written On ______________________________

1. ______________________________
2. ______________________________
3. ______________________________
4. ______________________________
5. ______________________________
6. ______________________________
7. ______________________________
8. ______________________________
9. ______________________________
10. ______________________________

Name ______________________________

QUICK? OR QUICKER?

As a researcher, you need to know which resource or reference gives you the fastest access to the information you need. Which of the following would be your first choice for locating the answer to each question below as quickly as possible?

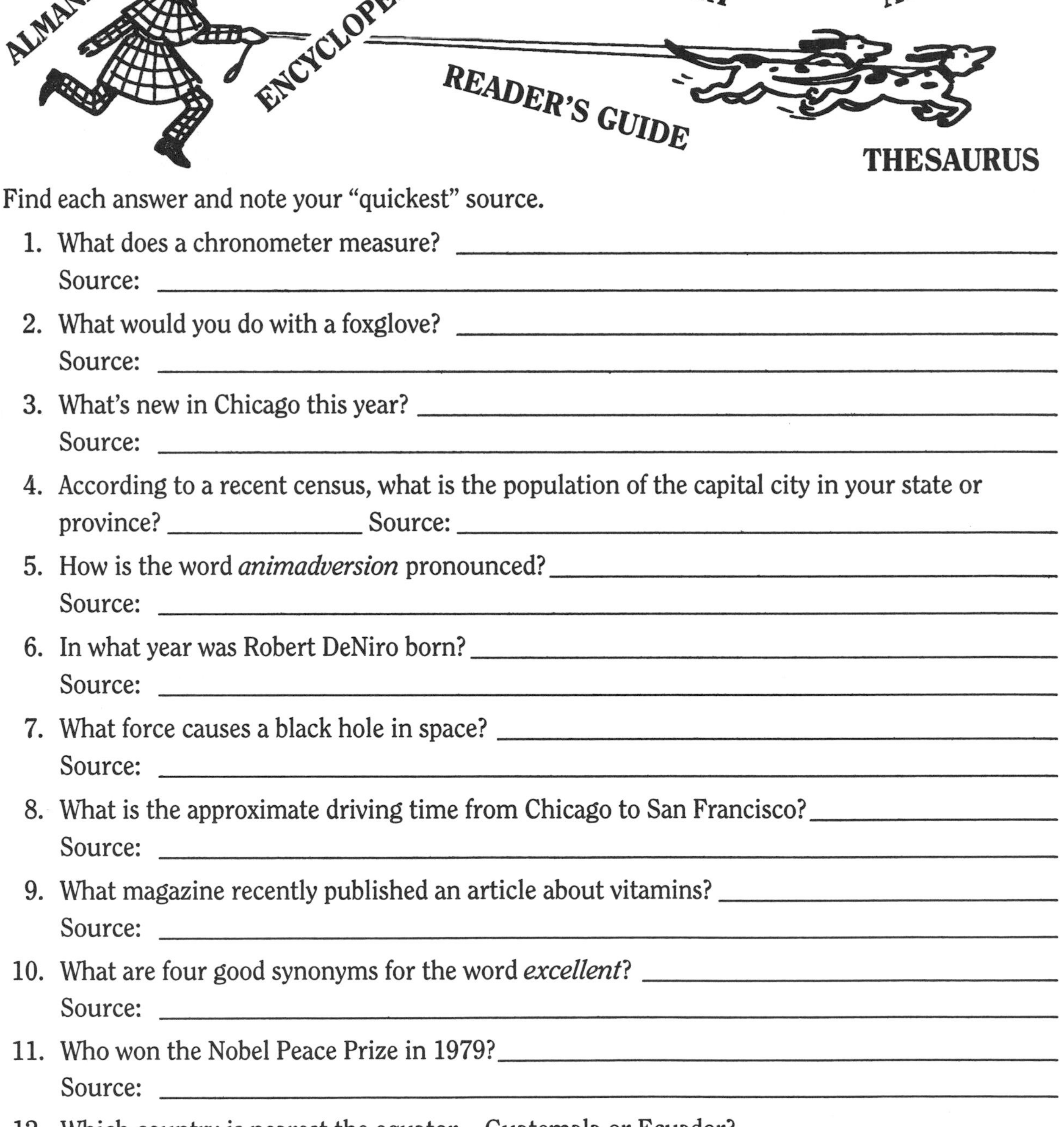
ALMANAC
ENCYCLOPEDIA
DICTIONARY
ATLAS
READER'S GUIDE
THESAURUS

Find each answer and note your "quickest" source.

1. What does a chronometer measure? ______
   Source: ______
2. What would you do with a foxglove? ______
   Source: ______
3. What's new in Chicago this year? ______
   Source: ______
4. According to a recent census, what is the population of the capital city in your state or province? ______ Source: ______
5. How is the word *animadversion* pronounced? ______
   Source: ______
6. In what year was Robert DeNiro born? ______
   Source: ______
7. What force causes a black hole in space? ______
   Source: ______
8. What is the approximate driving time from Chicago to San Francisco? ______
   Source: ______
9. What magazine recently published an article about vitamins? ______
   Source: ______
10. What are four good synonyms for the word *excellent*? ______
    Source: ______
11. Who won the Nobel Peace Prize in 1979? ______
    Source: ______
12. Which country is nearest the equator—Guatemala or Ecuador? ______
    Source: ______

Name ______

KIDNAPPED!

A famous entertainer of the mid 1900s was kidnapped from his or her New York hotel room. Your job is to find out who the entertainer was; exactly when, where, and why he or she was kidnapped; and where he or she was held in captivity until his or her release. Use the clues below to track your case.

HELP! I'M kidnapped.....

CLUE #1 The entertainer's first name is also the name of a U.S. state which is bordered by Georgia and six other states.

CLUE #2 The victim's middle name was shared by the famous American author who wrote A Farewell to Arms; however, it had been shortened to a nickname.

CLUE #3 The last name of the kidnapped person was the same as the last name of the famous industrialist who built a "Model T" automobile.

CLUE #4 He was abducted from a Manhattan hotel by the same name as a small Georgia town, located about 20 miles east of Dothan, Alabama, near the Chattahoochee River. The hotel also shares the first word in the name of one of the southern-most islands off the coast of South Carolina.

CLUE #5 The date of the kidnapping was the same month as the month in which the U.S. celebrates Veterans' Day. The day of the month was the same number as the longitude of Southport, England, and the year was the year that U.S. astronaut Neil Armstrong first set foot on the moon.

CLUE #6 He or she was held captive on an island located at latitude 58° S and longitude 27° W. (The island's name includes the name of an item commonly found on luncheon menus.)

CLUE #7 He or she was released when it was determined that he or she was a victim of mistaken identity. He or she was thought to be a playwright who won the Pulitzer Prize for drama in 1955 and was wanted for putting a cat on a hot tin roof.

TRACK YOUR CLUES:

Entertainer by the name of #1 ______________ #2 ______________ #3 ______________ was abducted from the #4 ______________ Hotel in New York on the #5 ______________ day of #5 ______________, #5____. He or she (circle one) was held captive on #6 ______________ Island, off the east coast of the #6 ______________ continent, and was released when it was discovered that because of a similarity in their names, he or she (circle one) had been confused with playwright #7 ____________________________________.

Name ____________________

SLEUTHING TOOLS

If you're going to be a good sleuth, you have to know when and how to use which tools and techniques to gather information and prove the facts of your case. Some tools are more efficient than others for a given task. Circle the BEST FIRST source to check in each of the following cases.

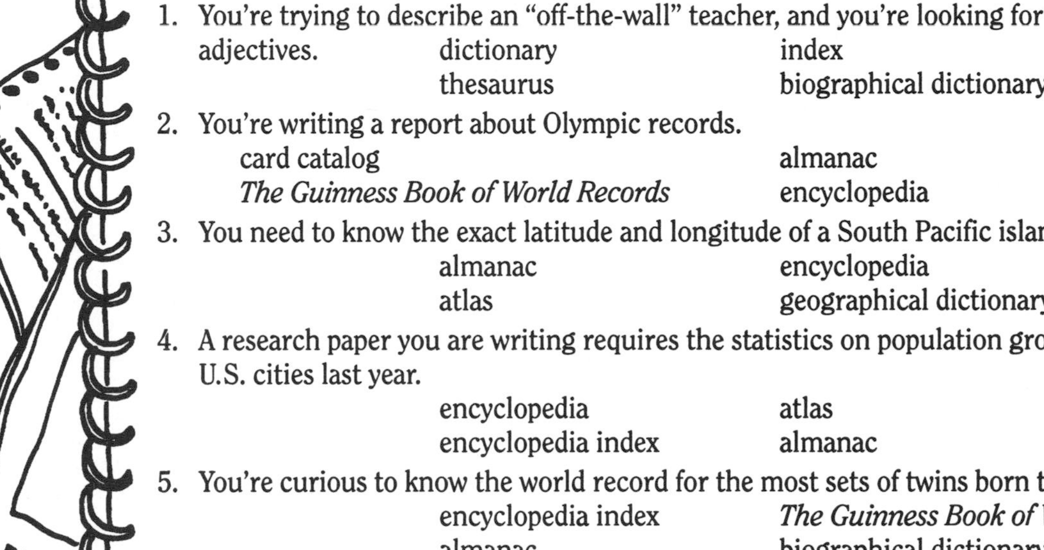

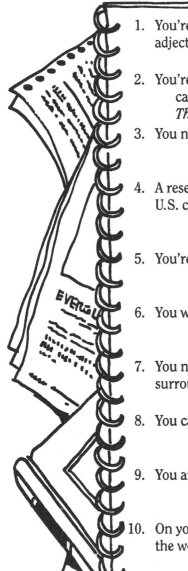

1. You're trying to describe an "off-the-wall" teacher, and you're looking for some unusual adjectives.
   dictionary — index
   thesaurus — biographical dictionary
2. You're writing a report about Olympic records.
   card catalog — almanac
   The Guinness Book of World Records — encyclopedia
3. You need to know the exact latitude and longitude of a South Pacific island.
   almanac — encyclopedia
   atlas — geographical dictionary
4. A research paper you are writing requires the statistics on population growth in major U.S. cities last year.
   encyclopedia — atlas
   encyclopedia index — almanac
5. You're curious to know the world record for the most sets of twins born to one family.
   encyclopedia index — *The Guinness Book of World Records*
   almanac — biographical dictionary
6. You want to make a replica of your state flag.
   atlas — encyclopedia
   card catalog — almanac
7. You need to make a list of the world's seven continents and note the bodies of water surrounding each.
   encyclopedia — atlas
   almanac — geographical dictionary
8. You can't remember how to pronounce the word *dichotomy.*
   biology text glossary — thesaurus
   dictionary — language text glossary
9. You are researching to find the name most commonly used for a U.S. city.
   almanac — atlas index
   geographical dictionary — encyclopedia
10. On your essay about art appreciation, your teacher has commented on the over-use of the word *beautiful.* You need to edit!
    almanac — dictionary
    thesaurus — language text glossary
11. You're trying to locate the section in your language text that discusses subject-verb agreement.
    text's table of contents — text's glossary
    text's index — text's preface
12. You are confused about whether to use the word *affect* or *effect* in a sentence.
    thesaurus — dictionary
    language text glossary — language text table of contents

Name ______________________________

FAST FIGURES

Your detective agency is located in a major city, but you must have quick access to other major cities if you are to be useful in solving crimes. How fast can you get to the scene? Below is a portion of the mileage chart located on your office wall. See if you can answer the following questions in record time. Get a friend to time you. Then invite your friend to do the same page and time him or her. Write your times at the bottom of the page. Which person would likely make the speediest reservations to get to the crime scene?

1. Of the following, which pair of cities is closer together? ____________________
   Albany, New York and Birmingham, Alabama or Boston, Massachusetts and Chicago, Illinois
2. What is the distance between Cleveland, Ohio and Boise, Idaho? ________________
3. Is Boise, Idaho closer to Atlanta, Georgia or closer to Cheyenne, Wyoming? __________
4. How far is it from Charleston, South Carolina to Charleston, West Virginia? __________
5. If you live in Billings, Montana, would you travel farther to a Boston Red Sox or Atlanta Braves home game? ____________________
6. Of the cities listed on this chart, which is closest to Buffalo, New York? ____________
7. Of the cities listed on this chart, which is the farthest from Baltimore, Maryland? ________
8. How many miles would you travel if you made a round trip between Albuquerque, New Mexico and Charlotte, North Carolina? ______________
9. What two cities on this chart are farthest apart? ________________________
10. Approximately how many miles would you travel if you made a trip from Boston to Atlanta to Chicago and back to Boston? ____________________

	Albany NY	Albuquerque NM	Atlanta GA	Baltimore MD	Billings MT	Birmingham AL	Boise ID	Boston MA	Buffalo NY	Charleston SC	Charleston WV	Charlotte NC	Cheyenne WY	Chicago IL	Cleveland OH
Arcadia N.P. ME	440	2459	1330	666	2468	1508	2958	274	733	1219	1039	1114	2221	1251	868
Albany NY		2041	1010	339	2098	1071	2518	169	301	880	636	772	1790	816	484
Albuquerque NM	2041		1404	1890	991	1254	940	2220	1773	1703	1600	1625	538	1312	1585
Atlanta GA	1010	1404		654	1799	150	2223	1108	907	291	501	240	1482	708	728
Baltimore MD	339	1890	654		1916	771	2406	427	365	568	362	418	1669	717	358
Big Bend N.P. TX	2239	586	1341	1907	1421	1192	1702	2297	1923	1623	1590	1583	966	1542	1732
Billings MT	2098	991	1799	1916		1775	606	2197	1721	2175	1721	1996	455	1231	1607
Birmingham AL	1071	1254	150	771	1775		2065	1226	902	441	561	391	1418	657	732
Boise ID	2518	940	2223	2406	606	2065		2685	2214	2493	2138	2345	734	1711	2026
Boston MA	169	2220	1108	427	2197	1226	2685		465	936	751	848	1923	1004	657
Buffalo NY	301	1773	907	365	1755	902	2214	465		925	446	707	1498	539	191
Charleston SC	880	1703	291	568	2175	441	2493	936	925		478	210	1710	906	726
Charleston WV	636	1600	501	362	1721	561	2138	751	446	478		268	1405	470	248
Charlotte NC	772	1625	240	418	1996	391	2345	848	707	210	268		1615	737	516
Cheyenne WY	1790	538	1482	1669	455	1418	734	1923	1498	1710	1405	1615		981	1326
Chicago IL	816	1312	708	717	1231	657	1711	1004	539	906	470	737	981		348
Cleveland OH	484	1585	728	358	1607	732	2026	657	191	726	248	516	1326	348	
Crater Lake N.P. OR	2926	1357	2632	2800	1023	2470	417	3099	2633	2856	2514	2744	1151	2111	2442

RECORDED TIME: Player I ____________________ Player II ____________________

Name ____

AT THE CRIME SCENE

Temperatures are often important pieces of evidence at crime scenes. You have been assigned as a partner to a pathologist who knows a lot about the qualities of blood at different temperatures. This partner needs to know what the temperature was at the crime scene for several hours. When she compares this information to blood found at the scene, it may help her to pin down the time of the crime. Your job is to chart and graph the temperature for each hour of the night up to the time the crime was discovered.

I. First, practice your graph reading skills so that you'll be ready to make your own graph.

1. What was the temperature at 10 P.M.?
2. At what time was the temperature below freezing?
3. At what two hours was the temperature the same?
4. Was the temperature lower at 1 A.M. or 11 P.M.?
5. At what time was the temperature 10 degrees higher than at 11 P.M.?
6. At what time was the temperature 45 degrees?
7. What was the lowest temperature before midnight?

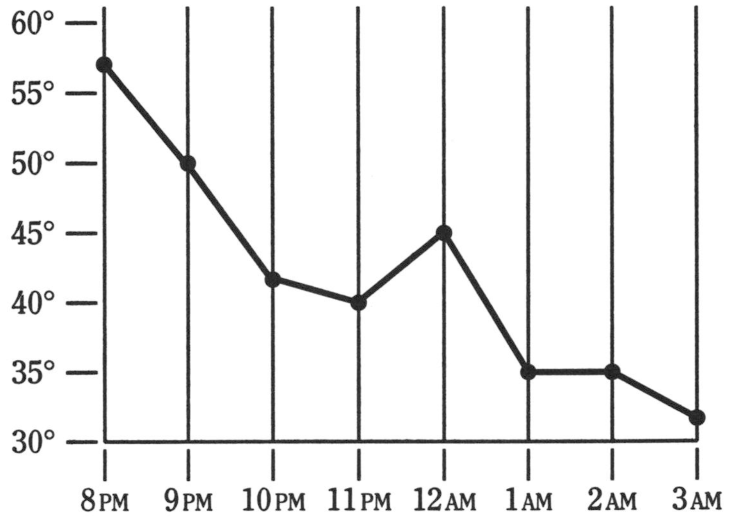
60°
55°
50°
45°
40°
35°
30°
8PM
9PM
10PM
11PM
12AM
1AM
2AM
3AM

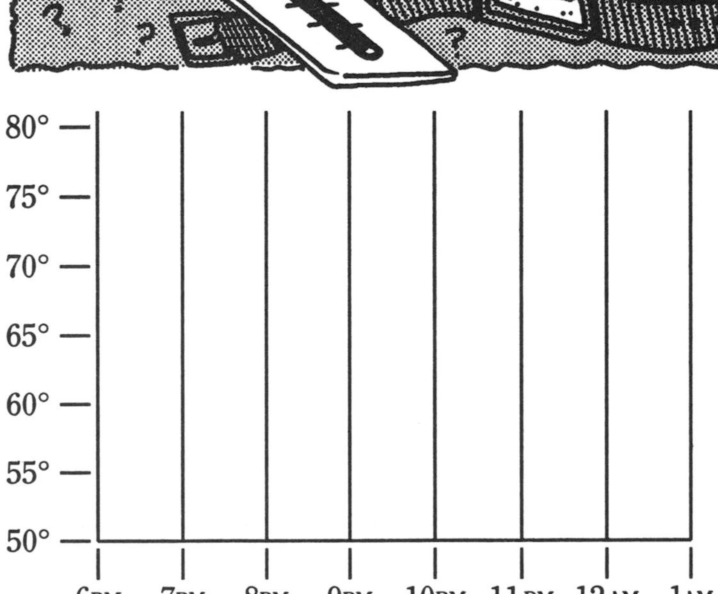
80°
75°
70°
65°
60°
55°
50°
6PM
7PM
8PM
9PM
10PM
11PM
12AM
1AM

II. Graph the information about the temperatures on the night of this crime. Use the graph on the left:

- At 6 P.M. the temperature was 75°.
- At 7 P.M. the temperature was 71°.
- At 8 P.M. the temperature was 60°.
- At 9 P.M. the temperature was 60°.
- At 10 P.M. the temperature was 55°.
- At 11 P.M. the temperature was 53°.
- At 12 A.M. the temperature was 50°.

Name

A DEADLY DIAGRAM

How good are you at reading diagrams? As a detective, you may be called upon at any time to read a diagram that demonstrates the exact location of a very important piece of evidence—such as a dead body!

Using the diagram below as your reference, see how quickly you can answer the following questions. Ask someone to time you. Then ask a friend to answer the same questions as you time him or her. Which of you is faster?

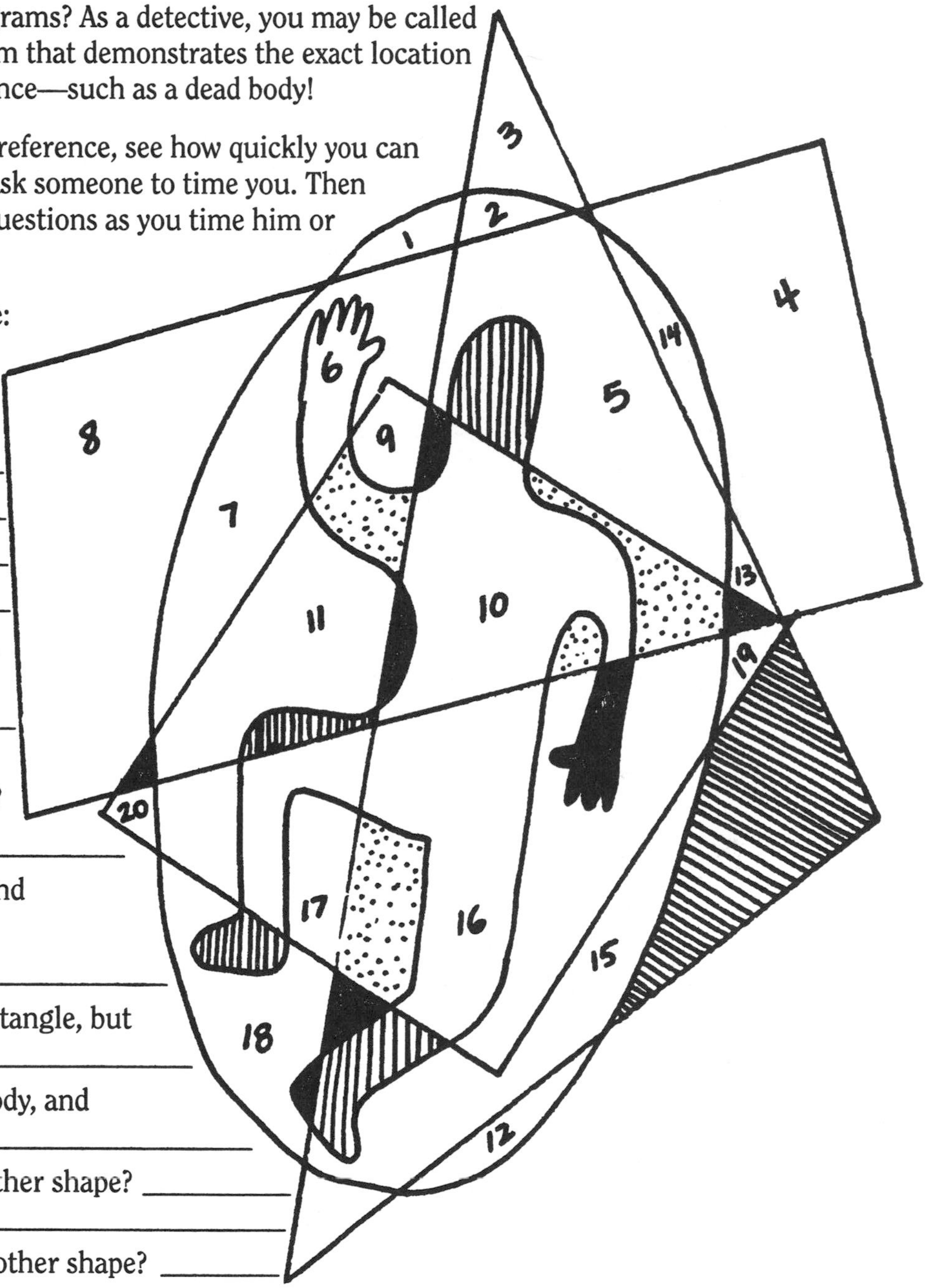

What numbers in the diagram are:

1. In both the triangle and rectangle, but not in the square or oval?
2. Not in the body?
3. In both the oval and rectangle, but not in the square or triangle?
4. In the rectangle, oval, and square, but not in the triangle?
5. In the square, triangle, body, and oval, but not in the rectangle?
6. In the triangle, square, and rectangle, but not in the oval?
7. In the triangle, square, oval, body, and rectangle?
8. In the square, but not in any other shape?
9. In the triangle, but not in any other shape?
10. In the body, but not in any other shape?
11. In the triangle, but not in the oval?
12. In the body, but not in the square?

Name

NOSING AROUND IN HISTORY

3500	Nile Civilization
3000	Sumerians write in cuneiform
	____ 365-day calendar invented
2500	Egyptian Pyramids
	Libraries open in Egypt Indus River Civilization Egyptian mummies made
2000	Percussion instruments added to Egyptian orchestra
	____ Code of Hammurabi
1500	Use of Iron; Egypt at height of glory
	____ Jewish exodus from Egypt ____ Ten Commandments given to Moses
1000	King David rules Israel
	____ First coins minted
500	Birth of Buddha
B.C.	____ Nebuchadnezzar II ____ Alexander the Great ____ Old Testament assembled
0	Birth of Christ
A.D.	

Archeologists and historians are kinds of sleuths who dig way back into ancient history to "nose out" facts. The timeline on the left shows some of the facts they have been able to gather through various means. Study the timeline carefully. Then see if you can answer the questions that follow.

1. Number the order in which these periods of history occured:
   _____ The rule of Alexander the Great
   _____ The beginning of civilization along the Nile
   _____ The time of the kingdom of Israel
2. Which leader lived first?
   Buddha
   Alexander the Great
   Hammurabi
   King David
3. What event took place about 2000 years before the birth of Christ?
4. How many years elapsed between the invention of the 365-day calendar and the first minted coins?
5. How many years passed between the use of cuneiform writing and the first use of iron?
6. At about what time did Nebuchadnezzar II rule the Babylonian Empire?
7. If he had lived long enough, how old would Buddha have been when Christ was born?
8. What event occurred about the year 2750 B.C. that affects every day of our twentieth-century lives?

Name

WANTED!

Four notorious criminals, who have changed their locations and evaded law enforcers many times, were recently caught and extradited to Washington, D.C. Carefully study the pictures and the news story below. Examine the clues within the story. With good detective work, you should be able to match each picture with the name of the fugitive, his most recent hiding place, and the nature of his crimes. Write the name, place, and crime in the space below each picture.

WASHINGTON (AP) Four of the FBI's top–ten wanted criminals were extradited today from their various hideouts to face charges here in Washington. A clever sting operation brought a forgerer, a jewel thief, a drug trafficker, and a cyber-terrorist to Dulles Airport within a four hour period. As Detective I.M. Clever watched the operation conclude, she reviewed the information on the four fugitives:

- Max is bald. Walter is not the forgerer.
- The jewel thief is allergic to birds.
- The forgerer has excellent eyesight.
- Archie is not the drug trafficker.
- Max never left the United States.
- Walter knows nothing about computers.
- Ivan was found hiding in a country known for watches, cheese, and mountains.
- Archie was hiding in a U.S. city called "The Windy City."
- The drug trafficker was apprehended trying to trade a pet bird for ski lift tickets.
- The cyber-terrorist is a former country singer who grew up on a Kentucky farm.
- The jewel thief hid in a country bordered by Belize, Guatemala, and the USA.
- The forgerer was caught in a state that is home to a famous mouse and famous dolphins.
- Walter was apprehended as he entered an optometrist's office.

HIC
BEARS
1.
2.
3.
4.

Name

EYEWITNESS REPORT

Something terrible has happened. Handsome Harry, on his way home from the library, was crushed by a load of bowling balls. The authorities found a scrap of paper clutched in his right hand—the last sentence of the novel *Moby Dick* by Herman Melville.

The scene looks like a tragic accident—but is it? You are the first detective at the scene. What questions will you ask the eyewitnesses? Will the clues lead you to the answer?

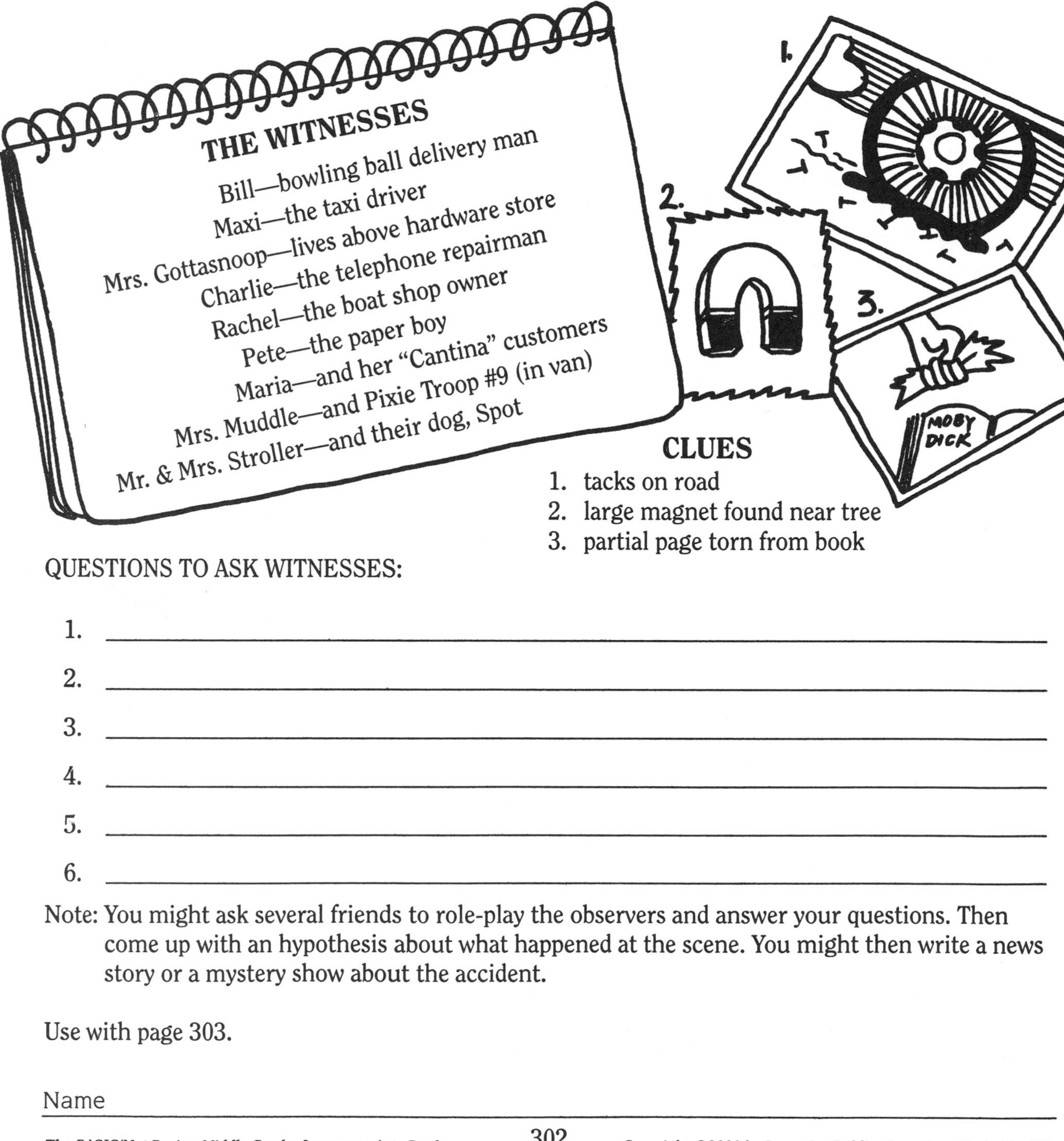
THE WITNESSES
Bill—bowling ball delivery man
Maxi—the taxi driver
Mrs. Gottasnoop—lives above hardware store
Charlie—the telephone repairman
Rachel—the boat shop owner
Pete—the paper boy
Maria—and her "Cantina" customers
Mrs. Muddle—and Pixie Troop #9 (in van)
Mr. & Mrs. Stroller—and their dog, Spot
1.
2.
3.
MOBY DICK

CLUES

1. tacks on road
2. large magnet found near tree
3. partial page torn from book

QUESTIONS TO ASK WITNESSES:

1. ____________________________
2. ____________________________
3. ____________________________
4. ____________________________
5. ____________________________
6. ____________________________

Note: You might ask several friends to role-play the observers and answer your questions. Then come up with an hypothesis about what happened at the scene. You might then write a news story or a mystery show about the accident.

Use with page 303.

Name ____________________________

EYEWITNESS REPORT, CONTINUED

Use with page 302.

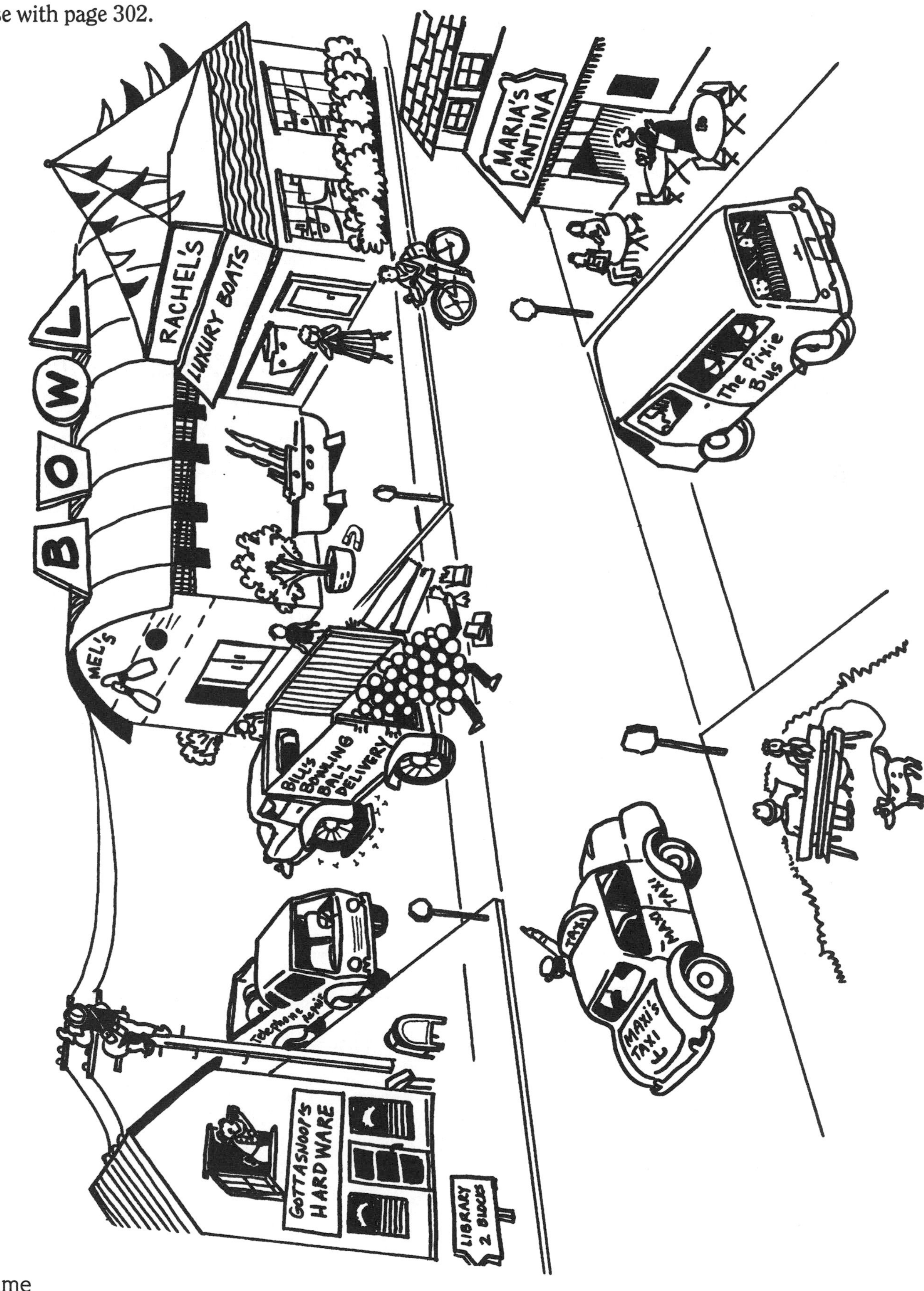
BOWL
RACHEL'S
LUXURY BOATS
MEL'S
BILL'S BOWLING BALL DELIVERY
MARIA'S CANTINA
The Pixie Bus
TAXI
MAXI TAXI
MAXI'S TAXI
Telephone Repair
GOTTASNOOP'S HARDWARE
LIBRARY 2 BLOCKS

Name ____________________

VOICES FROM THE PAST

"HIMSELF"
RED MAROON
b.
620
d.
695
A.D

Snooping for information and clues can take a detective to many places—maybe even to the cemetery. You'd be surprised at what you can learn about people, families, or even a whole community from a visit to the town cemetery.

Your job is to gather information about the people who lived in the past in the town where this cemetery is located (see page 305). Use these questions to help you gather some information from the cemetery. Write your answers here or on another piece of paper. Then organize the information to prepare a report about this community.

1. How many died before the age of 75?
2. How many died as children (16 or younger)?
3. How many gravestones have symbols, phrases, or epitaphs that are religious?
4. What kind of messages are found in the symbols or designs on the gravestones?
5. What clues do you find on the stones that let you know how some of these people wanted to be remembered?
6. What can you conclude about the Jackson family?
7. In what percentage of the family plots did the wife die before the husband?
8. What general statements about the community can you make from this picture?
9. Which gravestones do you find most interesting, and why?
10. By observing the general setting and appearance of the cemetery, can you make a generalization about the attitude of people in this community toward the care of their relatives after death?

Use with page 305.

Name

Use with page 304.

CEMETERY
MINNIE JACKSON 1899 1970 WIFE
SUE JACKSON 1925-1994 DEVOTED DAUGHTER
MOE JACKSON 1922-1945 BRAVE BROTHER
SAM JACKSON 1890-1985 HUSBAND
HY B. 1860 JOINED ETER-
SY D. 1915 FOR NITY
Baby Mary 1895-1897 R.I.P.
Mac Joy 1940-1989 "A GOOD LIFE"
1910-1985 BOZO JANGLE "He Loved To Clown Around"
MAYBELLE GOTT 1937- 1959 WE MISS 'GOTT' A LOT
1911 - 1925 ROSE BUDD
RUBY BLATT 1900-1975
SHE HAD A GREEN THUMB
1875 - 1925 MEHITABEL LEE SO SWEET
SOLOMON GOLD 1909-1980
FRANCES GOLD 1920-1989
EUBLE HIGGLE 1880 - 1937 HE FARMED THE LAND
BOW LEHR 1930 1990
MAY HE STRIKE '300' IN THE SKY
Doug Finn 1932 1994 "fisher-man"
MISHA MYNE 1971- 1975 WE MISS HIM SO—
JAYNE PLANE 1940- 1976 SPELUNKER
JAY B. PLANE 1933-1990 CLAUSTRO-PHOBIC EX-SPELUNKER

Name

STORY FOR CASES #33, #34, AND #35

CHANTICLEER AND THE FOX

Chanticleer was a clever but self-centered, conceited character whose chauvinistic attitude and foolish actions nearly resulted in great tragedy. He believed that he was, without question, the most gorgeous creature in the barnyard, and he strutted so proudly and crowed so loudly that no one would have dared to challenge him. In spite of his arrogance, his wives, the hens of the yard, rose early to preen and comb and prepare themselves to be chased by the most available and best looking husband in the feathered community. This chasing he did for his own pleasure and seemed not to notice if he scattered dust into the eyes of his wives or caused jealousies among them.

However, one young hen named Pertelote—the one most often favored by Chanticleer—was not entirely mesmerized by Chanticleer's charms. She recognized his arrogance and often reprimanded him for strutting too close to the edge of the forest where a sly fox lay in wait for a chance to de-feather a tasty meal.

"Who does he think he is?" retorted Chanticleer. "I am far too clever to be made into a mere snack for that silly fox!" But Pertelote continued to warn him, and he continued to ignore her. "I am more handsome than he, and my father has taught me to sing more beautifully than any forest animal. The fox is a second-class citizen!"

Then one day, as the hens were napping and Chanticleer sat preening on the fence near the forest, the sly fox saw his chance. He sneaked to the fence, cocked his head, and whispered in his sly voice, "Good day, Chanticleer!"

Chanticleer nearly fell off the fence in fright, but the fox hastened to assure him that he had come with no ill intentions.

"I came only to ask of you a favor, " he lied. "I have fond memories of the beautiful songs of your father, and I have heard some of those same glorious sounds in recent days. I only beg you to throw your head back and close your eyes tight as your father once did, and sing to me. I am made lame by your tender music."

So filled with his prideful arrogance that he could not detect the deceit in the fox, though he knew full well his reputation, he threw his head back and crowed his most glorious notes.

Immediately, the fox grabbed him by the throat and carted him off to the forest. The ruckus was heard in the farmhouse as well as in the barnyard, and when the farmer and his sons saw their beautiful rooster being towed away by the neck, they ran after him, pitchforks in hand.

Chanticleer recognized the fox's predicament and capitalized upon the situation.

"Oh, Sir Fox, " he croaked. "How embarrassingly low-class of you to run from those humans. They are not half as swift or skilled as you are, and now that you are safely in your forest domain, why not turn and scold them away? Are they not much more afraid of you than you are of them?"

The fox, as vain as the cock, could not resist showing his superiority. And when he opened his mouth to belittle the farmer, of course, Chanticleer escaped to the highest tree!

— (Paraphrased from Chaucer's *Canterbury Tales*)

Name

EYES-WISE

How fast can you pick up important clues and facts? A good detective needs to be able to get a quick overview of the most important information. You can check your skill at this by skimming the story "Chanticleer and the Fox" (found on page 306) and answering some questions to see if you picked up the important facts of the story.

A good method for skimming a story is to place your finger under each line and draw it across the page as you read. In doing this, your finger "pulls your eyes" across each line as quickly as possible. Do not look for details. Do not dwell on unfamiliar words. Just keep reading quickly!

I. Use the method above to skim the story. Ask someone to time you. When you're finished, write your "skim time" at the bottom of the page. See how many questions you can answer correctly without looking back at the story.

QUESTIONS

1. What kind of a character is Chanticleer? Recall some of the words that were used to describe him. ______________________________
2. How did Chanticleer treat the women in his life? ______________________________
3. Who is Pertelote? ______________________________
4. How did the fox trick Chanticleer? ______________________________
5. Who chased the fox? ______________________________
6. How did Chanticleer outwit the fox? ______________________________
7. Where did Chanticleer go after he escaped the fox? ______________________________
8. Where was the fox's home territory? ______________________________

II. Now, reread the story carefully. Have someone time you again. (Do not use your finger!) Write your reading time at the bottom of the page. Then use a pen or pencil of a different color to fill in any answers you could not answer after skimming.

Skim time ______________________________

Read time ______________________________

Name ______________________________

GET ORGANIZED!

In crime detection, as in any career, it is important to be able to organize information clearly so that other readers may have a precise understanding of the story. Practice your skills by organizing the main details of the story "Chanticleer and the Fox" into outline form for the purpose of exposing the character of Chanticleer. Your outline will help you write a precise report on what Chanticleer was like.

I. Main Idea (first outstanding characteristic)

____

A. Subtopic (first supporting statement)

____

1. Detail (first proof) ______________________________
2. Detail (second proof) ______________________________

B. Subtopic (second supporting statement)

____

1. Detail (first proof) ______________________________
2. Detail (second proof) ______________________________

II. Main Idea (second outstanding characteristic)

____

A. Subtopic (first supporting statement)

____

1. Detail (first proof) ______________________________
2. Detail (second proof) ______________________________

B. Subtopic (second supporting statement)

____

1. Detail (first proof) ______________________________
2. Detail (second proof) ______________________________

The above pattern may be continued to include a third or fourth idea if needed.

Name ____

SUCCINCTLY SPEAKING

When you and a partner are working on a mystery case, each of you has to be able to give the other a quick run-down—a succinct summary—of the information you have gathered separately.

Practice doing this by summarizing as completely, but as concisely, as possible, the story of "Chanticleer and the Fox." Pretend you were sitting in a tree above the barnyard, observing the entire turn of events. What happened?

Write the abridged version here!

CHANTICLEER AND THE FOX
A succinct summary
BY:

Name

FOLLOW THE NUMBERS

Slippery Numbers
#067-
NO-LIPS'
PICKELOK
VERY CRAFTY
#113
DANGEROUS
APPETITE
ATE A
!!

Every detective has a little black book of numbers. In the late 1800s, an American librarian named Melvil Dewey invented a system of numbers for keeping track of books—all the nonfiction books in a library. This numerical system divides all books into ten categories of knowledge, each of which has a specific set of numbers assigned to it.

Most school libraries are set up on the Dewey Decimal System. When a book is added to the collection, the librarian uses the Dewey Decimal system to assign it a "call number"—its own group of numbers within its classification category. This number is put on the spine of the book so it can be seen while the book is on the shelf. Since the numbers must follow the system guidelines, books about the same subject will always be found close to each other.

The chart below shows the ten groups and the numbers for each. Finish the third and fourth sections of the chart by finding books in your library that fit into each category. Write each title in its appropriate place. Then in the fourth section, write a simple phrase that tells what the books in each group are about.

Dewey Numbers	Group Name	Book Title	Description
000-099	General Works		
100-199	Philosophy		
200-299	Religion		
300-399	Social Studies		
400-499	Language		
500-599	Pure Science		
600-699	Applied Science		
700-799	Fine Arts		
800-899	Literature		
900-999	History, Geography, Biography		

Name

FINGER-FAST INFORMATION

The card catalog was created for finding information fast. It's a detective's dream. You can locate any book in a library by searching the card catalog under its title, its author, or its subject.

On the list below, there are items missing in two of the three columns. Use a card catalog or on-line catalog in your library to locate the missing pieces. Fill in each empty space under "author," "book title," and "subject."

CATALOG

	AUTHOR	BOOK TITLE	SUBJECT
1.		*Anne of Green Gables*	
2.	Louisa May Alcott		
3.		*The Illustrated Man*	
4.		*Huckleberry Finn*	
5.			Scotland Yard
6.	William Golding		
7.		*Pride & Prejudice*	
8.			Earthquakes
9.	Arthur Conan Doyle		
10.			Daniel Boone
11.	Jules Verne		
12.	Agatha Christie		
13.		*Great Expectations*	
14.			Mystery
15.	C. S. Lewis		
16.		*A Wrinkle in Time*	
17.			Crime
18.			Chemistry

Name ______________________________

STUDY & RESEARCH ASSESSMENT AND ANSWER KEYS

STUDY & RESEARCH
SKILLS TEST

Each correct answer is worth 2 points. Total possible score: 100 points.

1. Put these words in alphabetical order:
   1. perform ____________________
   2. prickly ____________________
   3. pharaoh ____________________
   4. pizza ____________________
   5. panic ____________________
   6. poorhouse ____________________

2. Put these words in alphabetical order:
   1. mystery ____________________
   2. mystify ____________________
   3. mysterious ____________________
   4. mystical ____________________
   5. mysteries ____________________
   6. mystic ____________________
   7. mystique ____________________
   8. mysticism ____________________

3. Which of the following topics would fall on an encyclopedia page which has the guide words *BERMUDA TRIANGLE* and *BIGFOOT*? Circle those words that would.

bicarbonate of soda	beta particle
Bill of Rights	binoculars
bighorn sheep	Bible
biathlon	Berlin, Irving
Bernhardt, Sarah	beeswax
Better Business Bureau	bronchitis

4. Where would you look in a book to find when it was first printed?
   a. title page　　b. table of contents
   c. index　　d. copyright page

5. Where would you find a listing of the sections of the book?
   a. index　　b. bibliography
   c. table of contents　　d. glossary

Use the map below to answer 6–10.

N
W
E
S
Belize
Guatemala
Honduras
El Salvador
Nicaragua
Gulf of Mexico
Pacific Ocean
Costa Rica
Panama

Name ____

　　

6. How many countries border Guatemala on the south and east? ______
7. How many countries border both the Pacific Ocean and the Gulf of Mexico? ______
8. What country borders Guatemala but not Honduras? ______
9. Which of these Central American countries do not border the Gulf of Mexico?

______

10. Which countries extend farther east than Honduras? ______

______

Use the chart below to answer 11-15.

MYSTERY CASE ASSIGNMENTS						
Case Type	**# Cases Given to Detectives**					
	J. Jolly	S. Snoop	U. P. Tight	I. V. League	S. Wiley	B. Sharp
Robberies	41	3	7	13	6	21
Missing Persons	7	4	9	2	6	11
Missing Animals	12	31	20	17	37	41
Assaults	6	12	16	22	19	11
Car Thefts	3	1	0	0	0	2
Break-Ins	4	0	17	6	22	18
Suspicious Noises	4	18	29	42	40	29

11. What kind of case did Detective Snoop investigate most frequently? ______
12. What kind of case was least common? ______
13. What kind of case was most common? ______
14. Which detective handled the most break-ins? ______
15. Which kind of case did Detective Jolly handle most frequently? ______
16. What kind of reference gives you synonyms for words? ______
17. What kind of reference supplies definitions and pronunciations of words? ______
18. What kind of reference contains a wide variety of facts that are up to date? ______
19. What kind of reference contains a lot of maps? ______
20. What kind of reference gives brief descriptions of important persons? ______
21. What kind of reference supplies histories of words? ______
22. What kind of reference supplies in-depth information about a wide variety of people, places, events, and other topics? ______

Name ______

Use the graph at the right to answer 23-26.

Unsolved Cases
J. J. Creep, P.I.

Numbers: 35, 30, 25, 20, 15, 10, 5
Year: 1990, 1991, 1992, 1993, 1994, 1995, 1996, 1997
cases closed
cases open

_____ 23. In what years did unsolved cases total over 50?

_____ 24. In how many years were there more cases closed than left open?

_____ 25. Between which two years was there the greatest drop in unsolved cases?

_____ 26. How many unsolved cases remained open in 1997?

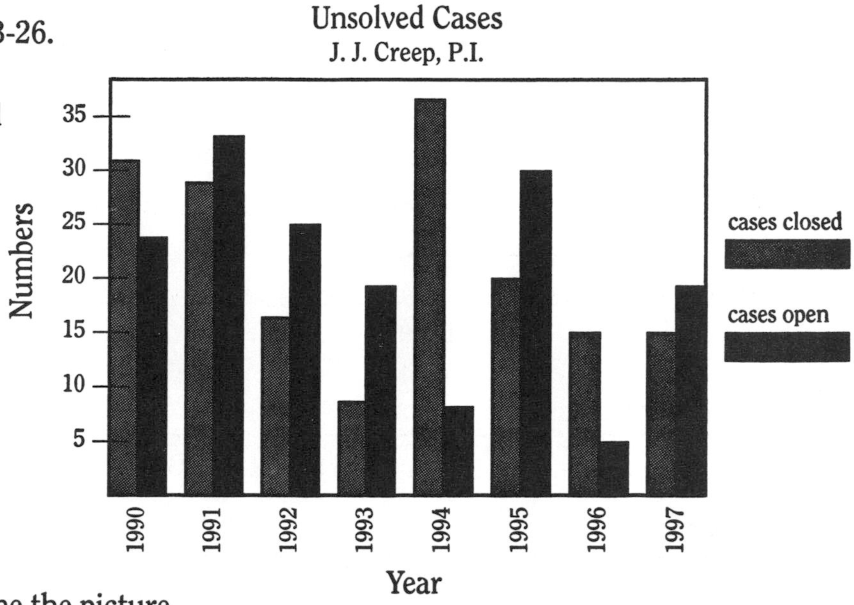

Use careful observation skills to examine the picture at the right. Describe four things you notice that give you information about clues to what has happened in this scene.

27. ____________________

28. ____________________

29. ____________________

30. ____________________

What word would you first look under in an encyclopedia to find each of the topics below? (31-34)

___ 31. President John Kennedy
- a. president
- b. John
- c. Kennedy
- d. government

___ 32. Temperatures in the English Channel
- a. weather
- b. England
- c. English Channel
- d. temperature

___ 33. Famous mystery radio programs
- a. radio
- b. mystery
- c. detectives
- d. programs

___ 34. Farthest planet from Earth?
- a. planets
- b. Earth
- c. space
- d. solar system

Name ____________________

Which reference book would be the best source in which to find each of these? (35-40)

___ 35. the best-selling mysteries of Agatha Christie
a. almanac b. thesaurus
c. *The Guinness Book of World Records* d. biographical dictionary

___ 36. the founder of the city of Chicago
a. encyclopedia b. atlas
c. dictionary d. card catalog

___ 37. the current population of California
a. atlas b. almanac
c. encyclopedia d. *The Kane Book of Famous First Facts*

___ 38. if it was Thomas Jefferson who said, "Give me liberty or give me death"
a. special encyclopedia b. quotation index on history
c. almanac d. gazetteer

___ 39. if *ambidextrous* is spelled correctly
a. thesaurus b. index
c. dictionary d. encyclopedia

___ 40. the first woman to climb Mt. Everest
a. *The Guinness Book of World Records* b. *The Kane Book of Famous First Facts*
c. atlas d. encyclopedia

In what section of the Dewey Decimal System would you find these? (41-45)

___ 41. A book of African poetry
a. 200-299 b. 800-899
c. 400-499 d. 300-399

___ 42. A biography of Walt Disney
a. 000-099 b. 500-599
c. 900-999 d. 600-699

___ 43. A book that has facts about shooting stars
a. 500-599 b. 700-799
c. 400-499 d. 200-299

___ 44. A book of puns
a. 200-299 b. 800 899
c. 700-799 d. 400-499

___ 45. A science encyclopedia
a. 000-099 b. 100-199
c. 300-399 d. 500-599

___ 46. What card in the card catalog would you search for to find a book on diseases?
a. subject card b. author card c. title card

___ 47. What card in the card catalog would you look for to find a book of spooky poems by Edgar Allen Poe?
a. subject card b. author card c. title card

___ 48. Which would you find in the *R* section of th Library of Congress classification system?
a. a book of chemistry experiments
b. a book about U.S. presidential elections
c. a book describing different medicines
d. a biography of a musician

___ 49. In which section of the Library of Congress system would you expect to find this book: *Black Holes and Wormholes: Mysteries of Deep Space?*
a. Section D b. Section V
c. Section H d. Section Q

___ 50. Which sentence best summarizes the paragraph below?
a. Detectives need special training for their work.
b. People hire detectives for some pretty strange jobs.
c. Detectives have to work odd hours.
d. A detective's job is dangerous.

The day began with a call from a Mrs. Squeal who was looking for a detective who could find the kittens her cat had given birth to and deserted. Detective Smogg went from that case to investigate a man's claim that his next-door neighbor was putting poison in his vegetable garden. The next case was to follow the trail of a brother-in-law who had disappeared along with his wife's seven wigs. After lunch, the detective finished some paperwork on a case where a family suspected a hobo was sleeping in their garage, and located a box of lost pet crickets. By dark, he was ready to resume his nighttime stake-out to locate the howling dog that was constantly bothering the Nervy family. Just when he thought he could quit for the night, a 2 a.m. call came, asking him to figure out why Mrs. Ears was hearing repeated sneezing in her house all night, when there was no one there but herself.

SCORE: Total Points ________________ out of a possible 100 points

Name ________________

STUDY & RESEARCH
SKILLS TEST ANSWER KEY

1. 1. panic
   2. perform
   3. pharaoh
   4. pizza
   5. poorhouse
   6. prickly
2. 1. mysteries
   2. mysterious
   3. mystery
   4. mystic
   5. mystical
   6. mysticism
   7. mystify
   8. mystique
3. bicarbonate of soda
   beta particle
   Bible
   biathlon
   Bernhardt, Sarah
   Better Business Bureau
4. d
5. c
6. 3
7. 5
8. Belize
9. El Salvador
10. Nicaragua, Costa Rica, Panama
11. missing animals
12. car thefts
13. suspicious noises
14. Detective S. Wiley
15. robberies
16. thesaurus
17. dictionary
18. almanac
19. atlas
20. biographical dictionary
21. dictionary
22. encyclopedia
23. 1990, 1991, 1992, 1995
24. 3
25. 1994-96
26. 19

27–30. Answers will vary. Give credit for any insightful observations students make about the scene. (e.g. open safe, picture on floor, window broken, glass lying outside, weather, shape of footprints, lack of water inside, keys on floor, broken necklace, broken lamp, direction of footprints, etc.)

31. c
32. c
33. b
34. d
35. d
36. a
37. b
38. b
39. c
40. b
41. b
42. c
43. a
44. d
45. d
46. a
47. b
48. c
49. d
50. b

ANSWERS

page 270

THE CHEF BAKED IT IN A PIE

page 271

TOP:	BOTTOM:
1. G	1. Zagreb
2. F	2. Zambezi
3. P	3. Zanzibar
4. C	4. Zapotec
5. D	5. Zedikiah
6. E	6. Zen
7. M	7. Zeppelin
8. N	8. Zeus
9. J	9. ziggurat
10. L	10. Zimbabwe
11. A	11. zinc
12. Q	12. zinnia
13. T	13. Zircon
14. I	14. zither
15. R	15. zodiac
16. K	16. zola
17. S	17. zoology
18. B	18. zoonosis
19. O	19. Zuider Zee
20. H	20. Zurich

pages 272-273

1. 33-37
2. 118-149
3. 150-175
4. 235
5. 190-194
6. 89-91
7. 16-31, 230
8. 43
9. 70-117
10. 140
11. 195–197
12. 100, 101, 123

pages 274–275

1. 100
2. 41
3. 287, 114
4. 28, 175
5. 264
6. 194–196, 204–209, 210-223
7. 19
8. 90–109, 288–289, 292
9. 250–251, 256–259, 266, 272
10. 120–135, 191, 211
11. 21
12. 52–53
13. 192–193, 224
14. 25
15. 199
16. 13
17. 47, 192–193, 202–203, 222
18. 216, 217
19. 154–160
20. 189, 201

page 276

(see below)

page 277

maps will vary

page 278

1. a right, granted by law, to a composer, author, or publisher to exclusive publication of a work
2. from the time it is created until 50 years after the author's death (75 years after creation if anonymous)
3. *Math in the Real World of Architecture* and *Brothers and Other Annoyances*
4. *Math in the Real World of Architecture*
5. Dr. I. Noahtall
6. *Training Your Pet Python, Brothers and Other Annoyances, Tales That Twist Your Tongue*
7. *Training Your Pet Python*
8. Bodyworks Press, Inc.
9. *Training Your Pet Python*
10. *Math in the Real World of Architecture*

page 279

1. Q	14. B
2. S	15. I
3. E	16. F
4. R	17. L
5. U	18. M
6. P	19. T
7. N	20. C
8. Y	21. D
9. O	22. G
10. J	23. K
11. X	24. W
12. H	25. A
13. V	

page 280

Answers will vary.

page 281

1. Boston, Budapest, Birmingham, Boise
2. Answers will vary.
3. Brazzaville
4. Bogotá
5. Baffin Island
6. Brisbane
7. Bulgaria
8. Bhutan
9. Bratislava & Budapest
10. Beirut
11. Answers will vary.

page 282

(see below)

page 276

LUCKY LAKE
CLOUD PIERCE MT.
FOREST
treasure
sunken ship
FOOTHILLS
SWAMP
N
W
E
S

page 282

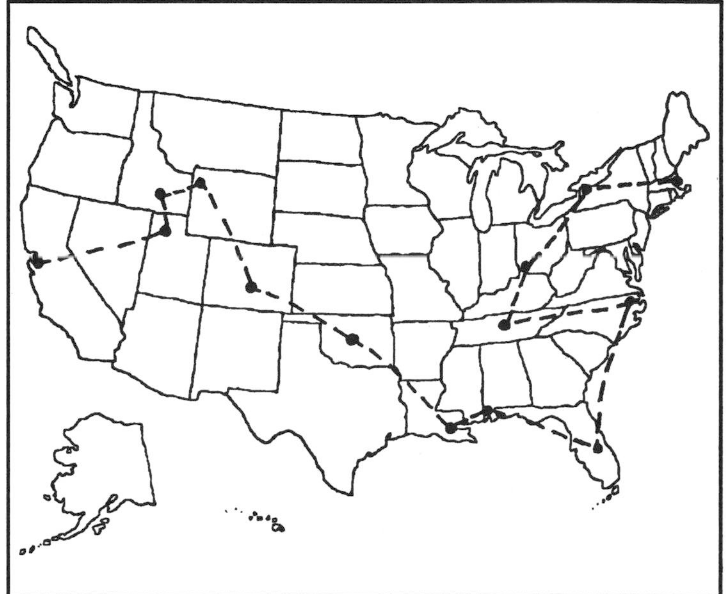

page 283

1. The brilliant detective in many of Agatha Christie's famous mysteries
2. A mystery of deep space— a hypothetical passageway in space and time
3. Volcanic island in the South Pacific that mysteriously appears and disappears
4. Well-known TV mystery-suspense series
5. Secret religious rites of ancient Greece
6. Also known as a "ghost" fish
7. Pilot who disappeared with her plane on an around-the-world flight in 1937—no trace was ever found.
8. The name of one of Agatha Christie's most famous mysteries, about a murder which takes place on the train "The Orient Express"
9. A fabled monster of Greek legend, with human head and a lion's body—legend is that the sphinx asked a mysterious riddle of anyone who passed it, and those who couldn't answer were killed.
10. Another of Agatha Christie's detectives—an old lady who solves crimes as a pastime
11. A lonely island west of Chile, with huge rock monoliths, the origin of which is a mystery
12. A mysterious disappearing ship
13. Detective main character of Mickey Spillane's mysteries
14. Playwright who wrote a famous play called "Ghosts"
15. A 1968 study of UFO sightings
16. An area in the Atlantic Ocean near Bermuda where about 70 ships and planes are said to have mysteriously disappeared leaving no trace
17. copies of old manuscripts of Biblical times, which were missing and searched for over centuries
18. American ship from which all passengers and crew mysteriously disappeared—a mystery never solved
19. 1952 U.S.Air Force Project to investigate the possibility of UFOs
20. French composer who created a piece of music called "The Mysterious Barricades"

page 284

1. c
2. c
3. b
4. c
5. d
6. d
7. a
8. e
9. a
10. c
11. b
12. c
13. c
14. a

page 285

Answers will vary due to differences in encyclopedia sets.

page 286

Answers will vary.

page 287

Answers may vary, as different sources list different "wonders." A possible set:

1. Mt. Everest — south central Asia
2. Victoria Falls — on Zambezi River in south central Africa
3. Grand Canyon —Arizona
4. Great Barrier Reef—Coral Sea, off east coast of Australia
5. Northern Lights—skies of the far northern hemispheres
6. Paricutin volcano —west of Mexico City
7. Harbor at Rio de Janeiro, Brazil—Brazil

page 288

1. Victor Petrenko
2. Seattle Slew
3. Rocky Marciano
4. Brazil
5. answers will vary
6. Martina Navratilova
7. Henie—figure skating
   Mantle—baseball
   Namath—football
   Becker—tennis
   Korbut—gymnastics
   Kersee—track & field
8. O. J. Simpson
9. United States
10. NASCAR—car racing
    NRS—shooting
    PGA—golf
    NFL—football
    NBA—basketball
    NHL—ice hockey

page 289

Susan Brownell Anthony: 1820–1906, Rochester, NY, school teacher, crusader for women's right to vote

Cesar Chavez, 1927– , Arizona, Migrant Worker, started National Farm Workers Association, a labor union for Mexican-American migrant workers' families

Hiram Fong, 1925– , Hawaii, laborer & lawyer & senator, worked to unite races

Shirley Chisholm, 1924– , Brooklyn, NY, educator and first black congresswoman, worked for laws raising standard of living for poor of all races

Gloria Steinem, 1934– , NY, NY, writer & speaker & feminist, worked for equal rights for minority groups, especially women

page 290

F—Charlie Chan
G—The Saint-Simon Templar
J—Perry Mason
B or H—Miss Jane Marple
A—Mike Hammer
H or B—Hercule Perot
C—Nero Wolfe
E—Father Brown
D—Cordelia Gray
I—Travis McGee

page 291

Answers will vary.

page 292

Answers will vary.

page 293

Answers will vary.

page 294

1. precise time—dictionary
2. plant it or put it in a flower arrangement—dictionary
3. answers will vary—Reader's Guide
4. answers will vary— almanac
5. dictionary
6. 1943—almanac
7. gravity—encyclopedia
8. 45 hours or 2175 miles—atlas
9. answers will vary—Reader's Guide
10. answers will vary—thesaurus
11. Mother Theresa—almanac
12. Ecuador—atlas

page 295

1. Tennessee
2. Ernie
3. Ford
4. Hilton
5. 3rd, November, 1969
6. South Sandwich
7. Tennessee Williams

page 296

1. thesaurus
2. almanac
3. atlas
4. almanac
5. *The Guinness Book*
6. encyclopedia
7. atlas
8. dictionary
9. atlas index
10. thesaurus
11. language text's index
12. dictionary

page 297

1. Boston and Chicago
2. 2026 mi
3. Cheyenne
4. 478 mi
5. Boston Red Sox
6. Albany, NY
7. Boise, ID
8. 3250 mi
9. Boston, MA and Crater Lake, OR
10. approx. 2820 mi

page 298

(see above right)

page 298

I. 1. 41°
2. 3 A.M.
3. 1 A.M. and 2 A.M.
4. 1 A.M.
5. 9 P.M.
6. 9:30 P.M. and 12 A.M.
7. 40°

II. Graph should look like this:

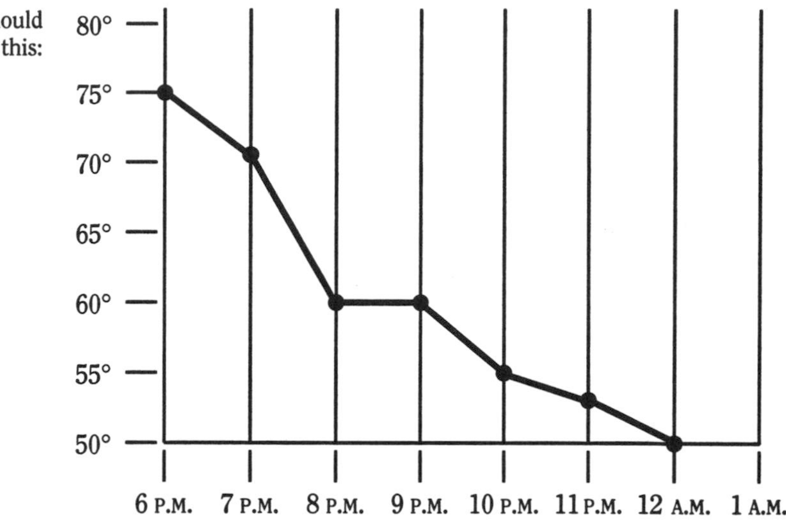
80°
75°
70°
65°
60°
55°
50°
6 P.M.
7 P.M.
8 P.M.
9 P.M.
10 P.M.
11 P.M.
12 A.M.
1 A.M.

page 299

1. 13
2. 1, 2, 3, 4, 5, 7, 8, 9, 11, 12, 13, 14, 15, 17, 18, 19, 20
3. 6, 7, 14
4. 9, 11
5. 16
6. 13
7. 10
8. 20
9. 3
10. none
11. 3, 13, 19
12. 6

page 300

1. 3, 1, 2
2. Hammurabi
3. Egyptians added percussion instruments to the orchestra
4. 2000 years
5. 1500 years
6. about 400 B.C.
7. 500 years old
8. 365-day calendar was invented

page 301

1. Walter, Mexico, jewel theif
2. Archie, Chicago, cyber-terrorist
3. Max, Florida, forgerer
4. Ivan, Switzerland, drug trafficker

pages 302–303

Questions will vary. Check to see that they are good questions that are based on the clues and picture.
A good answer to the mystery:
Any one of the eyewitnesses could have thrown the tacks on the road causing the bowling ball truck to suffer a flat tire. Only a few could have used the magnet to pull the hinges off the back of the truck just as Harry crossed the street. But only Rachel is named in the last sentence of *Moby Dick*. The last sentence of the Epilogue contains the phrase "It was Rachel."

pages 304–305

1. 18
2. 3
3. 8

Answers for 4–10 will vary.

page 307

1. Give credit if student writes a few of these: clever, self-centered, conceited, chauvinistic, proud, arrogant, best-looking, handsome
2. without respect
3. his favorite wife
4. by using flattery—complimenting his singing
5. the farmer and his sons
6. by appealing to his vanity
7. to the highest tree
8. the forest

page 308

Answers will vary.

page 309

Summaries will vary.

page 310

Answers will vary.

page 311

1. Author: Lucy Maude Montgomery
   Subject: life of an orphan
2. Answers will vary.
3. Author: Ray Bradbury
   Subject: science fiction
4. Author: Mark Twain
   Subject: adventures of teenage boy
5. Answers will vary.
6. Answers will vary.
7. Author: Jane Austen
   Subject: relationships; 18th century
8. Answers will vary.
9. Answers will vary.
10. Answers will vary.
11. Answers will vary.
12. Answers will vary.
13. Author: Charles Dickens
    Subject: adventures of an orphan boy
14. Answers will vary.
15. Answers will vary.
16. Author: Madeline L'Engle
    Subject: science fiction
17. Answers will vary.
18. Answers will vary.